NAS Monograph Series No. 4

Series editor Gerald Grainge

The Gresham Ship Project

A 16th-Century Merchantman Wrecked in the Princes Channel, Thames Estuary

Volume I: Excavation and Hull Studies

Edited by

Jens Auer and Thijs J. Maarleveld

with contributions by
Massimiliano Ditta, Antony Firth, Nigel Nayling,
Delia Ní Chíobháin, Christian Thomsen, and Cate Wagstaffe

BAR British Series 602

2014

Published in 2016 by
BAR Publishing, Oxford

BAR British Series 602

The Gresham Ship Project, Volume I

ISBN 978 1 4073 1210 1

© The editors and contributors severally and the Publisher 2014

The authors' moral rights under the 1988 UK Copyright,
Designs and Patents Act are hereby expressly asserted.

All rights reserved. No part of this work may be copied, reproduced, stored,
sold, distributed, scanned, saved in any form of digital format or transmitted
in any form digitally, without the written permission of the Publisher.

BAR Publishing is the trading name of British Archaeological Reports (Oxford) Ltd.
British Archaeological Reports was first incorporated in 1974 to publish the BAR
Series, International and British. In 1992 Hadrian Books Ltd became part of the BAR
group. This volume was originally published by Archaeopress in conjunction with
British Archaeological Reports (Oxford) Ltd / Hadrian Books Ltd, the Series principal
publisher, in 2014. This present volume is published by BAR Publishing, 2016.

Printed in England

PUBLISHING

BAR titles are available from:

	BAR Publishing
	122 Banbury Rd, Oxford, OX2 7BP, UK
EMAIL	info@barpublishing.com
PHONE	+44 (0)1865 310431
FAX	+44 (0)1865 316916
	www.barpublishing.com

Table of Contents

Foreword			iii
Acknowledgements			iv
1	Introduction		1
	1.1	Aims and Objectives	1
	1.2	Site Location	1
	1.3	Project Background	2
	1.4	The road to excavation	3
2	Excavation and Recording		7
	2.1	Logistics	7
	2.2	Methodology	8
	2.3	With the Benefit of Hindsight: a critical discussion of the 3D recording methodology	16
3	The Ship		19
	3.1	The Princes Channel Wreck: An Overview	19
	3.2	Site History: The Princes Channel Wreck in situ	20
	3.3	Construction	22
	3.4	Some Thoughts on the Sequence of Construction	39
	3.5	Oak Dendrochronology	43
	3.6	The Ship's Anchor	46
4	Armament		47
	4.1	Structural Evidence	47
	4.2	PC1, A Cast-Iron Falcon	48
	4.3	PC2, A Cast-Iron Minion	49
	4.4	PC3, A Cast-Iron Falcon	51
	4.5	PC4, A Wrought-Iron Perrier	53
	4.6	Carriages for Cast-Iron Ordnance	53
	4.7.	Mountings for Wrought-Iron Ordnance	54
	4.8	Shot	54
	4.9	Discussion of the Armament Assemblage	55
5	From Record to Model		56
	5.1	The Record	56
	5.2	The Methods	56
	5.3	Preparing the Data	57
	5.4	Wood and Cardboard	58
	5.5	Selective Laser Sintering (SLS)	59
	5.6	Modelling Problem Areas	61
	5.7	Alignment of the Hull Sections	61
	5.8	The Model	65
6	Analysing the Model of the Princes Channel Ship		66
	6.1	The Master Frame	66
	6.2	The Bow	66
	6.3	The Stern	67
	6.4	Recording the Model	68
	6.5	A Lines Plan, Adjustments and Shape	68
	6.6	The Design of the Master Frame	69
	6.7	Tonnage	71
	6.8	More proportions and ratios	73
7	Furring in the Light of 16th Century Ship Design		75
	7.1	Mainwaring on Furring	75
	7.2	Thomas Harriot	75
	7.3	Matthew Baker and Phineas Pett	76

TABLE OF CONTENTS

7		Furring in the Light of 16th Century Ship Design (cont.)	
	7.4	John Smith and Nathanial Butler	77
	7.5	Later References	78
	7.6	Other References	79
	7.7	Early Modern Ship Design in England	79
8		The Ship from the Princes Channel: A typical 16th Century Merchant Vessel?	81
	8.1	From Princes Channel Wreck to Gresham Ship: A Summary	81
	8.2	The Gresham Ship in the Context of Early Modern Ship-building	82
9		In Conclusion: Looking Back and Looking Forward	86
	9.1	Results	86
	9.2	The Archaeological Process	87
	9.3	The Role of Universities	89
	9.4	Final Remarks	90
Appendix: Princes Channel Wreck – Dendrochronological Data			91
Glossary			93
Bibliography			103
Index			108

Foreword

As I write this, the proposed recovery of a unique Second World War German bomber from the Goodwin Sands is being jeopardised by a run of bad weather; despite all the technical resources being available, the cost of repeated delays is clearly causing concern. The Goodwin Sands are just round the corner, in a sense, from the Princes Channel in the outer Thames Estuary and the planned recovery of the bomber is a reminder both of the extraordinary discoveries that can still be made in this part of the world and of the enormous difficulties of working in that environment.

The Princes Channel Wreck was not too exacting as an exercise in underwater archaeology itself; the site was not especially deep for diving and it comprised a range of material such as timber structure, concretions, larger artefacts and small finds that have been found on numerous other sites. The circumstances of the site made all the difference, however. On the one hand the low visibility, strong tides, intemperate weather and distance from port added complexity and disruption; on the other, this was development-led work for a client whose capacity to provide support was sympathetic, but not limitless at a time when there were few comparable investigations from which to borrow.

The result was that the recovery and recording of the Princes Channel Wreck was necessarily innovative in the way in which techniques were used and combined, seeking to obtain the best possible results within the constraints that applied. The experience fed directly into other development-led work in the Thames, recently published as *London Gateway: Maritime Archaeology in the Thames Estuary*, and into research initiatives such as projects funded by the Aggregate Levy Sustainability Fund. For these reasons, the investigations of the Princes Channel Wreck have an important place in the history of maritime archaeology in the UK.

Nonetheless, evaluation of the success of the investigations in 2003–2004 depends upon what happened subsequently: on the conservation, understanding and public access that the initial work helped – it is to be hoped – rather than hindered. It is important to see, therefore, this project in its entirety, including the current publication – and the analyses it presents – as an inherent and essential component of the whole endeavour. All the people who have contributed to and supported this publication are to be congratulated for bringing it to press, for adding in such a major way to the growing body of archaeological literature that is arising from marine development. Working with the sea is never easy, but the archaeological rewards are so very worthwhile.

Antony Firth
June 2013

Acknowledgements

It took seven years for the Princes Channel Wreck to reach the stage of publication, seven years during which a wide variety of professionals, researchers, students and specialists from various institutions participated in the project. As a result the names of those involved are almost too many to be mentioned.

In chronological order, thanks are due to Wessex Archaeology staff involved on all levels in the series of smaller projects and investigations that led up to the excavation of the wreck in 2004. The excavation team in 2004, composed of Wessex Archaeology staff and divers from the Port of London Authority Marine Services, worked hard during long hours in order to recover the remains of the Princes Channel Wreck from the Thames. The excavation team was supported by the PLA Marine Services under Captain Peter Steen, as well as by staff from the surveying section and the drawing office of Wessex Archaeology. The help and advice received from various specialists and researchers directly after the excavation was greatly appreciated. Here the editors would like to name Nicholas Hall, Keeper of Artillery at the Royal Armouries, who helped to identify the armament of the wreck, Damian Goodburn, with whom one of the editors spent a long and inspirational day, looking at tool marks and trying to understand constructional features, and Douglas McElvogue, who greatly helped with advice and comparative material.

In later stages of the project, numerous students of the Maritime Archaeology Programme at the University of Southern Denmark endured rainy field schools in Portsmouth, while recording the remains of the Princes Channel Wreck under the strict security regime in Horsea Lake and dealt with aspects of post-processing in their coursework. The editors would like to specifically thank Sylvia Bates, Delia Ní Chíobháin, Christian Thomsen and Cate Wagstaffe, who wrote their master theses on subjects related to the project. The Royal Navy diving school provided a hospitable use of some of their facilities.

Further thanks are due to the authors who submitted chapters for this publication and who perhaps find these changed in the editing process. Massimiliano Ditta not only contributed to the text, but also produced a series of illustrations in an extremely short amount of time and applied his 3D modelling skills to the digital reconstruction of the wreck. Katrin Auer contributed indefatigably in the tiresome process of digitizing of the overall plans as well as proof reading and general editing.

In the order of appearance in the text, the editors are grateful to Dr Antony Firth, former head of Wessex Archaeology Coastal & Marine section, for contributing to this volume and providing a foreword. Many thanks also go to Nigel Nayling, who not only participated in the excavation, but also carried out the analysis of the dendrochronological samples. Ian Tyers and Cathy Groves kindly gave access to unpublished data for the dendrochronological analysis.

Advice and suggestions on the study of the armament were provided by Rudi Roth, Ruth Rynas Brown, Nico Brinck and Jan Piet Puype. Patrik Höglund, Niklas Eriksson, Johann Rönnby, Staffan von Arbin, Alice Overmeer, Pjotr Bojakowski and Lin Annerbäck all helped by pointing out comparative material. Further thanks go to staff of the Royal Armouries at Fort Nelson and at University College London for providing access to the armament related material from the wreck and accommodating the recording. During the building of the physical reconstruction model of the wreck, Frederik Hyttel, now at the Viking Ship Museum, and Toby Jones of the Newport Ship Project provided assistance and technical advice. Dr Ian Friel FSA, Dr Wendy van Duivenvoorde and Dr Fred Hocker greatly helped with information regarding the study of furring and many other colleagues provided valuable feedback and discussion in relation to preliminary presentations. The editing was greatly helped by the critical and constructive reviews by Seán McGrail and Richard Barker. The latter's deep understanding of the period's documentary evidence contributed considerably to the fine-tuning of the context in which the evidence from the Princes Channel Wreck needs to be integrated; it did not change our view on the specific role of archaeological observations in understanding the technological changes of the period that were only partly informed by formal debate and learning.

On an organisational level, thanks are due to the Steering Group of the Gresham Ship Project, which co-ordinated the research carried out by the different institutions.

And last, but certainly not least, the editors are indebted to the Port of London Authority for financially supporting the analysis of the wreck and this publication. Our last thanks go to Gerald Grainge, who did a formidable job in keeping us keen all through the editing process.

Jens Auer
Thijs J. Maarleveld
December 2013

Chapter 1: Introduction
by Jens Auer and Antony Firth

1.1 Aim and Objectives

This volume presents the results of the analysis of the Princes Channel Wreck, a 16th-century merchant vessel, later to be termed the Gresham Ship, a working name assigned to the wreck after the English merchant and financier Sir Thomas Gresham, the owner of the gun foundry which produced one of the guns found on board.

As yet, little is known about the voyages this ship undertook in its lifetime or the events that led to its loss in the Thames Estuary, but its final journey, from excavation to its current and hopefully last resting place, was certainly long and adventurous. Between 2004 and 2012 the wreck travelled from the Port of London Authority docks in Gravesend to Horsea Lake in Portsmouth and later to the Stoney Cove National Diving Centre in Leicestershire.

This journey is also reflected in the long and just as adventurous process of analysis and finally publication. The current volume is the result of a series of field schools and surveys, university courses and student projects as well as specialist analyses, involving students, staff and researchers from a wide range of institutions, including the University of Southern Denmark and University College London.

This volume describes the discovery, and the sequence and methodology of the archaeological interventions, as well as the wreck and related armament. Some aspects, such as reconstruction and hull design, as well as a comparative analysis of the ship and its construction, are dealt with extensively, while others, such as archival research into the history and loss of the ship still remain to be considered and offer potential for future research.

1.2 Site Location

The Princes Channel forms part of the southern approaches to the Port of London in the southern Thames Estuary (Figure 1-1). It runs in an east-west direction at a distance of approximately 13 km parallel to the coastline of Kent. The channel is bordered by shallows and sandbanks, such as the Shivering Sands and the Girdler to the North and Pan Sand and the Southern Girdler to the South.

The wreck was located at the western end of the channel near the navigational marker Princes No 7, just

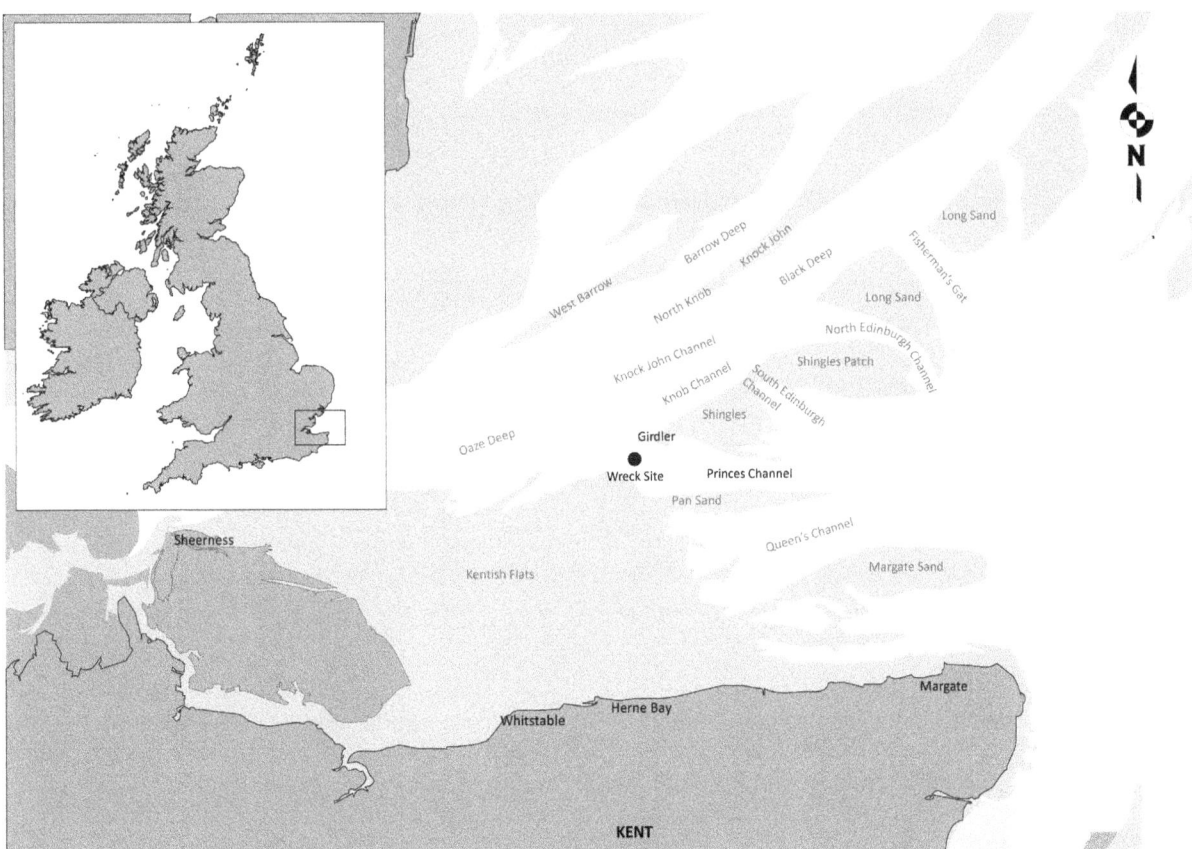

Figure 1-1: Simplified map of the Thames estuary showing the location of the wreck site and major sandbanks and channels (J. Auer)

INTRODUCTION

south of the Girdler sandbank. The depth in this area is 5–6 m below Chart Datum, with water depth on site during diving varying between 7 m and 10 m, depending on the tide. The seabed in the vicinity of the wreck site consists of hard grey clay with a thin veneer of sand.

1.3 Project Background

The Princes Channel Wreck came to the attention of archaeologists in July 2003 through a telephone call to Wessex Archaeology (WA) from the River Regime and Environment Manager of the Port of London Authority (PLA), Nicola Clay. An old cannon and an anchor had been recovered; so arrangements were made to carry out a brief inspection of the items. The inspection confirmed the anchor and the cannon, a possible second cannon and numerous timbers and iron bars (see generally Firth, 2006; Auer and Firth, 2007).

The recovery of this material was the culmination of a series of investigations by the PLA in the spring and early summer of 2003. In April, prior to planned dredging for navigational purposes in the Princes Channel, the PLA undertook a magnetometer survey that highlighted an area of debris. PLA divers established in May that the source of the anomaly was an old wreck. In June iron bars were recovered and an attempt was made to disperse the wreck. Subsequent diving showed that the wreck had not been dispersed; so a grab barge was employed in July 2003, leading to the recovery of the material reported to WA.

Undoubtedly, the Princes Channel Wreck would have been in a more complete and coherent condition at the start of its archaeological investigation, if appropriate expertise had been sought at an earlier stage of its discovery. Had the survey in April 2003 been carried out with archaeological advice and interpretation, according to specifications then current for other forms of marine development, then the potential of the anomaly as a historic wreck is much more likely to have been recognized. The involvement of archaeologists in the inspection dives in May 2003 or shortly thereafter might have avoided the dispersal and salvage attempts in June and July. Nonetheless, once the archaeological potential of the wreck became plain, the PLA's actions with respect to the Princes Channel Wreck started to create a whole set of new practices for marine development-led archaeology in the UK that went on to influence other major schemes (Firth *et al.*, 2012).

As highlighted previously (Firth, 2006; Auer and Firth, 2007) the Princes Channel Wreck is important not only in itself – for what it reveals about many aspects of ships and seafaring in the 16th century – but also for its place in the development of marine archaeology in England. Specifically, the investigations of the Princes Channel Wreck were an early example of development-led marine archaeology, i.e. marine archaeology prompted by the development and use of the sea – in this case, dredging to improve navigation – rather than by archaeological enquiry. The Princes Channel Wreck was the first example in English waters of shipwreck remains in their entirety being recorded and recovered by archaeologists to enable further dredging to take place. This work was funded and supported by the developer, the PLA. Whilst this arrangement had become commonplace on land long before the investigations in the Princes Channel took place, supported by planning law and policy, the application of equivalent provisions to archaeology at sea were still at an early stage. This is not to say that marine developers had never encountered archaeological material on the seabed in earlier years. In fact the broadly contemporary Cattewater wreck was discovered during navigational dredging in 1973. It is just to say that principles with respect to archaeology and development had only started to extend to the sea from the late 1990s.

Matters were complicated because the PLA is not a typical developer. Most developers – on land and at sea – have to apply for permission from the relevant authority to carry out the activities they propose. Archaeological requirements can be placed on the application process or attached as conditions when permission is granted. The PLA is itself the relevant authority and in this case was carrying out activities that are consistent with its own statutory powers under the Port of London Act 1968, which include carrying out dredging (section 60 of the Port of London Act 1968).

Although it does not require permission from an outside body, the PLA operates an Environmental Management System (EMS) through which it carries out its own assessment of the environmental consequences of its activities. It was during this assessment that the original magnetometer survey was carried out in April 2003.

Under section 120 of the Port of London Act 1968, the PLA also has an obligation with respect to vessels that are sunk. Specifically the PLA is obliged to raise, remove, blow up or otherwise destroy vessels that are sunk, stranded or abandoned and which are (or are likely to become) an obstruction, impediment or danger to the safe and convenient navigation of the Thames. There are many wrecked vessels and other obstructions in the Thames and the PLA has both a long history of removing such impediments to navigation and much of the necessary equipment and expertise to carry it out.

The obligation on the PLA with respect to sunken vessels contains no restriction as to the age or potential archaeological importance of the vessel; they are referred to in the 1968 Act only in terms of their implications for navigation, not their potential archaeological interest. However, under section 48A of the Harbours Act 1964 all harbour authorities have a duty to have regard to 'the desirability of maintaining the availability to the public of any facility for visiting or inspecting any building, site or object of archaeological, architectural or historical interest'. This duty is not especially demanding – requiring only that harbour authorities 'have regard to the desirability of' – and it refers principally to maintaining public access; so its application to the removal of sunken vessels is tangential. Nonetheless, the PLA considered that this duty created a degree of archaeological obligation upon their handling of the Princes Channel Wreck once its archaeological character was made plain.

It is worth noting here that the PLA's powers under section 120 of the 1968 Act include disposing of any wreck that has been removed. This means that, although there is a duty to report any wreck that has been found to the Receiver of Wreck under the Merchant Shipping Act 1995, the PLA's vessel removal activities are regarded as not subject to this duty. The PLA was not, therefore, obliged to inform the Receiver that it had found and recovered wreck material in the spring and early summer of 2003, which might have resulted in it coming to the attention of archaeologists at an earlier stage.

Once the presence of an archaeologically important wreck becomes known, it has often been the case that the site has been assessed for designation under the Protection of Wrecks Act 1973 (PWA 1973). Two points had a bearing on this possibility. First the PWA 1973 contains a saving whereby no offence occurs if a person is exercising 'functions conferred by or under an enactment (local or other) on him or a body for which he acts'. That is to say, designation of the Princes Channel Wreck under the PWA 1973 would have no legal effect on the PLA's activities under the Port of London Act 1968. Secondly over recent decades the PWA 1973 has usually been used to protect wrecks in situ rather than as a means of regulating their recovery. In the case of the Princes Channel Wreck, the remains had to be removed in order to enable navigation from the southern approaches of the Thames; so an 'in-situ' solution was not considered feasible. In consequence the option that was pursued was to manage the recovery of the Princes Channel Wreck through development-led processes.

Although English Heritage had no formal curatorial role, the PLA entered a dialogue with them and plans for dealing with the wreck were set out in a formal Mitigation Strategy. The Mitigation Strategy took the form of a Project Design for excavation, recovery, recording and post-fieldwork processing that was informed by an explicit research framework. Proposals for subsequent phases – post-excavation assessment, analysis, conservation, publication and deposition of the archive were also outlined. The Mitigation Strategy was agreed with English Heritage in advance of the main phase of fieldwork in August 2004.

1.4 The road to excavation

After the initial discovery of the Princes Channel Wreck by the Port of London Authority, Wessex

Figure 1-2: Wessex Archaeology staff recording the anchor and wooden stock in August 2003 (Wessex Archaeology)

Archaeology was commissioned to carry out a series of archaeological investigations relating to the wreck. This section is based on the original Wessex Archaeology Reports (Thomsen, 2003; Auer and Baggaley, 2004; Auer and Steyne, 2004; Auer, 2005) and outlines the various stages of the archaeological fieldwork. It describes the sequence of events, as well as the process of decision-making, which led to the excavation of the site in August 2004.

Remedial Recording

In August 2003, Wessex Archaeology was commissioned to carry out remedial recording and an assessment of the timbers and metal objects that had been recovered during the wreck removal operations by the Port of London Authority. The main aim of the assessment was to establish the character and date of the wreck site from which the material derived.

Over two days, Wessex Archaeology personnel provisionally recorded a total of 47 timber fragments, a large number of iron bars, an anchor with a wooden stock (Figure 1-2) and a cast-iron gun, as well as a wrought-iron breech-loader. All the material was photographed and important timbers, as well as the iron guns and the anchor, were drawn at a scale of 1:10. The timbers were suggested to derive from a vessel of approximately 200 tons burthen. Curatorial staff at the

INTRODUCTION

Figure 1-3:   Screen capture taken during the sidescan survey between inspection dives in October 2003. The capture shows the principal wreck site (left) and the dived anomalies (right) (Wessex Archaeology)

Royal Armouries at Fort Nelson dated the cast-iron gun to the late 18th/early 19th century, while the wrought-iron breech-loader was determined to be of 16th century date. The iron bars were thought to have been cargo. The project report (Thomsen, 2003) considered the wreck to be of archaeological importance and suggested that the wreck site should be held under observation during future works.

Further Surveys

At this point the Port of London Authority assumed that the wreck had been removed in its entirety. However, during a survey of the dredged channel in October 2003, further anomalies were noted approximately 30 m from the original wreck position. After a short diving inspection, it became clear that wooden structures remained on the seabed.

Consequently, Wessex Archaeology was commissioned to carry out an inspection dive in the same month. When the wooden structures could not be found at the given position during the first dive, a short sidescan sonar survey was conducted with the aim to relocate them. The survey was successful, producing evidence of a larger, seemingly coherent wreck site in situ (Figure 1-3). During a second dive, the Wessex Archaeology diver described two sections of a curved hull structure, a smaller and a larger one (Auer and Steyne, 2004).

Recovery

The larger of the two newly discovered structures was considered a navigational hazard in the shipping channel by the Port of London Authority and it was lifted by PLA divers with Wessex Archaeology staff in attendance on 20 November 2003. The lifting was carried out using strops and the section was hoisted on board the PLA salvage vessel *Hookness* with a crane. Once out of the water, the timber structure came apart and was recovered as two separate sections, named section 1 and section 2 (Figure 1-4). Both were stored at Denton Wharf in Gravesend and covered with plastic sheeting awaiting further recording (Auer and Steyne, 2004).

Another inspection dive and further recording

After the sidescan sonar survey in October 2003 had shown what appeared to be extensive structures in the position of the original wreck site, another inspection dive was commissioned in December of the same year. The aim of the dive was to establish whether there were indeed coherent structures left on the seabed and, if this were the case, to assess their extent, condition and character. The Wessex Archaeology divers found two large sections of wreckage in situ. The smaller section had a length of 3–4 m, while the larger section measured 8 m in length. The scantlings of the timbers in these sections corresponded to those in the previously lifted wreck parts. Furthermore, a large number of iron bars were observed and a single pottery sherd of a Spanish olive jar was recovered (Auer and Steyne, 2004).

At this point it was clear that substantial parts of a potentially significant archaeological site remained on the seabed in the Princes Channel.

Figure 1-4: *The recovered hull structure breaking into two sections during the lift in November 2003 (Wessex Archaeology)*

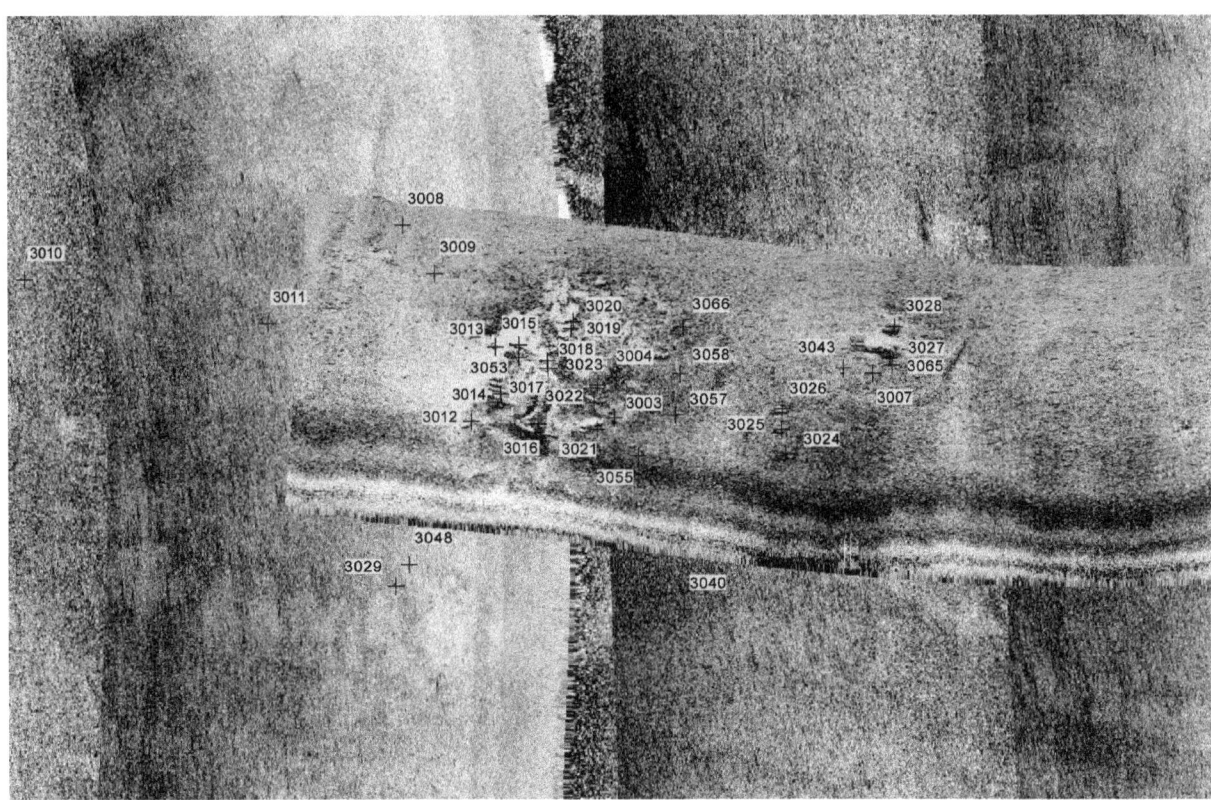

Figure 1-5: *Results of the sidescan survey in May 2004. All targets have been marked and labelled. There is a concentration of targets on the main site and towards the east of the site (right in the image) (Wessex Archaeology)*

Introduction

In order better to characterize the wreck in question, the previously recovered sections, section 1 and section 2, were recorded in January 2004. Constructional details seemed to indicate an early modern dating and thus high archaeological potential (Auer and Steyne, 2004).

Preparing the excavation

In order to inform a suitable mitigation strategy, dendrochronological dating of the recovered sections was commissioned in May 2004 (Auer and Baggaley, 2004). As a result a sample with bark edge could be dated to AD 1574, with the timber likely to have originated from Eastern England (see Chapter 3.5, pages 43–6). This confirmed earlier suspicions of an early modern date for the wreck.

Later in the same month, Wessex Archaeology conducted a high-resolution sidescan sonar survey of the wreck site in order to obtain a geo-referenced image of the area and to establish the full extent of the site. The sonar data also served as a basis for further diving inspections (Auer and Baggaley, 2004). The data clearly showed the wreck site in situ and allowed the identification of 34 targets, the majority of which was concentrated on and around the main site. A trail of targets was observed to the east of the site (Figure 1-5).

The geophysical survey was supplemented with another short diving inspection in June 2004. This was to identify the extent of the surviving structural elements, to assess the degree of sediment cover and to explore the feasibility of lifting the surviving wreckage (Auer and Baggaley, 2004). As a result the remains on the seabed could be characterized as two separate sections, termed section 3 and section 4. Section 3 was thought to be a section of the lower hull 6.5 m long and 5.6 m wide, while section 4 was now described as a part of the ship's bow or stern 5.6 m long and 3 m wide. While section 4 seemed to be clear with the exception of a few stones, section 3 was almost entirely covered by iron concretion, possibly the remains of the cargo (Auer and Baggaley, 2004).

Based on this information, a project design for the excavation of the wreck was produced and submitted to the English Heritage Maritime Team by the Port of London Authority in July 2004. The project design was approved in early August 2004 (Auer, 2005).

Chapter 2: Excavation and Recording
by Jens Auer and Christian Thomsen

The excavation of the Princes Channel Wreck took place between August and October 2004. The objectives were to record all the archaeological material on the seabed and to excavate and recover the two large hull sections (section 3 and section 4) as well as associated artefacts and disarticulated timbers. Furthermore, all recovered structures were to be recorded. The excavation resulted in a report (Auer, 2005) which summarized the immediate results and presented possibilities for further work. However, the excavation of the wreck was the last phase of work carried out by Wessex Archaeology. This section is based on the initial fieldwork report (Auer, 2005) and outlines excavation logistics, methodology and results. In addition, the recording methodology employed after excavation and during previous fieldwork stages is presented and critically discussed.

2.1 Logistics

The excavation and subsequent lifting of the wreck remains was planned as a co-operation between Wessex Archaeology and the Port of London Authority. Underwater operations were scheduled for a period of 20 dive days starting 16 August and split into two 10-day slots. Shore-side recording was planned to take place after all diving on site was completed.

However, the project was severely delayed by adverse weather conditions. As a result, diving stretched over a period of nine weeks with the last dive completed on 19 October 2004. In this time 30 dives with a total bottom time of 89 hours were conducted. In order to make use of diving downtime, shore-side recording was started on 14 September and concluded on 22 October. At this point the project team was under extreme time pressure and did not manage to finish the recording of all structures to the same standard (see section 2.2).

Project staff was made up of four diving archaeologists from Wessex Archaeology, as well as a skipper and diving supervisor, a standby diver and a tender from the Port of London Authority. While all recording and excavation was undertaken by the archaeological divers, PLA Marine Services were responsible for the preparation of the dive site and the lifting of coherent ship structures. For digital shore-side recording the team was joined by an additional two Wessex Archaeology staff members.

With the wreck site located at the edge of a busy shipping channel, project logistics were challenging. Because of the position of the site it was not possible to establish a permanent mooring system or to use a jack-up platform or similar rigid structure as a basis. Consequently all diving was carried out from diving support vessels, which were based at Whitstable and later Gravesend. Until 11 October, the PLA river tug *Impulse* was used as the main diving support craft. The

Figure 2-1: The Port of London Authority river tug Impulse *was the main diving support vessel for the excavation (J. Auer, Wessex Archaeology)*

tug was equipped with a one-ton crane and provided ample deck space for an airlift compressor and the low-pressure diving air supply compressor (Figure 2-1). After 11 October diving was conducted from the PLA Marine Services dive boat *PLA Diver*. As this boat was not equipped with a crane and had insufficient deck space for the airlift compressor, diving after this date was limited to seabed searches and recording.

The coherent timber structures were lifted by the purpose-built PLA salvage vessel *Hookness*.

One of the greatest logistic challenges was to find an efficient solution for mooring the diving support vessel above the wreck site. The site location in the shipping channel did not allow for the presence of surface markers, as these were seen as possible hazards to navigation.

To overcome this problem, two sinkers, of two and three tons respectively, were positioned at a distance of 6 m to 10 m upstream and downstream of the wreck site. Two steel cables were connected to the sinkers and led to a guide cable, long enough to reach the edge of the shipping channel. The cable was held down by a weight and marked with a buoy outside the channel.

The guide cable could be picked up at the beginning of each diving day. It was then hauled in, until the two mooring wires were reached. These were split and attached to bow and stern respectively. This system allowed the diving vessel to be moored in the same position, almost directly above the wreck site, every day.

Dive vessel positioning could be checked with the help of Differential GPS data, which was projected over a high resolution sidescan sonar image of the site in the navigation software ESRI Arcpad.

Figure 2-2: A diver from Wessex Archaeology being prepared for a dive (F. Mallon, Wessex Archaeology)

However, this system turned out to be problematic in winds stronger than force four Beaufort. The long guide cable and the mooring wires got entangled around each other and the shipwreck on a number of occasions and the wires broke in heavy swells.

These problems could be solved by restricting diving to wind conditions of force three Beaufort and less and by using heavier grade mooring wires. Before mooring the vessel a diver was deployed to make sure the cables were clear.

Although time consuming, these measures helped to make the mooring procedure more efficient and less destructive. Nevertheless, the mooring system caused damage to the wreck on two occasions, when passing vessels picked up the guide cable and dragged mooring wires and sinkers through the site. The first time section 3 broke in two and the second time one of the resulting halves, termed section 3b, was dragged and ultimately flipped over.

With no, or at best very low, visibility and strong tidal currents on site, all diving was conducted using surface supplied equipment. The air supply was provided by a low-pressure compressor with a number of high-pressure cylinders as backup. The diving control panel and diver communication were set up in the wheelhouse of the respective diving vessels.

Because of the tidal current diving could only be undertaken during slack periods when the tide turned.

To maximize work efficiency, two divers were deployed simultaneously. The first diver was equipped with a Kirby Morgan Superlite 27B helmet with attached surface-powered light and digital video camera (Figure 2-2), while the second diver wore a Kirby Morgan 18 band mask with a battery-powered light. The divers either descended along the mooring wires or used a separate shot line to locate the site. A diving ladder provided a safe exit.

Artefacts and cargo were lifted from the site using a large metal basket, which could be lowered with the vessel's crane. The basket was often left on the seabed for the whole day and provided a safe tool storage as well as an orientation point for the divers.

A large warehouse was rented in Whitstable harbour in order to store the material lifted from the site. All artefacts were stored in temporary holding tanks, constructed from wood and pond liner. Larger objects and coherent ship structures were transported to the Port of London Authority Marine Services facilities in Gravesend at Denton Wharf, where they could be stored in water-filled barges until time for recording could be found.

2.2 Methodology

Underwater Recording

The underwater recording served two main objectives. Recording the timber structures in situ would help to devise a strategy for the planned recovery. Additionally it was important to document the location of the individual structures in relation to each other, as well as the location of cargo, disarticulated timbers and artefacts in relation to the surviving wreck remains. This information could then be used to compile a basic plan of the wreck structures (Figure 2-3). Considering the adverse environmental conditions on site, it was decided to carry out all detailed recording of the timber structures after the recovery. Based on the results of shore-side recording, a more detailed underwater site plan was produced during post-processing (Figure 2-4).

The original plan foresaw the use of a Sonardyne ultra short baseline (USBL) acoustic positioning system for the positioning of objects on the seabed. The system was set up at the beginning of the project, but could not be used because of a number of hardware and software failures, which could not be resolved by the manufacturer. Because of the time constraints of the project, it was decided to demobilize the system and resort to more traditional recording methods.

The strong tidal currents made it impossible to use grid-based recording systems, as any tape measures, datum lines or wires would be swept away or ripped apart in between dives. Thus a simple network of datum points was established on and around the timber structures. Based on this, a combination of offset measurements and trilateration, as well as distance and bearing measurements, was used to plot the structures and

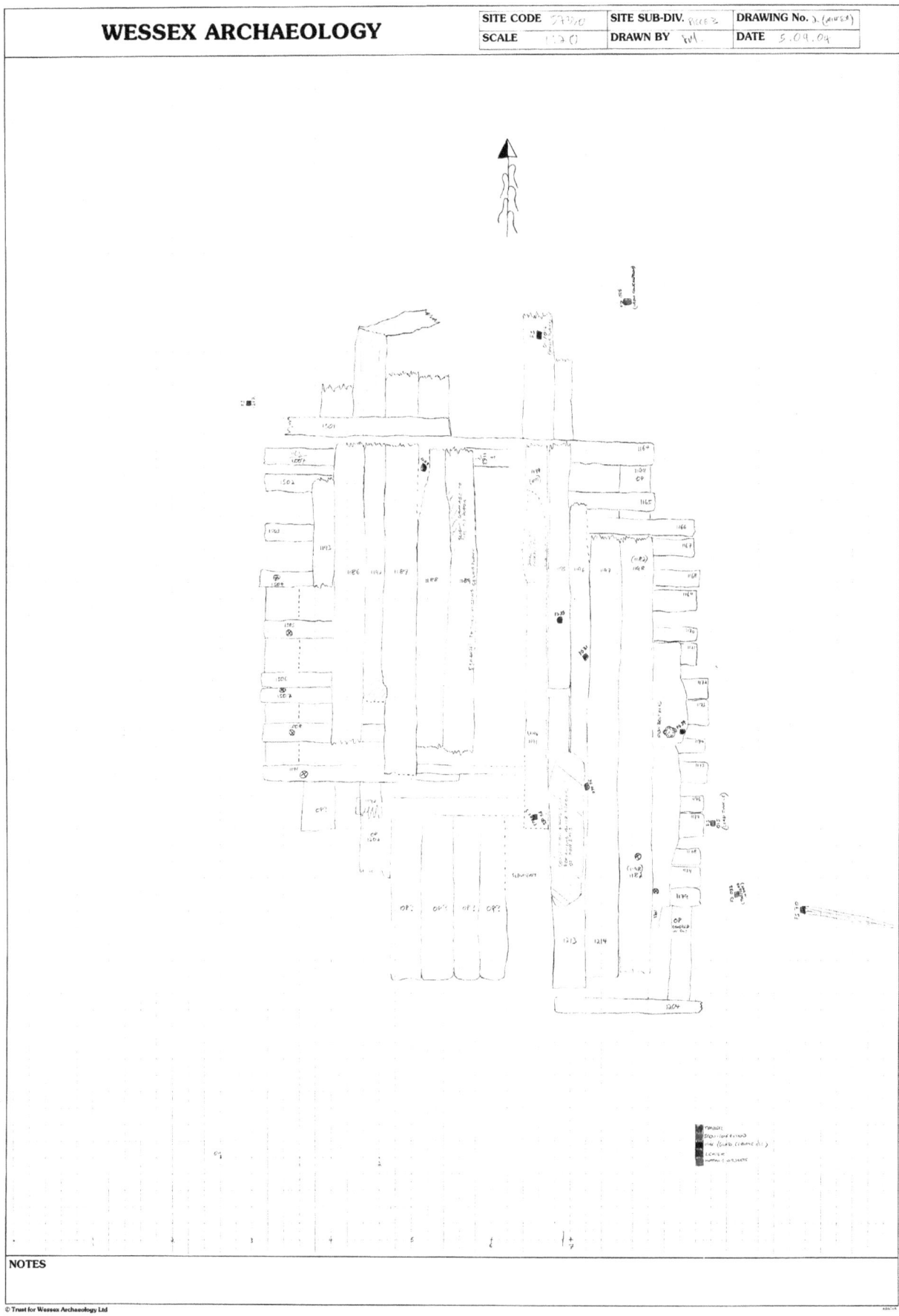

Figure 2-3: Temporary plan of section 3. The plan was plotted on the surface, based on measurements relayed by the divers (F. Mallon, Wessex Archaeology)

EXCAVATION AND RECORDING

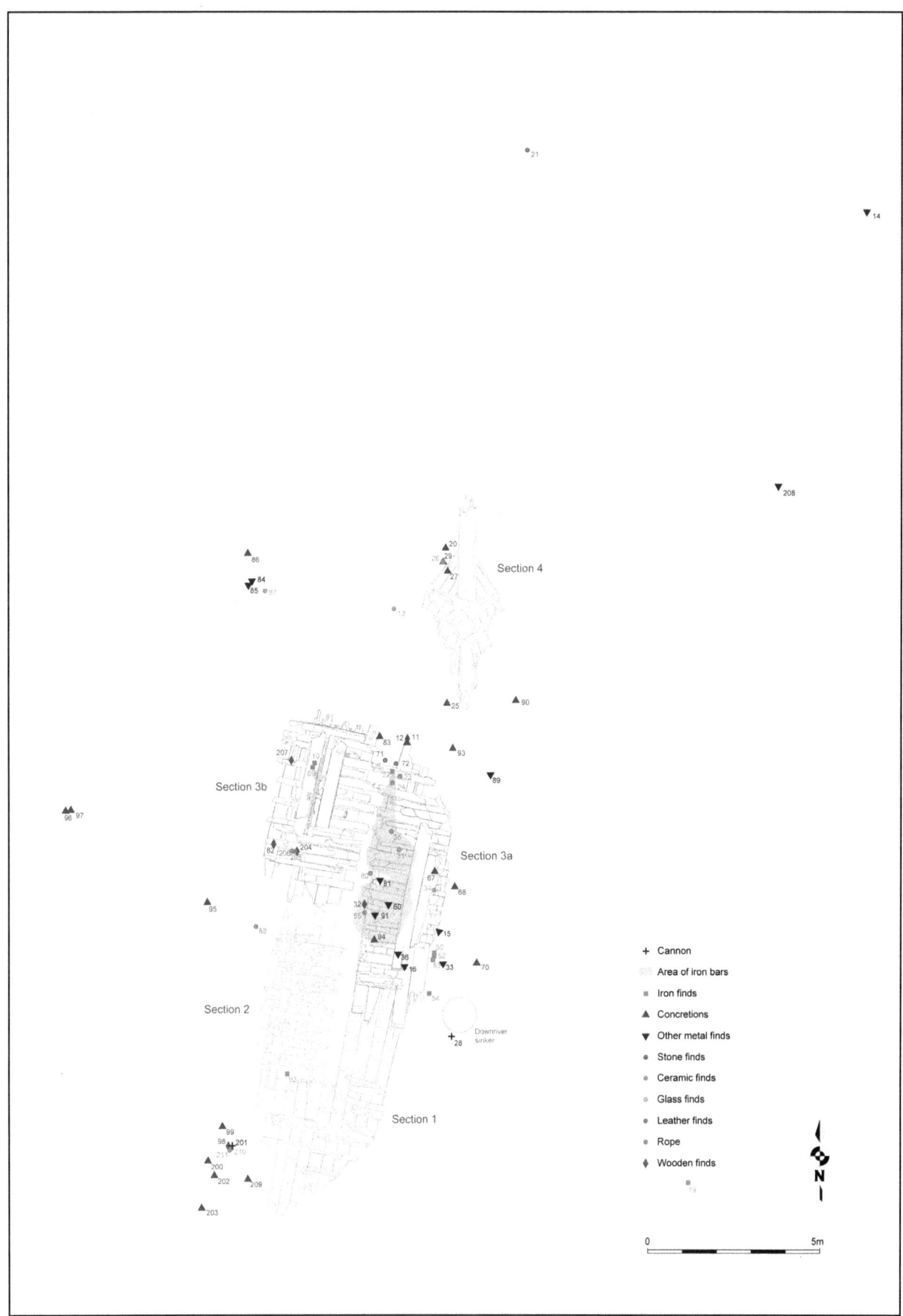

Figure 2-4: Reconstructed site plan of the Princes Channel Wreck, based on the results of shore-side recording. Timber sections, which were lifted prior to the excavation, are greyed out (K.J. Brandon, Wessex Archaeology)

surrounding artefacts. However, this system had to be re-established and altered several times, when the wreck structures moved around on the seabed because of interference with the mooring system. The reconstructed site plan in Figure 2-4 shows the datum points established around the moved wreck structure towards the end of the project.

After setting up the datum system, all the timbers and objects that could be seen or felt on site were tagged with yellow survey markers engraved with unique numbers. Subsequently, their position was measured and relayed to the surface, where an archaeologist plotted them out on a temporary site plan. This plan allowed the definition of contexts, for example for visible gaps between frames, which could be used to locate smaller artefacts during the excavation (Figure 2-4).

Excavation

In preparation for lifting, the inside of section 3, the largest coherent timber structure on the seabed, was excavated by airlift. Two divers worked simultaneously and cleared the gaps between frames moving from north to south. Mesh bags attached to the end of the airlift prevented the loss of smaller artefacts. In order to prevent confusion, the mesh bags were exchanged for each new context. The bags were then sealed underwater and brought to the surface, where the content was sieved. On the eastern side of section 3, iron bars were concreted to the preserved ceiling planks. These had to be removed in order to facilitate the recovery of the timber structure. A pneumatic chisel was used to loosen concretion. Whenever it was possible to separate larger parts of the concretion, these were lifted using the ship's crane.

Recovery and recording of artefacts

After fixing their position, all artefacts, disarticulated timbers and remains of the cargo were recovered from the seabed. Larger objects, such as iron bars and guns were raised individually with the one-ton crane on board the diving support vessel *Impulse*. Smaller artefacts and more delicate items were stored in sealed containers or plastic bags and collected in the metal basket for lifting. Immediately after recovery, all artefacts were labelled, photographed and recorded on recording sheets. The data was later transferred into a purpose-built MS Access database. Very well preserved or functionally important disarticulated timbers were also drawn at a scale of 1:10. After recording, all artefacts were stored in the temporary freshwater holding tanks before being transferred to the Wessex Archaeology head office in Salisbury. Only the best preserved examples of bulk finds, such as, for example, the iron bars, were kept in wet storage. The remainder were stacked on pallets and left to dry out. The scientific results of the artefact analysis, as well as the associated methodologies are presented in Volume II of this monograph.

Figure 2-5: Recovery of the bow section (section 4) by the PLA salvage vessel Hookness *on 2 September 2004 (J. Auer, Wessex Archaeology)*

Raising the timber structures

The original project plan intended the wreck structures to be lifted individually after the in-situ recording was completed and all overlying sediment had been removed during the excavation. This also meant that the results recorded could inform the construction of lifting frames or cradles.

However, during the first days of the excavation, section 4, the presumed bow section, could not be found in the surveyed position. After extensive circular searches, the bow section was discovered 25 m north-east of its original location. Attempts to establish guide lines between it and section 3 failed, as section 4 kept moving on the seabed. Finally, the decision was made to lift section 4, although the underwater recording was not complete. The PLA survey vessel *Verifier* located the hull section with the help of multibeam sonar. Section 4 was then stropped and lifted to the surface by the PLA salvage vessel *Hookness* on 2 September 2004 (Figure 2-5). The section was supported with wooden chocks and transported to Gravesend, where it was unloaded into a flooded barge to prevent it from drying out.

The remaining section 3 consisted of a coherent timber structure approximately 8 m long and 5.5 m wide, which was partially buried in the underlying clay. The structure was assessed as being sufficiently stable for a recovery in one piece. Plans were made to lift it with the help of a purpose-built steel frame with wide, heavy-duty ratchet straps attached. The straps would either be tunnelled or slid underneath the structure. Subsequently the lifting frame would be suspended above the wreck section so that the straps could be attached to the frame. This would ensure an even distribution of the weight and prevent undue distortion or breakage of the timbers.

The design of the lifting frame was discussed with the Port of London Authority and an external contractor was commissioned to construct and test the frame.

Figure 2-6: Section 3a on board of the salvage vessel Hookness *after recovery (J. Auer, Wessex Archaeology)*

However, on the first dive after a long spell of bad weather on 15 September 2004, the divers found section 3 broken in half. The eastern side of the wreck section (section 3a) had been turned upside down and was located approximately 3 m to the west of the other half (section 3b), which remained in its original location. As section 3a was now entangled in the mooring arrangement for the diving support vessel, it had to be lifted to allow *Impulse* to moor above the wreck site. It was lifted using a conventional strop arrangement on 30 September 2004. It was transported to Gravesend on board the salvage vessel *Hookness* and deposited on the quayside, where it was covered and kept wet with a leaky hose system (Figure 2-6).

As the lifting frame was now obsolete, plans were made to recover the only remaining structure, section 3b, with the use of strops and a spreader bar.

On 7 October 2004 the project experienced another setback. A passing cargo vessel had picked up the mooring wires with its propeller and dragged the whole mooring system, including sinkers, along the seabed. In the process, section 3b had been removed from its original position and flipped upside down. Now being exposed to tidal currents, it was moving around the seabed. Consequently, the decision was taken to recover it immediately. Section 3b was stropped and lifted by the PLA salvage vessel *Hookness* on the same day. It was also transported to Gravesend, where it was stored in a flooded barge.

The results of the excavation

Despite the difficulties described above, all of the project objectives could be met. The two coherent timber structures were, as far as possible, recorded in situ, excavated and lifted. A hundred and one artefacts were raised and recorded during the excavation, bringing the total number of objects related to the Princes Channel Wreck up to 110. The majority of these (42) were iron bars, which probably formed part of the cargo. Three boat-shaped lead ingots and two small tin ingots are also likely to have been cargo.

Concretions form the second largest group of artefacts from the wreck. The 22 concretions were left intact and stored for further treatment. All artefacts were analysed by the Institute of Archaeology at University College London, and are described in Volume II of this publication.

Furthermore, two cast-iron guns were recovered. These are analysed and presented in Chapter 4. In the course of the excavation 12 disarticulated timbers were raised and individually recorded. As the majority of these resulted from the interference with the timber structures on the seabed, they could be placed back into context and have been included in the analysis of the ship timbers in Chapter 3.

Following the excavation, Wessex Archaeology published a summary report which outlined the work that was carried out on site and suggested a post-excavation programme (Auer, 2005). This factual report was supplemented by a more extensive article in *Post-Medieval Archaeology*, giving an interim report on the archaeological results of the project (Auer and Firth, 2007).

Initial Shore-Side Recording Methodology and Results

The choice of recording methodology in archaeology is heavily influenced by the intended outcome and the availability of time and resources. Another important factor is the preservation strategy for the material to be recorded. A shipwreck, which is going to be fully conserved, will almost certainly be recorded in a different manner to one that is going to be discarded and thus preserved by record only. Between discovery in 2003 and final excavation in 2004 the Princes Channel Wreck project consisted of a number of smaller investigations or stages, each of which added pieces of information to the final picture (see Chapter 1.4, pages 3–6). The date and character of the wreck were not known during the first phase of remedial recording and the future of the wreck remained unclear, even after the excavation in 2004.

When recording the first material recovered from the site in the Princes Channel, the archaeologists were faced with a large container full of loose timbers. These were briefly sketched, photographed and described (Thomsen, 2003). However, the primary recording method used during the remainder of the project was developed when recording the two coherent hull sections 1 and 2 in January 2004. Both sections were relatively complex and retained a considerable amount of their original shape. At this point the future of the wreck was unclear, which meant that interference with the timbers had to be minimized in order to allow for the possibility of full conservation. The archaeologists were thus faced with the conundrum of extracting the maximum amount of information with minimum

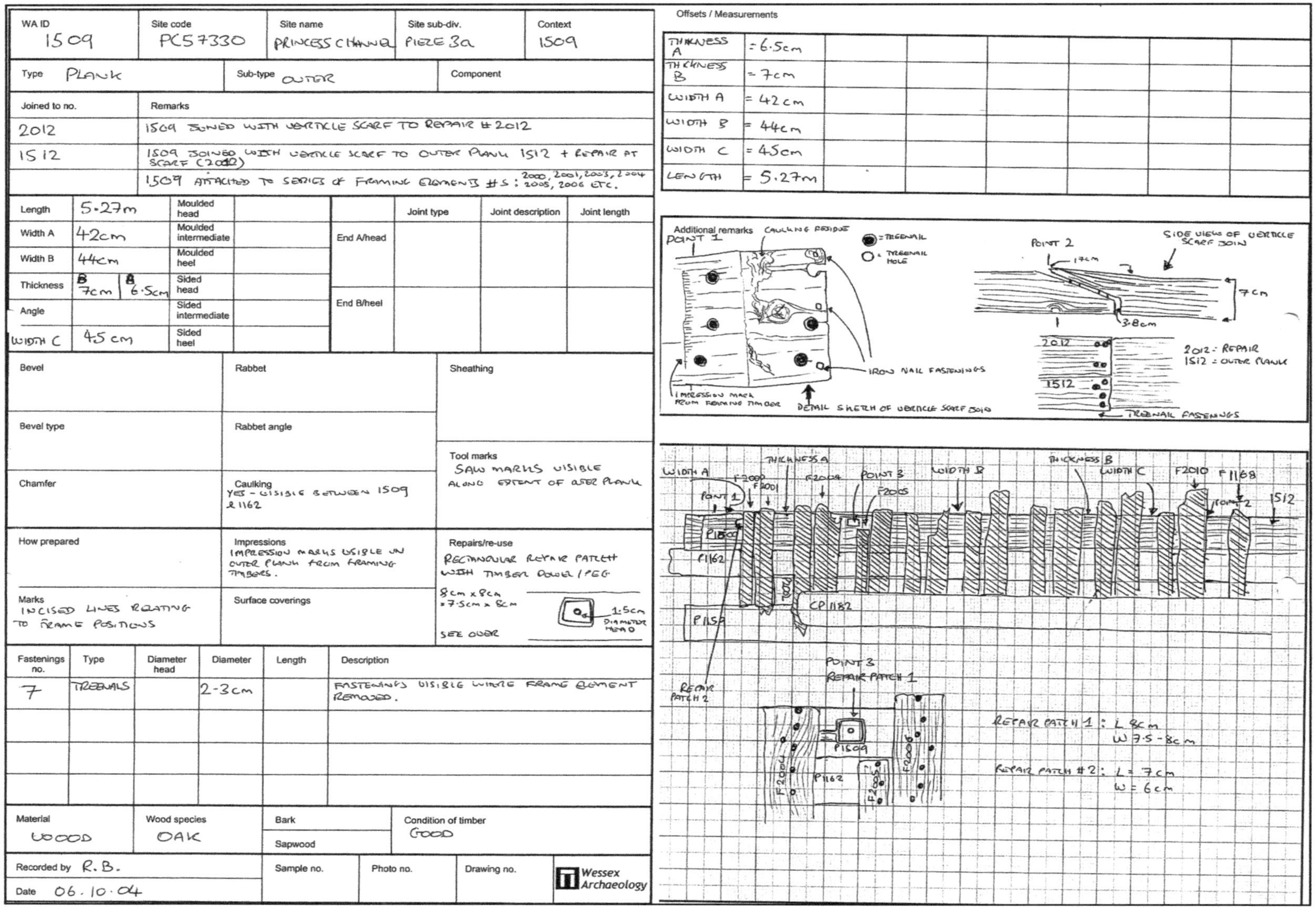
WA ID: 1509
Site code: PC57330
Site name: PRINCESS CHANNEL
Site sub-div.: PIEZE 3a
Context: 1509

Type: PLANK
Sub-type: OUTER
Component:

Joined to no. / Remarks:
2012 — 1509 JOINED WITH VERTICLE SCARF TO REPAIR # 2012
1512 — 1509 JOINED WITH VERTICLE SCARF TO OUTER PLANK 1512 + REPAIR AT SCARF (2012)
1509 ATTACHED TO SERIES OF FRAMING ELEMENTS #S: 2000, 2001, 2003, 2004, 2005, 2006 ETC.

Length	5·27m	Moulded head	
Width A	42cm	Moulded intermediate	
Width B	44cm	Moulded heel	
Thickness	B 7cm / B 6·5cm	Sided head	
Angle		Sided intermediate	
WIDTH C	45 cm	Sided heel	

	Joint type	Joint description	Joint length
End A/head			
End B/heel			

Bevel:
Rabbet:
Sheathing:
Bevel type:
Rabbet angle:
Tool marks: SAW MARKS VISIBLE ALONG EXTENT OF OUTER PLANK
Chamfer:
Caulking: YES – VISIBLE BETWEEN 1509 & 1162
How prepared:
Impressions: IMPRESSION MARKS VISIBLE ON OUTER PLANK FROM FRAMING TIMBERS.
Repairs/re-use: RECTANGULAR REPAIR PATCH WITH TIMBER DOWEL / PEG. 8cm x 8cm, 7·5cm x 8cm. 1·5cm DIAMETER HEAD. SEE OVER
Marks: INCISED LINES RELATING TO FRAME POSITIONS
Surface coverings:

Fastenings no.	Type	Diameter head	Diameter	Length	Description
7	TREENAILS		2-3cm		FASTENINGS VISIBLE WHERE FRAME ELEMENT REMOVED.

Material: WOOD
Wood species: OAK
Bark:
Sapwood:
Condition of timber: GOOD
Recorded by: R. B.
Date: 06.10.04
Sample no.:
Photo no.:
Drawing no.:
Wessex Archaeology

Offsets / Measurements

THICKNESS A	= 6·5cm
THICKNESS B	= 7cm
WIDTH A	= 42cm
WIDTH B	= 44cm
WIDTH C	= 45cm
LENGTH	= 5·27m

Additional remarks

Figure 2-7: Example of the refined timber-recording form, which was used during the excavation (Wessex Archaeology) interference or damage to the structure. The recording method of choice also had to be cost-effective, relatively fast and suitable for large three-dimensional objects.

Initially three different methods were considered (Auer, 2012):

1. traditional recording using offsets or 3D-trilateration or a combination of both;
2. total station recording;
3. laser scanning.

Of the three methods, laser scanning was thought to be the most rapid in the field, but also the most time consuming in post-processing and the most costly. Laser scanning can probably be described as an indirect recording method, as the data acquisition process leaves no room for interpretation and the resulting point cloud has to be interpreted during post-processing. In practice this would have meant supplementing the laser scan with detailed sketches and photographs that would later allow the identification of small features in the point cloud, such as tool marks, markings or repairs. In addition the small gaps between many of the timbers were expected to be a problem for this method.

Traditional recording methods were excluded because they were thought to be too time consuming considering the allotted time frame.

This left total station recording as the method of choice. The ability to generate a digital three-dimensional record relatively quickly, while – it was hoped – still retaining full control over the type and amount of detail recorded, was seen as the main advantage of this method.

Consequently the recording was carried out using a Leica TCR 705 reflectorless total station connected to a laptop running AutoCAD with the TheoLT 2.1 plug-in. This permitted connecting recorded points in real time, which was fast and allowed for continuous monitoring of the survey progress and results (Figure 2-8).

In preparation for the total station survey, all individual hull components were cleaned and labelled with unique identifiers. Features such as fastenings, tool marks and repairs were then marked with chalk and coloured drawing pins to prevent them from being missed. Each timber, including related fastenings, was recorded on an individual layer in AutoCad. Tool marks, markings and surface coverings were recorded on separate layers. The total station was mostly used in the reflectorless red laser mode, unless a mini prism was required to survey inside narrow gaps between timbers or other locations out of reach of the laser.

As both wreck sections had to be turned over with a crane to allow recording of the outside and inside respectively, large nails were used as reference points

Figure 2-8: Total station setup for the recording of section 1 and section 2 (J. Auer, Wessex Archaeology)

on the sections. This ensured that both sides could later be combined in AutoCad to form a single 3D model.

In addition, each timber was described and sketched on a timber-recording form in order to provide as full a record as possible and to include details such as hidden joints which would not be visible in the digital record (Figure 2-7).

Furthermore annotated and partially measured sketches of the coherent sections were made. The recording was supplemented with digital photographs of the sections, of individual timbers and of details.

With the exception of some minor changes and refinements, the shore-side recording of sections 3a, 3b and 4 was planned based on the same recording methodology. The timber sections were lifted onto the quayside to enable access and were carefully cleaned. The underwater labels were checked for consistency and replaced or supplemented where necessary. The visible fastenings, tool marks and other features of interest were then marked with chalk or drawing pins, following a colour coding system based on functional differences.

Prior to total station recording, timber forms (Figure 2-7) were filled in for each recognisable individual timber. When completing the timber forms, the archaeologists were prompted to check carefully for any features that might have been overlooked during the marking phase. Additional sketches were made in order to reconstruct the original location of disarticulated timbers and the composition of the individual wreck sections (Figure 2-9). The total station recording was intended to form the last phase in the recording process.

In practice, however, this was not always the case. When the diving fieldwork was delayed, shore-side recording of the lifted structures started and was conducted by a separate team simultaneously with the underwater work. This meant that individual timber records were not always completed before total station

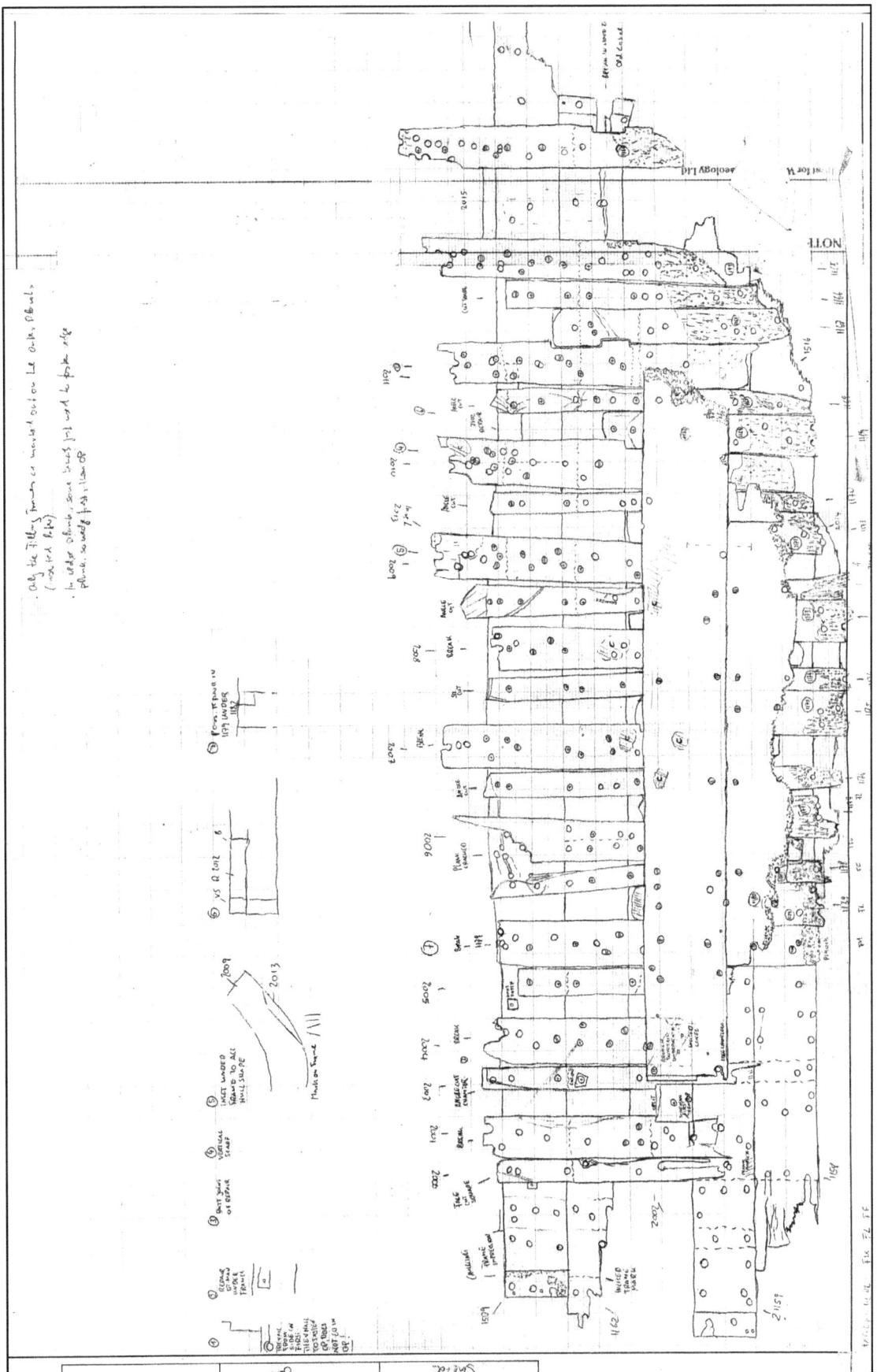

Figure 2-9: Field sketch drawn to supplement the total station recording; field sketches were used to reconstruct how individual wreck sections were joined before breakage (J. Auer, Wessex Archaeology)

recording started, which could lead to features being missed or misinterpreted.

Nevertheless, both section 4 and section 3a were fully recorded in the available timeframe. Recording of section 3b started, but had to be aborted when the project ran out of time. Accordingly, only the outlines of major timbers were recorded on one side of this hull section.

Further Documentation

After the excavation, the fate of the five hull sections of the Princes Channel Wreck remained unclear. Eventually, the Nautical Archaeology Society took custody of the wreck. In 2005 all hull sections were moved to Portsmouth and deposited in Horsea Lake, a man-made lake located on Horsea Island in Portsmouth Harbour. Here the wreck served as a training site for archaeological divers. The scientific analysis of the Princes Channel Wreck and its contents was put on hold until 2007, when the Gresham Ship Project was established. This five year research programme was a collaboration between the University College London Institute of Archaeology, the University of Southern Denmark Maritime Archaeology Programme, Gresham College, the Museum of London Group and the Nautical Archaeology Society. The project was financially supported by the Port of London Authority. Wessex Archaeology was represented in the steering group as it still had custody of the project archive. English Heritage and the Receiver of Wreck assisted in their respective capacities.

The Maritime Archaeology Programme at the University of Southern Denmark assumed responsibility for the study of the hull remains and the artillery. Following an approach of research-based teaching, this study was integrated into the course schedule in the form of field schools, coursework and a series of student dissertations.

The first field school took place in August 2007 and had the aim of checking the state of the wreck, re-tagging the timbers with more durable labels and recording sections through the wreck structures in order to supplement previously acquired total station data. Preliminary research had shown that the complexity of the coherent structures and the narrow gaps between individual frames had limited the detail of the total station record.

Sections were recorded with vertical offsets from a tape measure running along each frame. The data was processed by Maritime Archaeology Programme students and added to the project archive.

In July 2008 another group of students returned to Horsea Lake to conclude the fieldwork aspect of the hull study programme. The aim was to finish the surface recording of the partially recorded hull section 3b and to analyse parts of the bow section in order to understand its composition and construction. This was achieved using simple offset drawing techniques.

The 2008 field school represented the last stage of archaeological recording of the hull timbers of the Princes Channel Wreck.

2.3 With the Benefit of Hindsight: a critical discussion of the 3D recording methodology

The recording methodology of choice and the reasons for choosing it were outlined in section 2.2 above, but how well did it work? Would it be chosen again? With some eleven years between the initial discovery of the wreck and the publication of this final report, the hull study programme had the luxury of being able to discuss critically the recording results obtained in 2004 and to assess the recording methodology with the benefit of hindsight. This section is an updated version of a paper presented at the IKUWA conference in London in 2008 (Auer, 2012).

In general, the recording strategy adopted in 2004 provided satisfactory results. All wreck sections could be recorded as three-dimensional line objects on the basis of which an accurate overview plan was produced. It was also possible to join most of the broken sections retrospectively so that the state of the wreck before interference could be reconstructed. In conjunction with timber-recording forms, sketches and digital photographs, the total station record also allowed for a description of the main constructional features of the wreck (Auer and Firth, 2007; Auer *et al.*, 2009).

However, two limiting factors quickly became apparent in the field and are also revealed in the resulting digital record. These were the time constraints and a lack of consistency in the digital record. Recording always started with the timber outlines of each section and then moved on to the details on individual timbers. As the survey progressed and the survey team was more pressed for time, fewer details were recorded and with less accuracy. To give an example, trenails were recorded as three-point circles at the beginning of the survey, while towards the end only a single centre point was surveyed for each nail. Also the detail in markings, repairs, surface coverings, etc. decreases significantly on the wreck sections recorded towards the end of the project to the point where no surface detail was recorded on parts of section 3b.

Another reason for data inconsistencies was change of personnel. When diving fieldwork started to be delayed because of the weather, the recording of some of the lifted sections occurred simultaneously with the diving fieldwork. In practice this meant that the dive team, which had become very familiar with the wreck sections, could not be present during the recording fieldwork. Although attempts were made to mark relevant details on the timbers, recording results varied considerably.

Often, the survey was slowed down when modern breaks in the outline of planks were carefully recorded, with the result that less time was available for details on the timber surface. Finding the ideal compromise between recording speed, accuracy and detail turned out to be a very subjective process in spite of a clear recording methodology and the marking of sections before recording.

A first assessment of the excavation archive at the start of the Gresham Ship Project in 2007 revealed a number of problems that would arise from using the available recording data for the planned hull study.

As the timber sections were left assembled, a considerable amount of detail could not be recorded in the field. Ceiling planks covered framing timbers and a number of framing elements were sandwiched in the construction, so that they did not appear in the digital record. In addition many timber surfaces were inaccessible even when using a mini prism, so that for some frames only one or two sides could be recorded.

In its original format the digital three-dimensional line- and point-data did not allow the creation of cross sections either. Although this issue could partially be solved in post-processing with the modelling package Rhinoceros 3D (see Chapter 5.3, page 57–8), it remained a problem where timber surfaces were missing in the digital record.

Finally, the quality of the digital data was generally found insufficient for a detailed analysis of the construction and building sequence, mainly because covered details could not be recorded.

However, the supplementary record, namely timber-recording forms, sketches and digital photographs were very useful – essential even – in solving issues like the ones mentioned above. In addition, the two recording sessions in Horsea Lake were planned to help fill some of the gaps in the data.

Nevertheless, the decision to leave the wreck sections assembled and the resulting lack of detail 'led to frustrating moments during the digital reconstruction and preparation of data', as Christian Thomsen noted during his attempt at reconstructing the lines of the wreck. He states that 'the amount of interpretation could have been drastically reduced, had only selected elements been removed to allow recording of the hidden construction' (Thomsen, 2010, 111 – see also Chapter 5.3, pages 57–8).

Another aspect that seriously influenced the quality of the recording was the way the large wreck sections were suspended and moved to allow total station recording of both inside and outside. As the sections were simply placed on the quayside during recording, their own weight caused considerable distortion and changes in shape. While this was not noticeable when looking at individual sides, it became very apparent as soon as inside and outside were merged into a single file (Thomsen, 2010, 111).

Lessons learned:
or what should be done differently next time?

It is common for development-led archaeological projects to be steered by factors such as time and financial limitations. Development-led projects generally require compromises by both archaeologists and developers and such compromises will undoubtedly also affect the choice of recording methodology and strategy. However, what influenced the recording strategy more than time constraints or financial limitations in this particular case was the lack of a final decision about the future management of the lifted wreck. Full conservation as well as temporary or permanent reburial or even disposal remained viable options throughout the project and as a result the recording strategy employed was a compromise between recording as much detail as possible and impacting the coherent sections as little as possible.

Bearing in mind the background of the project, the lack of such a decision before excavation is not surprising. The Princes Channel project was a very early case of marine development-led archaeology in the UK, further complicated by the fact that the developer in this case was a port authority with an obligation to remove wrecks that might present a hazard to shipping. Such removal is not subject to planning permissions and overrides statutory heritage designations. Firth rightly points out that the Princes Channel project was a steep learning curve for all parties involved and that it highlighted a number of existing problems related to the curation of shipwreck material in the UK (Firth, 2006).

However, as a decision on the future management of any excavated archaeological material always has a major effect on the recording strategy, the importance of such a decision can only be stressed again in this instance.

On a more practical level, what could be done differently next time? It is clear that full dismantling and subsequent recording of all individual timbers would have produced a much better record and avoided the problems encountered during the hull study programme. It is also clear that this is not always feasible, but the dismantling and full recording of a selected sample section through the wreck would have kept destruction to a minimum and would probably have answered many of the open questions related to the construction and building sequence analysis.

The fieldwork on wreck site SL4 encountered during a large scale marine dredging project in the Netherlands showcases the impressive amount of information that can be learned through the detailed study of a section of wreckage recovered by grab (Adams *et al.*, 1990).

On a practical level the total station recording produced good results, although it could be optimized by streamlining the survey organization and by training recording personnel in order to ensure more consistent data quality.

The recording of all details with the total station proved to be a lengthy and time consuming process. Here it is interesting to take a look at the recording methodology employed by Lemée during the excavation of a number of wrecks on the Burmeister and Wain shipyard site in Copenhagen (Lemée, 2006). Lemée surveyed timber outlines with a total station, plotted these to scale, traced them onto drafting film and filled fastenings and details in by hand. This method, or a variation thereof, would probably have been useful as it would have been faster than the recording of detail by total station. In addition, the time consuming post-processing task of combining the digital data with the information contained in sketches and on recording forms would have become unnecessary. Recent recording projects have also shown the effectiveness of combining total station recording with photogrammetry and hand sketches (Auer *et al.*, 2012). The one thing that cannot be stressed enough is that ample photography of details and simple descriptions in text, in diary form or as entered on the timber recording sheets remains a crucial addition to make the most of any recording strategy.

Chapter 3: The Ship
by Jens Auer and Nigel Nayling

This chapter aims to present the results of the recording process outlined earlier. However, before proceeding with a technical description of the individual hull components, it is important to carry out a first reconstruction, not of the ship in this case, but of the wreck. The first section provides an overview of the preserved wreck parts and their initial arrangement. Based on this and earlier survey results, as well as historical sources, an attempt will also be made to reconstruct the history of the site and the processes it was subjected to before the first archaeological surveys and subsequent recoveries in 2003. This not only helps the understanding of the distribution of artefacts and cargo, but also had a bearing on decision-making during the model building (see Chapter 5).

The description of the ship's hull is followed by an analysis of construction methods and sequence as well as a discussion of the dendrochronological dating.

3.1 The Princes Channel Wreck: An Overview

Altogether, five coherent hull sections of the Princes Channel Wreck survive. Of these, two were lifted in November 2003 (sections 1 and 2, see Chapter 1.4, page 4) and three were recovered during the excavation in 2004 (sections 3a, 3b and 4, see Chapter 2.2, pages 11–12). The wreck remains include a part of the bow (section 4), as well as a run of the port side approximately 14 m long from just above the turn of the bilge to the level of the deck (from bow to stern: section 3a and 3b and section 1 and 2). The most likely original layout of the pieces was reconstructed by matching up the edges of broken timbers (Figures 3-1, 3-2 and 3-3 for details). The bow section could not easily be linked to the port side. Based on the results of a sidescan sonar survey in May 2004, as well as diver observations, it was then located approximately 2 m away from the forward most part of the port side (see Chapter 3.2, pages 20–1). As none of the broken plank edges match up, it was assumed that this gap was caused by interference with a grab in an early attempt to remove the wreck and that the bow section remained close to its original position. The alignment of the individual hull sections is discussed in more detail in Chapter 5.7 (pages 61–5).

Section 4 forms the lower part of the ship's bow. It has a height of 4.9 m and is approximately 2.2 m long. It consists of a fragment of the keel, which is joined to the stempost. The joint is reinforced by a massive apron, which is secured to the inside. Two v-shaped rising floor timbers are in their original position, with part of a futtock surviving on one side. The remains of seven strakes of outer planking, including the garboard strake, are preserved on the port side, while the more exposed starboard side has six eroded outer planks still in place.

The foremost part of the port side is represented by sections 3a and 3b. As described earlier, these were still joined on the seabed and came only apart during the later stages of the excavation. The lower part, section 3a, measures 8.2 x 2.32 m. It consists of six strakes of outer planking. On the inside, the surviving upper ends of floor timbers are joined to eleven futtocks, which were all broken where section 3b joined section 3a. Between floor timbers and futtocks, smaller filling frames were inserted. Two ceiling planks that survive are still connected.

Section 3b represents the remainder of the ship's side from just above the turn of the bilge to the level of the gunports on the lowest continuous deck. It is 6.3 m long and 3 m high. On the outside, four strakes of planking lead up to a wale, composed of five strakes. Above the wale, a complete gunport is visible, with the edge of another gunport preserved 2.5 m aft of the first. On the inside of the section, the deck construction is apparent below the gunport. Deck beams and planks are missing,

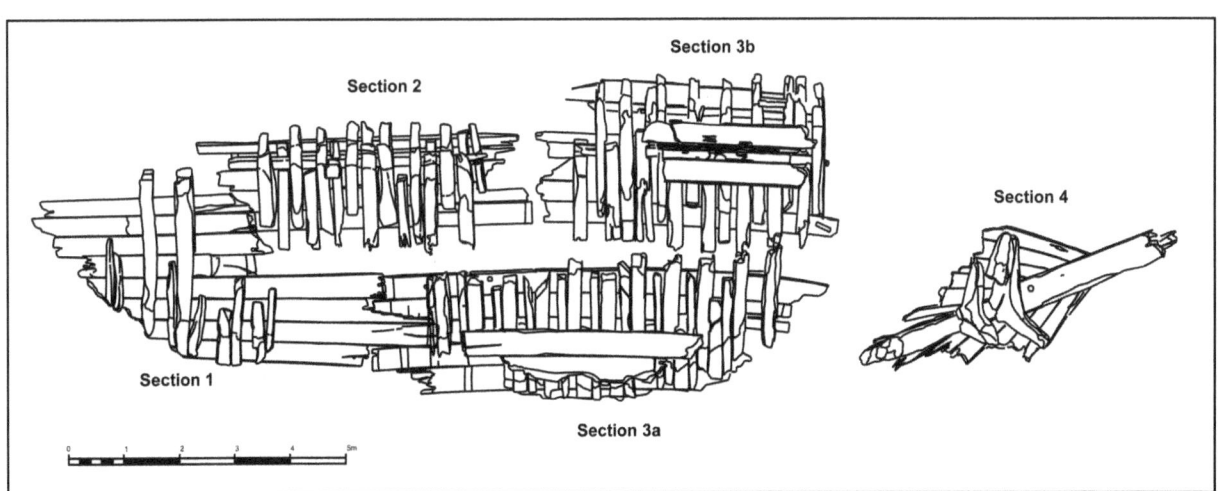

Figure 3-1:   *Overview plan of all wreck sections showing their approximate location and relation to each other (drawing J. Auer, based on data acquired by Wessex Archaeology)*

THE SHIP

but the beam shelf as well as a half-beam clamp and part of the waterway survives.

The aftermost preserved part of the ship's port side is made up of sections 1 and 2. The two sections were originally joined, but came apart during recovery. Section 1 measures 7.48 x 3.34 m and has eight strakes of outer planking preserved. On the inside the upper ends of three floor timbers remain in place. Two futtocks and a number of filling frames are also visible. The adjoining section 2 measures 6.11 x 2.29 m. It is composed of five strakes of outer planking, two of which form part of the wale, which continues on section 3b. The only preserved end of a deck beam is located on this section.

3.2 Site History: The Princes Channel Wreck in situ

What was excavated in 2004 was a heavily disturbed site, believed to have been cleared before the archaeological involvement in the project. Chapter 1 gives an indication of the disturbance associated with the pre-dredging work in the Princes Channel, but what did the site look like before that? What was preserved on the seabed prior to the first wreck removal attempts in June and July 2003?

A short history of the wreck site

Nothing is known about the events that led to the loss of the ship on the Girdler Sandbank in the Thames Estuary. Depending on the nature of those events, it is very possible that parts of the wreck were visible above the surface of the water, in which case it is probable that any accessible goods would have been salvaged right then.

The wreck might, however, have left traces in the contemporary or later historical record. On 2 May 1846 the *Whitstable Shipping and Mercantile Gazette* reported:

> A wreck apparently sunk many years ago has been discovered near the Girdler by the divers of this place. They have landed six guns, 4 and 6 pounders, a few bars of solder or block tin, a few bars of iron and two casks of red lead, the wood of which is nearly gone.

A short note in the *Journal of the British Archaeological Association* (1846, ii, 47–8) is more specific. At a meeting on the 9 December 1846, a tin ingot 'stamped with the royal mark', a knife, a leather shoe and a silk doublet 'of a kind in fashion in the time of Elizabeth' from the said wreck were presented. The note continues to state that the salvage operations were conducted under the orders of the Duke of Wellington, Lord Warden of the Cinque Ports at the time, and that tin ingots, iron, lead in pigs and 'red lead in cast iron casks covered with wood' had been recovered. Furthermore stone shot and iron guns are mentioned. Although the exact quantity of the recovered items remains unclear, the note mentions that about 2700 ingots were lifted, but that the divers were still at work. The wreck is said to be located on the Girdler Sand in four fathoms (7.3 m) at low water mark and had apparently been known for some time.

Could this be the Princes Channel Wreck? The stated depth and the location seem to match, as do the description of the salvaged cargo (see Volume II of this monograph) and the observation of the Elizabethan date. The presence of a rope around the lifting rings of the wrought iron gun when recovered from the site could also be evidence of an earlier salvage attempt (see Chapter 4.5, page 53).

Although there is no proof, it is highly probable, that the salvage of 1846 took place on the Princes Channel Wreck. Previous salvage would also explain the relatively small number of artefacts and cargo found on the site. However, such salvage would also have had an impact on the preserved timber structure and the distribution of cargo and contents of the ship.

One of the items recovered during clearance work in 2003 was the iron skid from one side of a beam trawl that presumably snagged on the wreck. This means the wreck was probably known to fishermen and was exposed enough to represent an obstruction on the seabed.

The wreck may also have been known to the PLA in earlier decades. A reference in 1967 mentions a diving inspection of a previously uncharted wreck that is 'fairly large … and rises about 15 ft (4.6 m) above the seabed' in the Princes Channel, where 'the changeable nature of the Girdler Sand presents special problems' (*PLA Monthly*, 1967).

The wreck site before clearance attempts

In June 2003, a Port of London Authority salvage craft made the first attempts to disperse the wreck site by dragging an anchor through the site and using a heavy-duty grapple. On finding that this had not been sufficient to clear the wreck, the UK Dredging hopper dredger *Cherry Sand* was ordered in for more extensive salvage operations. A cactus grab was used to recover the material that was later subject to remedial recording by Wessex Archaeology (see Chapter 1.4, page 3–4). When comparing sidescan data acquired in October 2003 with those obtained before the excavation in May 2004, the effect of the clearance attempts becomes visible (Figure 3-4). The aftermost part of the port side, composed of sections 1 and 2, was broken off and dragged across the seabed to a location approximately 20 to 30 m away from the main site. This was most probably a result of dragging an anchor and grapple through the wreck. The impact of the hopper dredger is harder to assess, although the recovered material offers some clues. The timbers recorded in August 2003 included planks with well preserved, angled hood-ends and a breasthook (Thomsen, 2003). These probably derive from the upper part of the bow section, where fresh breaks indicate

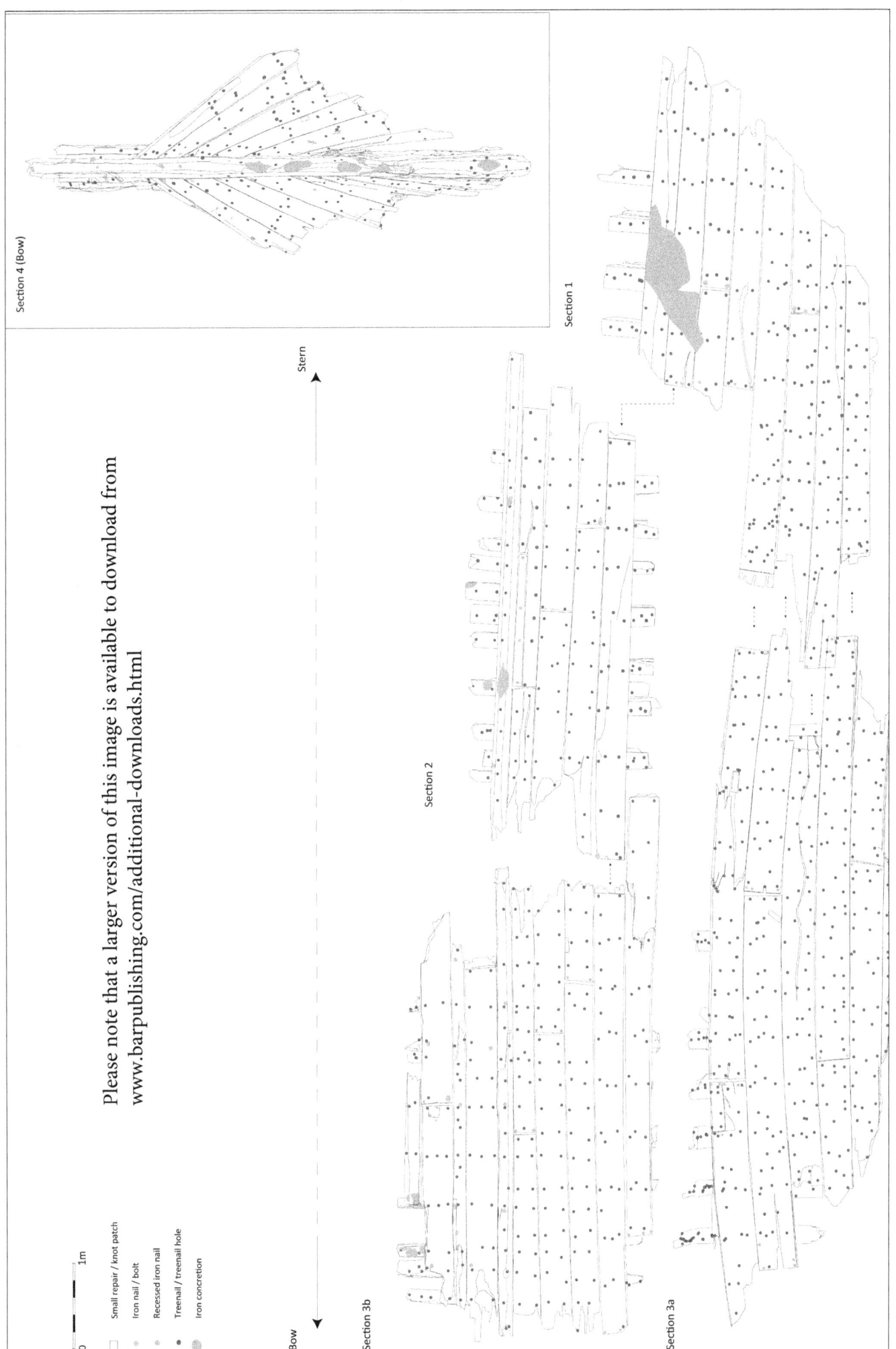

Figure 3-2: Plan of the wreck sections, outside view (J. Auer, based on the original recording results and illustrations by Wessex Archaeology); section 4 (inset) was originally located forward of sections 3a and 3b

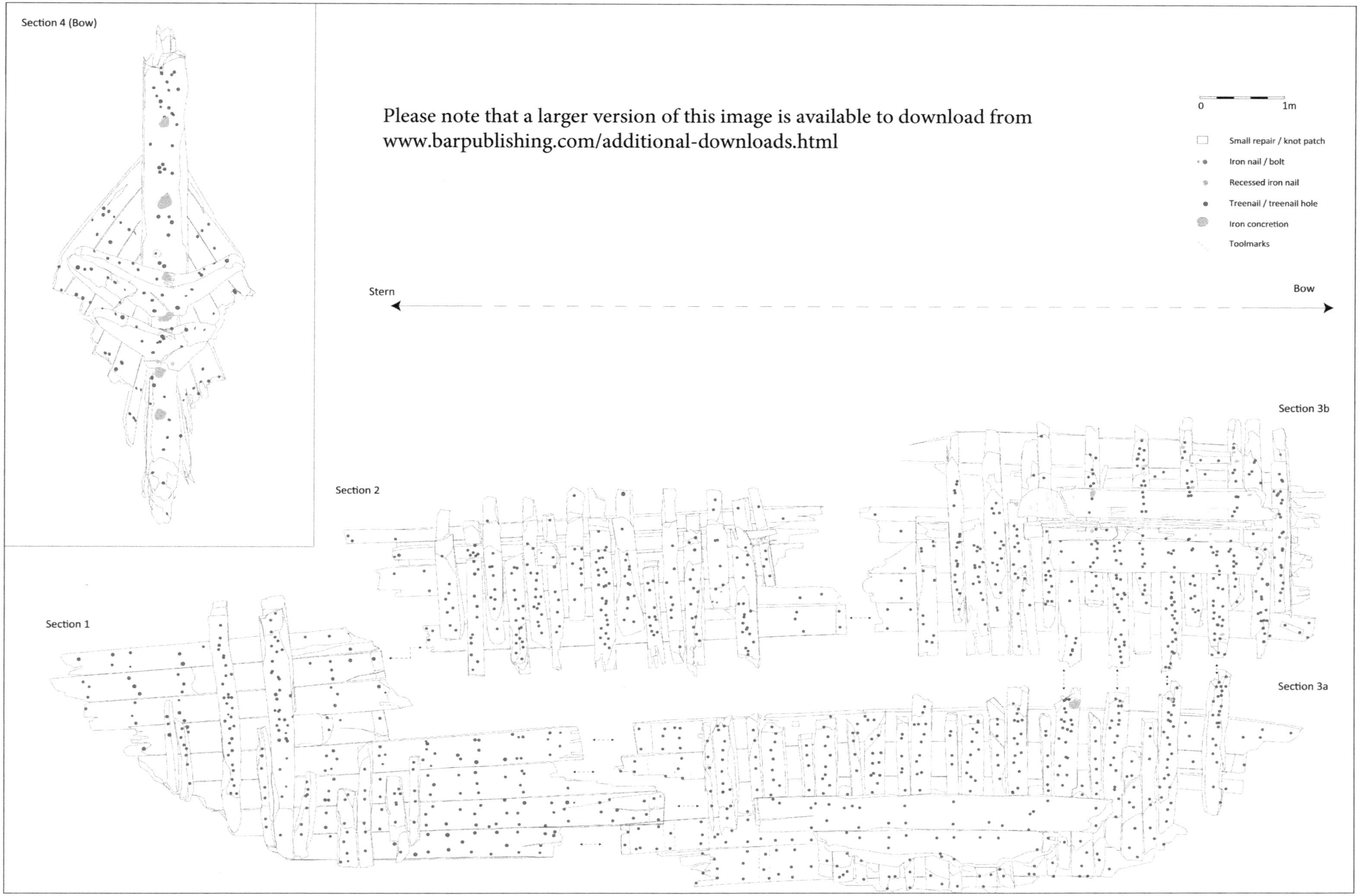

Figure 3-3: Plan of the wreck sections, inside view (J. Auer based on the original recording results and illustrations by Wessex Archaeology); section 4 (inset) was originally located forward of sections 3a and 3b

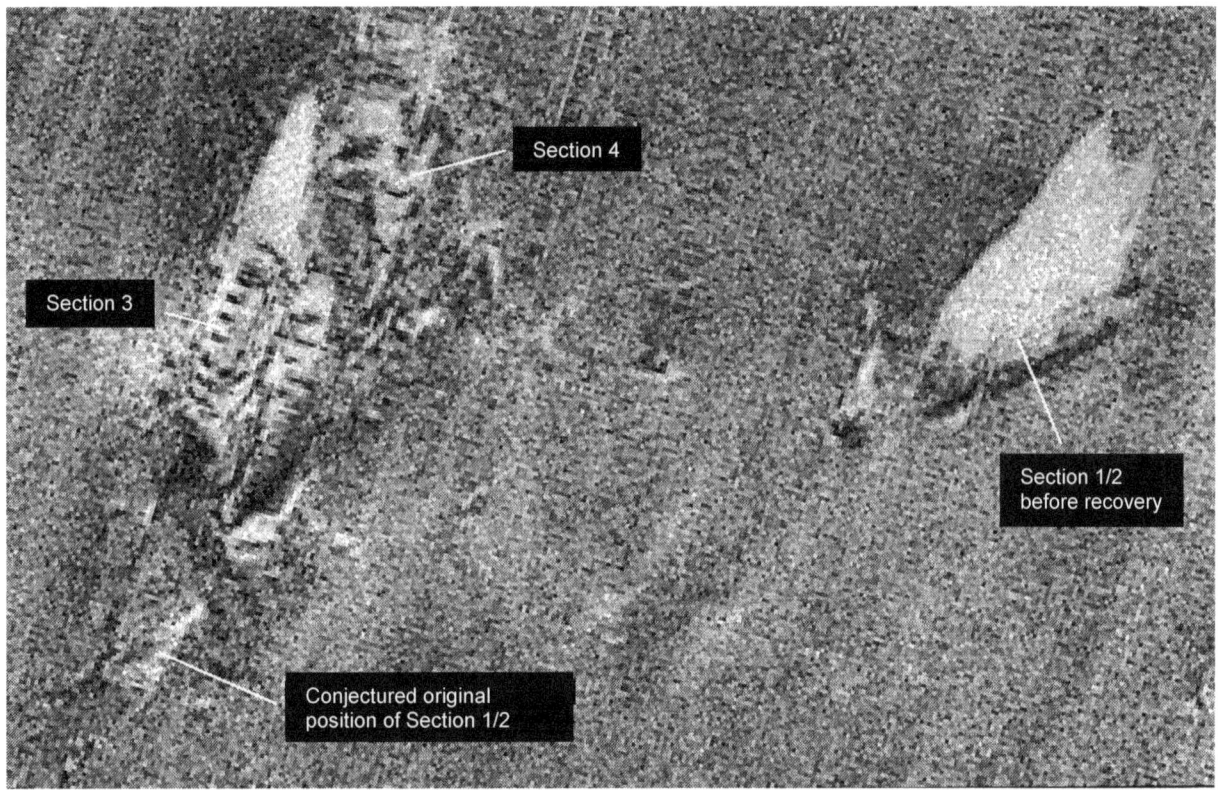

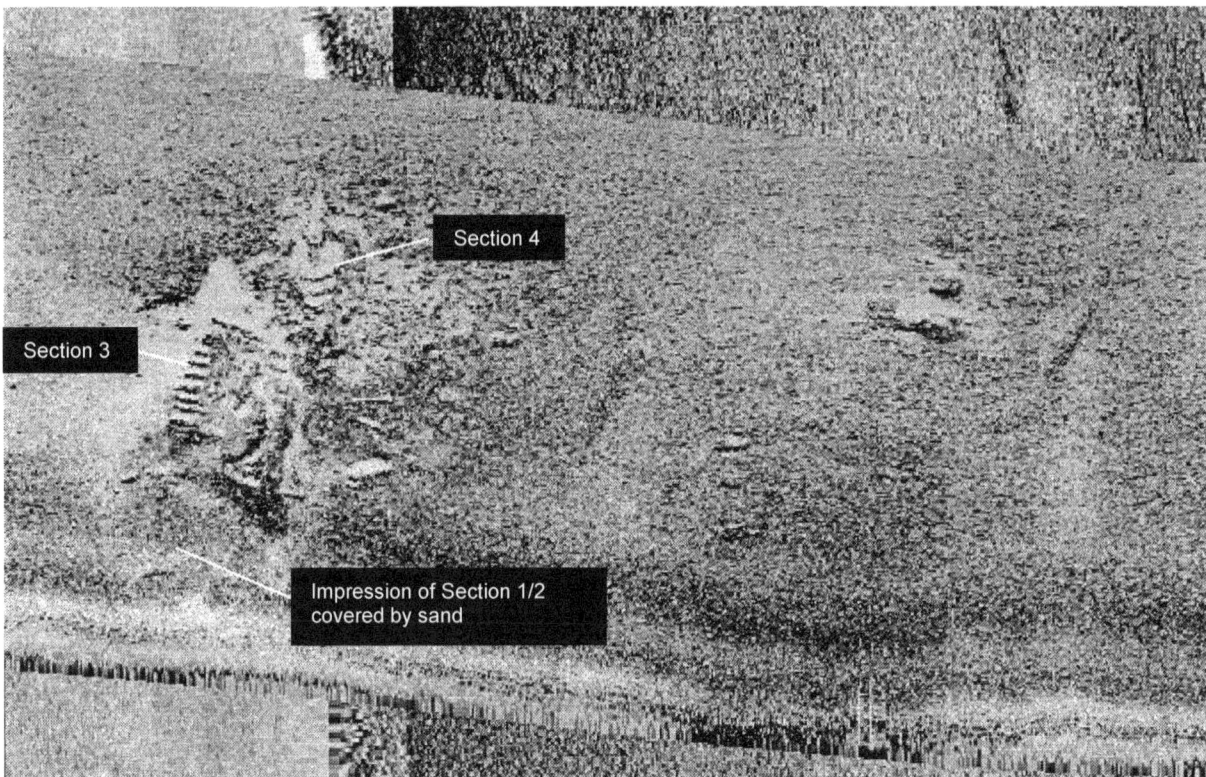

Figure 3-4: Sidescan images showing the wreck site in October 2003 (above) and May 2004 (below). The results of the dispersal attempts are clearly visible (K.J. Brandon, Wessex Archaeology)

recent damage. Further material, such as a v-shaped floor timber and a keel fragment were probably torn away from the lower part of the bow section, where recent damage is also apparent. It would therefore seem that the grabbing operations mainly impacted the bow section and its connection to the port side.

This would mean that the reconstructed wreck remains presented in the previous section are a good reflection of the level of preservation prior to the dispersal attempts. The area where most information was lost is the bow, which was probably better preserved and also linked to the lower part of the port side (section 3a).

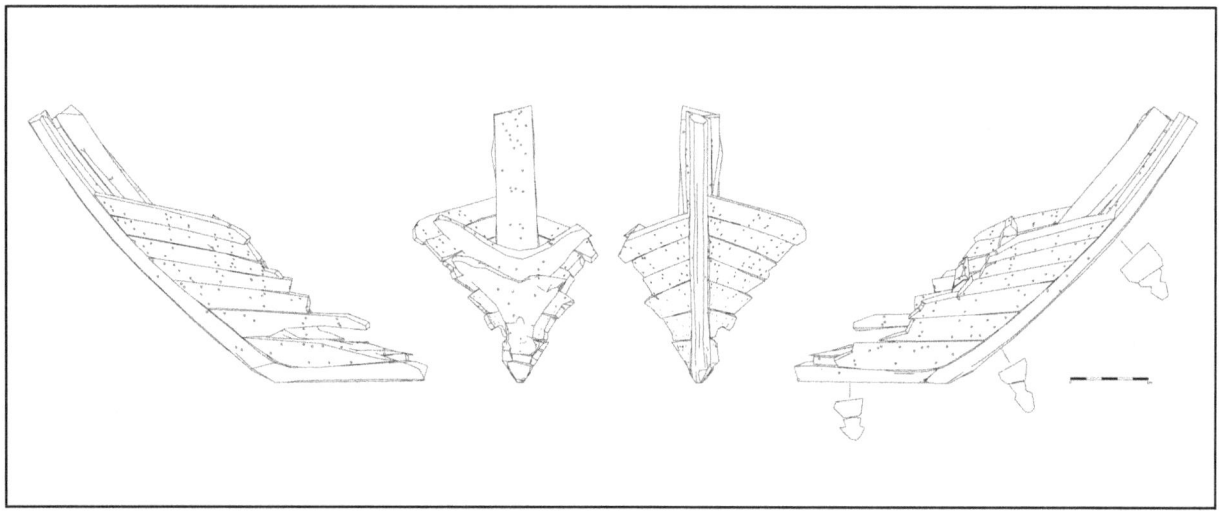

Figure 3-5: Different views of the bow (section 4) of the Princes Channel Wreck (M. Ditta, based on the original recording data by Wessex Archaeology). The scale is 1 metre

3.3 Construction

Bow Assembly

Despite the damage caused by clearance attempts in 2003 (see section 3.2 above), the bow of the Princes Channel Wreck is extremely well preserved (Figure 3-5). Relatively well preserved comparable contemporary bow assemblies are otherwise only known from the Basque whaler *San Juan* found in Red Bay (Grenier *et al.*, 2007) and from the *Mary Rose* (Marsden, 2009). The bow, also termed section 4, consists of stempost and keel, a large apron, outer planking and framing timbers, as well as a breasthook (Figure 3-7). This section focuses on the principal timbers in the bow, while framing and planking elements are discussed in the respective sections below.

Keel and stempost

Both keel and stempost are made of oak. As the bow section was left assembled and the ends were broken or eroded, it was not possible to observe how the timbers were shaped.

Neither keel nor stempost survives in its entirety. Of the keel only the forward 1.82 m are preserved. One end is joined to the stempost, while the other end is broken. The keel is heavily eroded. It measures 25 cm sided and 30 cm moulded. The starboard and port side rabbets 6 cm to 6.5 cm deep form the upper 9 cm of the moulded sides.

The keel is joined to the stempost with a flat vertical scarf joint at least 37 cm long (Figures 3-6 and 3-8). Three trenails of 3 cm diameter and three square shafted iron nails were driven horizontally through the joint to secure it.

A further four trenails were observed in the moulded face of the keel well below the rabbet. These were driven horizontally through the full width of the keel and were cut off flush with the outer face of the keel on both sides. Their function is unclear; it is currently assumed that they are associated with temporary fastenings during the construction process.

On the lower face of the keel, five vertically driven trenails and two heavily concreted iron bolts were observed. While the trenails secured the apron to the keel, the iron bolts were used to fasten the rising floor timbers in the bow. Due to the concreted state, it was difficult to obtain accurate measurements of the bolt diameter, but one bolt measured approximately 25 mm.

The preserved part of the stempost has a total length from tip to tip of 4.86 m. The upper part shows signs of a fresh break, presumably a result of the clearance attempts, while the lower part is joined to the keel. The post has an average sided dimension or breadth of 20 cm to 25 cm on the outside and 25 cm to 30 cm on the inside. The average moulded dimension is 30 cm. Stem rabbets with an average depth of 65 to 70 mm and an angle of 36° are located between 12 cm and 15 cm from the outside face of the post. In the lower part of the post, the hood-ends of a series of outer planks are fastened in the rabbet with a combination of trenails and square shafted iron spikes (Figure 3-5). Tool marks and cut trenails show that the rabbet angle was modified to reflect the ship's increase

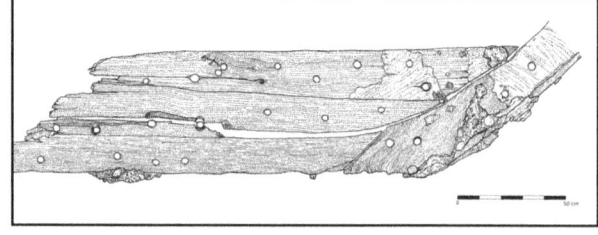

Figure 3-6: The joint between keel and stempost seen from the starboard side; the garboard strake is also depicted (R. Bangerter)

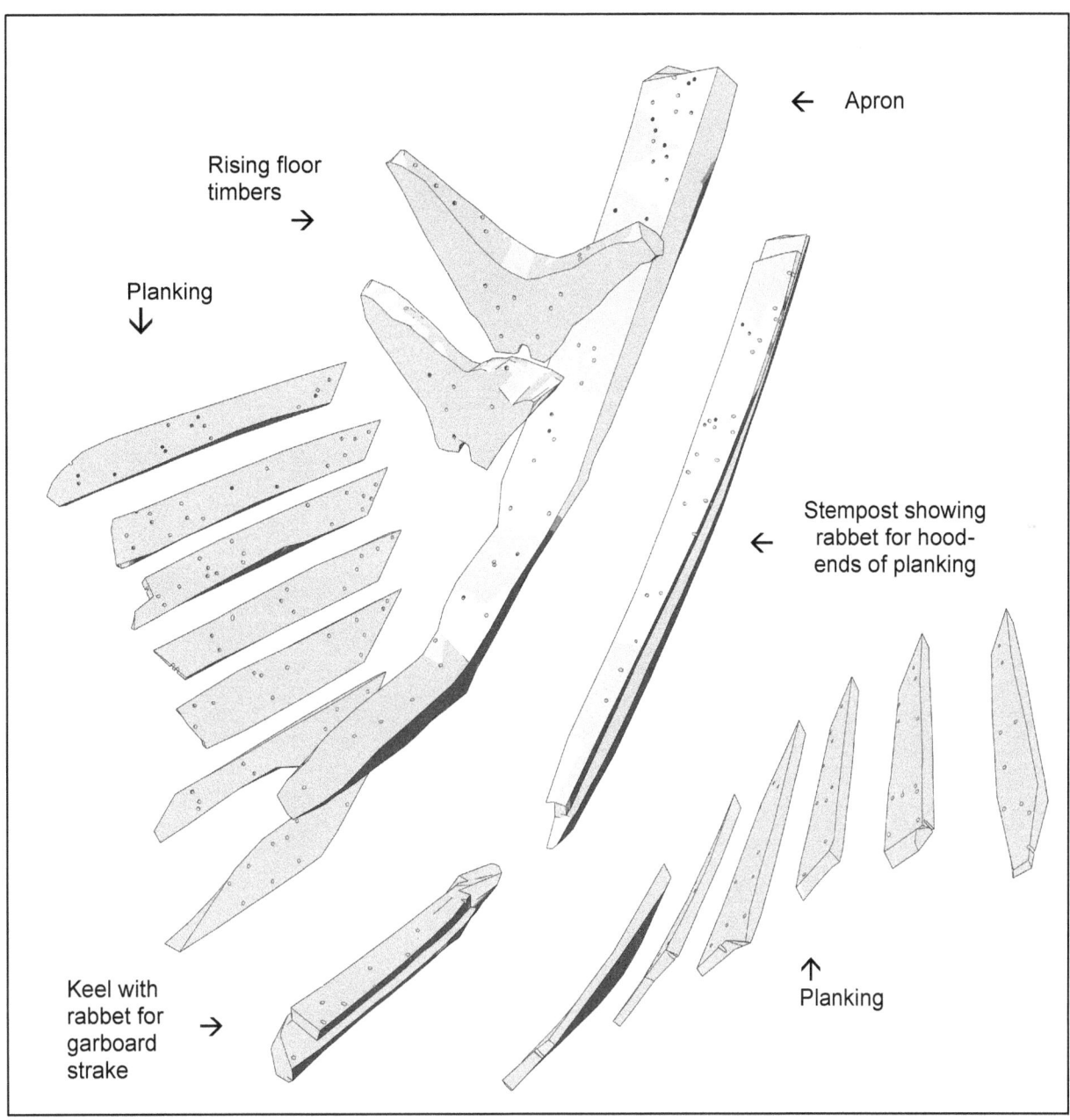

Figure 3-7: Exploded isometric view of the bow section showing the principal components (M. Ditta, based on data generated by M.H. Thomsen)

in beam caused by furring (Figure 3-9) (see Section 3.4. pages 41–3).

Just as in the keel, a number of trenails of about 32 mm diameter were observed running horizontally through the full width of the post. These are likely also to be associated with the construction process.

Trenails driven through the sided face of the post fastened the apron to it and rising floor timbers and breasthooks were held in place by iron bolts, of which only concretions remain.

In the eroded outer sided face of the stempost a number of 1 cm x 1 cm square iron holes were observed. Their distribution is irregular and it is unclear whether they were originally associated with some kind of sheathing or result from the construction process.

Apron

The joint between keel and stempost is reinforced by the apron, a massive knee, which is fastened to the inboard face of both elements. The preserved part of the apron consists of a single curved oak timber, which ends in a fresh break in the upper part and is eroded at the bottom end. The timber was box-halved with sapwood still evident at the inboard edges. The apron was originally thought to consist of two timbers (Auer and Firth, 2007; Auer *et al*., 2009), but the removal of a garboard strake during the field school in 2008 has shown it to be a single element. It measures 4.7 m from tip to tip. The sided dimension tapers from 55 cm in the upper part to approximately 36 cm above the keel. The depth or moulded dimension is 24 cm in the upper portion, but tapers to 20 cm above the keel (Figures 3-5 and 3-7).

Figure 3-8: The joint between keel and stempost seen from underneath (J. Auer)

Figure 3-9: Cut trenails and tool marks indicate a change of the rabbet angle in the stempost (J. Auer). The scale is 10 cm

To provide a smooth surface for the outer planking, the gap between apron and stempost was filled with small, wedge-shaped pieces of wood and caulking material (Figure 3-10).

Framing

The framing timbers are the main element of transverse reinforcement in a wooden ship. But in frame-based construction they also define the shape of the outer hull. Frames are built up of a number of individual components, which are either joined or laid beside each other. The lowest of these components, which span

Figure 3-10: The gap between apron and stempost (at the bottom) was filled with wedges to form a smooth surface for the outer planking (J. Auer). The scale is 5 cm

the bottom of the hull are the floor timbers. Joined to these are futtocks, which are named sequentially after their position in the hull, for example first futtock, second futtock, etc.

On the Princes Channel Wreck, the preserved hull sections include all three types of framing components.

The ends of ten floor timbers are preserved on sections 1 and 3a. In addition, two rising floor timbers were left in structural cohesion in the bow section. Although not a framing timber as such, a breasthook, deriving from the bow of the ship, will also be discussed here.

Joined to the floor timbers are the first futtocks. A total of 18 of these framing components are preserved on all four sections forming the port side. The first futtocks originally spanned a substantial part of the preserved height of the port side and broke when the hull sections came apart.

Second futtocks can only be found on the upper hull sections 2 and 3b. Of these 16 remain in place.

The space between floor timbers and first futtocks was filled with smaller 'filling frames' around the turn of the bilge. Of these, 14 are preserved on sections 1 and 3a (Figure 3-11).

The Princes Channel Wreck was subject to a major rebuild, which resulted in the ship becoming wider or beamier. This was achieved by doubling up the framing timbers from the turn of the bilge upwards. Timbers relating to this alteration are left on sections 1, 2 and 3b (Figure 3-12).

Floor timbers

Along the port side, only the outermost ends of floor timbers are preserved. However, in the bow section, two rising floor timbers remain connected (Figure 3-11).

Figure 3-11: Inside view of the hull sections with the different framing elements marked (J. Auer, based on the original recording results and illustrations by Wessex Archaeology). Section 4 (inset) was originally located forward of sections 3a and 3b

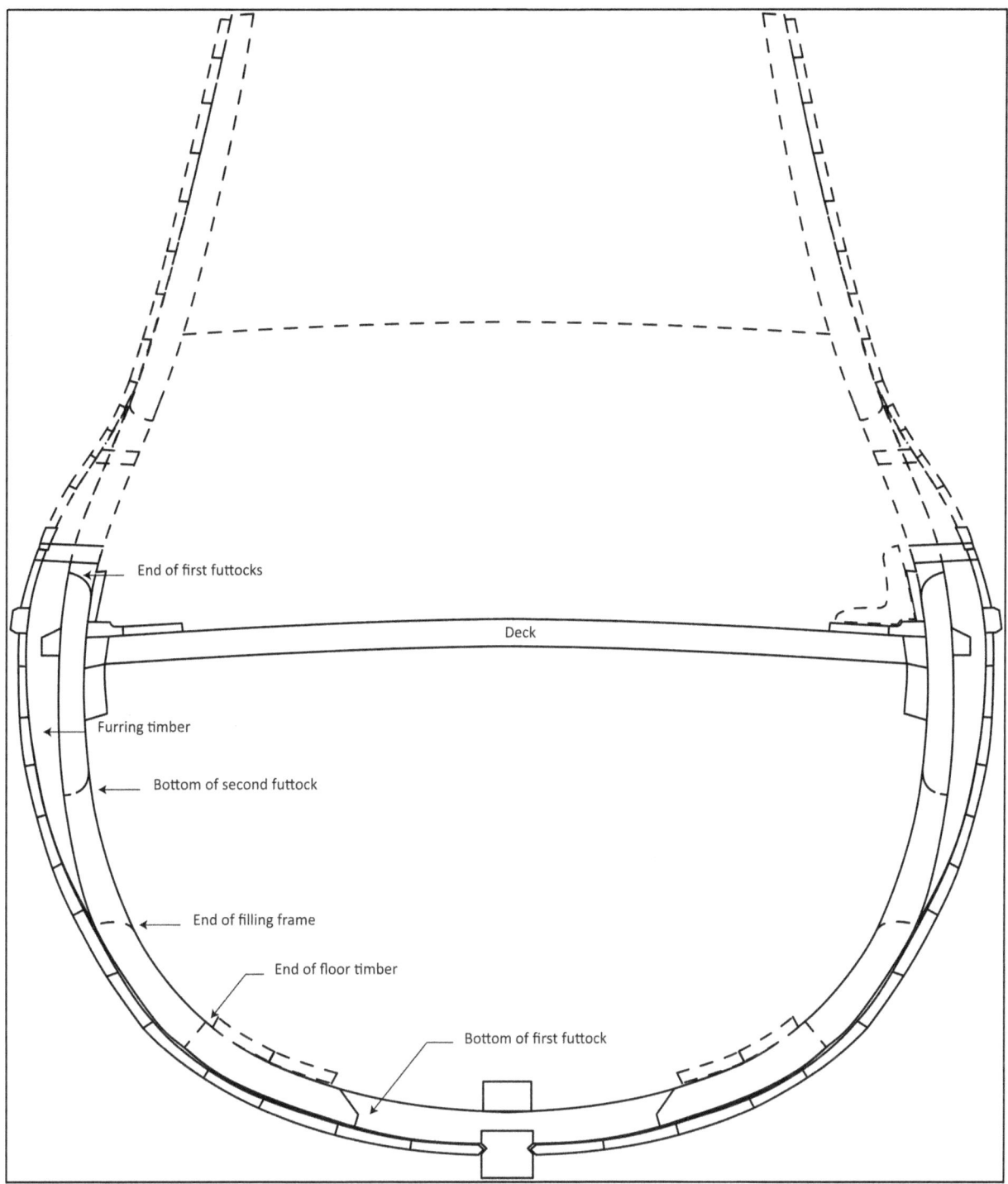

Figure 3-12: Reconstructed midships section showing the layout of framing timber (M. Ditta)

Like the remainder of the framing components, all floor timbers are made of oak. They were shaped with a saw and axe and carefully dubbed with an adze where it was deemed necessary. However, in many places, sapwood or even bark edge was left in situ. The patterning of saw marks suggests the use of a pit saw. The ends were either sawn off or cut with an axe, leaving marks up to 11 cm wide (Goodburn, 2004). The two rising floor timbers in the bow are natural crotches, which were shaped with saw and axe. They have a considerable amount of sapwood left on the forward face.

Because of the state of preservation, it is unclear how long the floor timbers were and whether they crossed the keel. The only two fully preserved floors are the two crotches in the bow (Figure 3-13). These were v-shaped and placed on the apron at increasing angles. They have semi-circular grooves or channels in their upper face and roughly worked central limber holes at the bottom.

Moulded dimensions vary between 19 cm and 22 cm, with the crotches in the bow being up to 50 cm high due to their angle and shape. The floor timbers are sided to between 18 cm and 25 cm.

Figure 3-13: Inside view of the bow section with the two rising floor timbers in place (J. Auer)

Figure 3-15: Floor timber and first futtock on section 3a connected with a double dovetail joint (J. Auer)

Figure 3-14: Broken dovetail joint in a first futtock on section 3a. The joint was secured with a trenail (J. Auer)

Figure 3-16: Possible breasthook, which would have fitted over the apron on section 4 (C.H.R. Thomsen)

The spacing between the floor timbers is a fairly regular 60 cm between centres throughout the length of the port side and between the two crotches in the bow.

Floor timbers and first futtocks are laid side by side, with the futtocks positioned aft of the floors throughout the preserved part of the port side. Both timbers overlap by at least 1 m. The exact length of the overlap could not be determined, as the lower ends of floor timbers and futtocks are eroded. With the exception of the bow, where futtocks are not attached to the crotches, all floor timbers are joined to first futtocks with double dovetail joints, in which mortise and tenon are located both on floor timber and futtock. The shape of these joints is irregular, some are trapezoidal, while others are almost rectangular. The mortises are up to 5 cm deep and vary in length between just under 20 cm to more than 30 cm.

The total length of the joints can be up to 60 cm. All visible joints were secured with either a single 3-cm trenail driven vertically through the centre of the joint or two trenails, one through each mortise-tenon connection (Figure 3-14 and 3-15). The ends were cut flush with the surface of the timber. In one case, a rectangular wedge was observed in a trenail.

Breasthook

Among the timber recovered during the first clearance attempts by the Port of London Authority, two parts of what was interpreted as a breasthook were found (Thomsen, 2003). As the timber was disposed of after recording, the following description is based on the notes taken during remedial recording. The timber was roughly shaped from a large oak branch and was almost circular in section. It had a large central rebate 60 cm long and 15 cm deep. The overall length was 1.84 m and moulded and sided dimension were approximately 30 cm. Both ends were cut at an angle. Several trenails of 3 cm diameter were observed in the ends and the central rebate. The breasthook would have fitted over the apron above the rising floor timbers in the bow. It was fastened to the apron and the outer planking with trenails (Figure 3-16).

First Futtocks

Of the 18 first futtocks which are preserved, 16 broke when the port side of the Princes Channel Wreck came apart into four separate sections (Figure 3-11). Just like the floor timbers, all first futtocks are made of oak and were shaped with saw and axe. They span from below the joint with floor timbers up to a level just above the lowest deck in the vessel. The maximum preserved

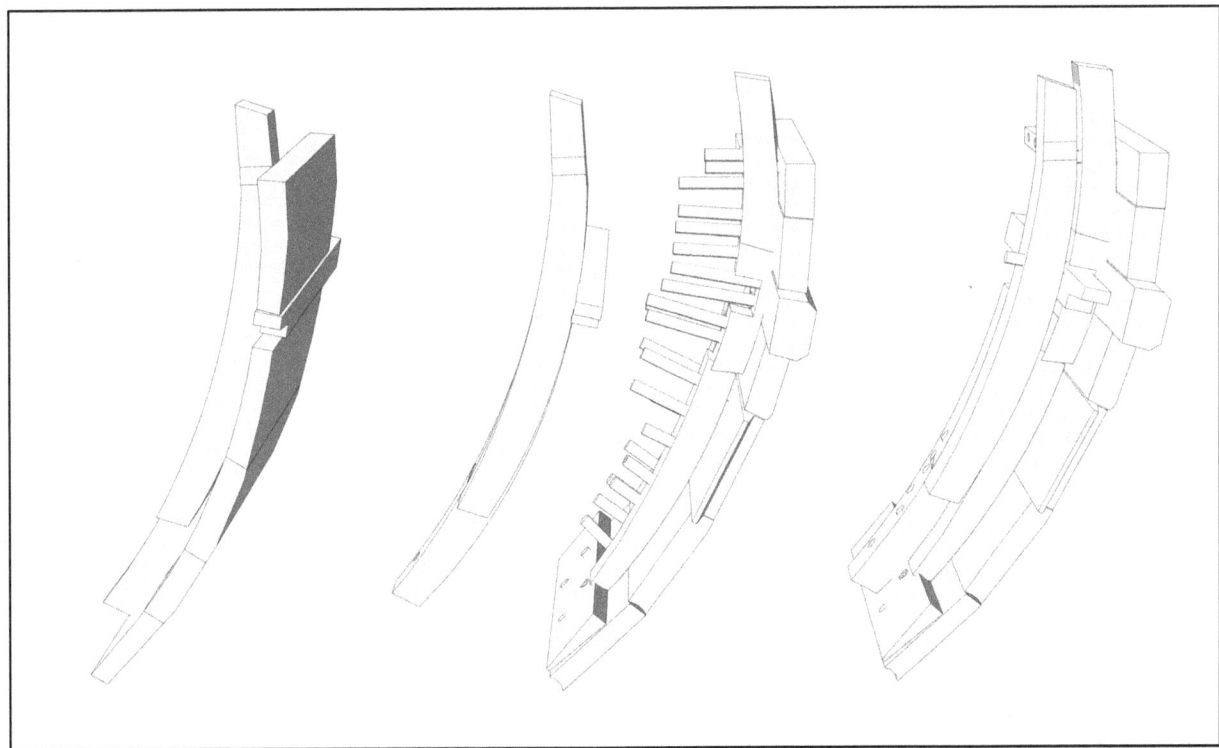

Figure 3-17: *Diagram showing how furring timbers were applied to the outside of the existing frames on the Princes Channel wreck (drawing J. Auer)*

First Futtocks

Of the 18 first futtocks which are preserved, 16 broke when the port side of the Princes Channel Wreck came apart into four separate sections (Figure 3-11). Just like the floor timbers, all first futtocks are made of oak and were converted with saw and axe. They span from below the joint with floor timbers up to a level just above the lowest deck in the vessel. The maximum preserved length is 3.85 m, but as the lower ends are eroded, the original length cannot be determined. The futtock heads are generally either sawn off or cut square with an axe. Moulded dimensions vary between 20 cm and 22 cm, and the average width or sided dimension is 25 cm. In one case, the broken upper end of a first futtock is missing, but a 1-m long wedge-shaped filling piece still remains in place. This must have been set into the outer sided face of the futtock, probably to replace a defective area of wood.

Second Futtocks

Sixteen second futtocks are left on the two uppermost hull sections 2 and 3b (Figure 3-11). All are made from oak and were converted in the same way as the other framing components. They are located between first futtocks with their heels extending to a level of approximately 1 m below the level of the lowest deck. The upper ends are eroded. The heels are sawn off square or at an angle or cut with an axe. The scantlings of the second futtocks are more irregular than those of floor timbers or first futtocks. While the moulded dimension is 18 cm on average, sided dimensions range from 16 cm to 30 cm. Some timbers were box-quartered, while others were box-halved or boxed. The second futtocks are not attached to first futtocks, although in one case a second futtock was rebated to fit around the head of a first futtock. Some empty fore-and-aft holes through the futtocks might be related to hoisting or clamping them into place during the construction process (Goodburn, 2004).

Filling timbers

The upper ends of 14 so-called filling frames or filling timbers survive on the lower sections 1 and 3a. These timbers do not form part of the framing assemblies, but were inserted between the joined pairs of floor timbers and first futtocks to fill the space and to form a continuous band of timber around the turn of the bilge (Figure 3-11). Filling timbers are also of oak and were converted with saw, axe and adze. Most of them are box-quartered. Their lower ends are eroded and the heads are located at a level of approximately two strakes above the wrongheads. The scantlings of the filling timbers are governed by the space between frame pairs. The average moulded dimension is 20 cm and the average siding is 14 cm. The filling timbers are not attached to other framing components.

Marks on framing timbers

The inner sided face of floor timbers, futtocks and filling timbers was in some instances marked with a series of roughly hacked lines. This was observed on section 3a and section 3b. These lines were most probably cut with an axe and seem to indicate the location of ceiling planks, which are now missing.

The Ship

Figure 3-18: First futtock on section 1 with furring timber attached. The lower end of the furring timber would have rested on the triangular plank (photo J. Auer)

Figure 3-19: Wedges and filling timbers are used to achieve the desired moulded dimension on section 3b (photo J. Auer)

Furring

One of the most striking aspects of the construction of the Princes Channel Wreck is the doubling of framing timbers from the turn of the bilge upwards. The investigators did not fully understand the purpose of this doubled framing until the explanation of the term 'furring' was found in Sir Henry Mainwaring's *Seaman's Dictionary*:

> The other [kind of furring], which is more eminent and more properly furring, is to rip off the first planks and to put other timbers upon the first, and so to put on the planks upon these timbers. The occasion of it is to make a ship bear a better sail, for when a ship is too narrow and her bearing either not laid out enough or too low, then they must make her broader and lay her bearing higher. They commonly fur some two or three strakes under water and as much above, according as the ship requires, more or less. I think in all the world there are not so many ships furred as are in England, and it is pity that there is no order taken either for the punishing of those who build such ships or the preventing of it, for it is an infinite loss to the owners and an utter spoiling and disgrace to all ships that are so handled (Perrin and Manwaring, 1922, 153).

The Princes Channel Wreck was furred by applying the furring timbers from a level below the waterline, six strakes below the lowest deck and continuing past the limit of preservation of the port side. Compared to the common extent of furring, quoted by Mainwaring above – 'two or three strakes underwater and as much above' – the hull shape of the Princes Channel Wreck was heavily altered (Figure 3-17).

The heels of the lowest furring timbers, which are applied to the first futtocks, have a moulded dimension of only 5 cm and rest on a 41-cm wide plank with triangular section. The thickness of this plank tapers from 5 cm at the top to 5 mm at the bottom. It fills the gap between the heel of the outer framing timbers and the surface of the first futtocks and thus provides a smooth surface for the application of outer planks (Figure 3-18). Above the triangular plank, all first and second futtocks are doubled or furred with furring timbers.

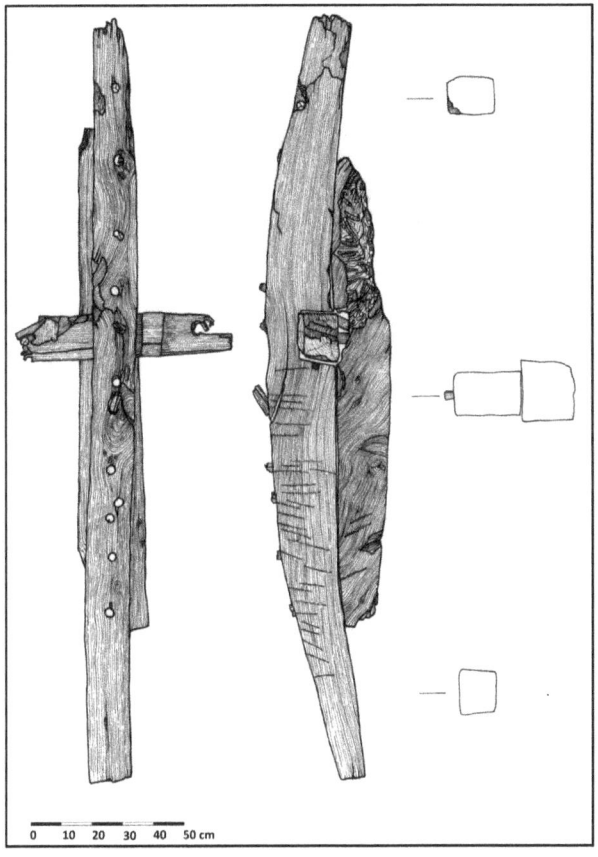

Figure 3-20: Drawing of a loose second futtock, which has a furring timber attached. The furring timber is recessed to fit around the former wale (R. Bangerter)

The furring timbers are of oak and were converted in a similar way to the original framing timbers. Where timbers of the right size were not available, smaller, sawn filling pieces and wedges were used to achieve the desired moulded dimension. This was especially the case with furring timbers applied to the heads of first futtocks at the level of the lowest deck (Figure 3-19).

Some of the furring timbers were extremely sappy and waney and at least two had substantial heart rot before being used. As the furring timbers were hidden from view by outer planking and ceiling, this might be an indication of cost saving, where it is invisible (Goodburn, 2004).

While the siding of furring timbers is guided by the underlying futtocks, the moulded dimension is up to 30 cm in the widest part at the level of the lowest deck. This would have added a good 60 cm to the original beam of the vessel.

The furring timbers were fastened to the futtocks with wooden trenails of 30 mm diameter.

At the height of lowest deck, a longitudinal oak timber was left trenailed to the original futtocks. The timber consists of several components, which are scarfed to each other. It is almost square in section and measures 16 cm x 6 cm. All furring timbers are rebated to fit

Figure 3-21: Break in a first futtock on section 3a. The integrity of the timber was compromised by the number of trenails driven through it. Trenails which were cut flush with the frame (marked with a drawing pin in the picture) are associated with the original construction (J. Auer)

around this timber, indicating that it was left in place during the furring process. Based on its location and dimensions, the timber could be part of the original wale, which was left in place as a ribband during the furring process. It is also possible that it was meant to provide additional longitudinal strength (Figure 3-20).

Framing pattern: Some thoughts

A closer look at the pattern of framing in the Princes Channel Wreck shows a number of oddities. While the framing in the lower part of the hull is very dense and regular, with floor timbers and first futtocks securely joined and forming a continuous band of timber together with the filling frames, the upper part of the hull gives a different impression. The second futtocks are not joined to first futtocks and there are gaps between these timbers. In addition there are substantial gaps of more than one metre long between the heads of filling frames and the heels of second futtocks. These are only bridged by first futtocks, which are spaced approximately 60 cm apart in this area. This means that two sections of relatively dense framing are linked by a one-metre high section with widely spaced frames, thus introducing a weak point in the hull structure (Figure 3-22). The addition of furring timbers in this weaker section might have increased this problem by compromising the strength of the existing futtocks as a result of the addition of further trenails. It is also along this weaker line, that the recovered hull pieces came apart either on the seabed or during lifting (Figure 3-21).

Planking

The outer planking of a ship is applied to the outside face of the frames and forms a waterproof skin. It consists of

The Ship

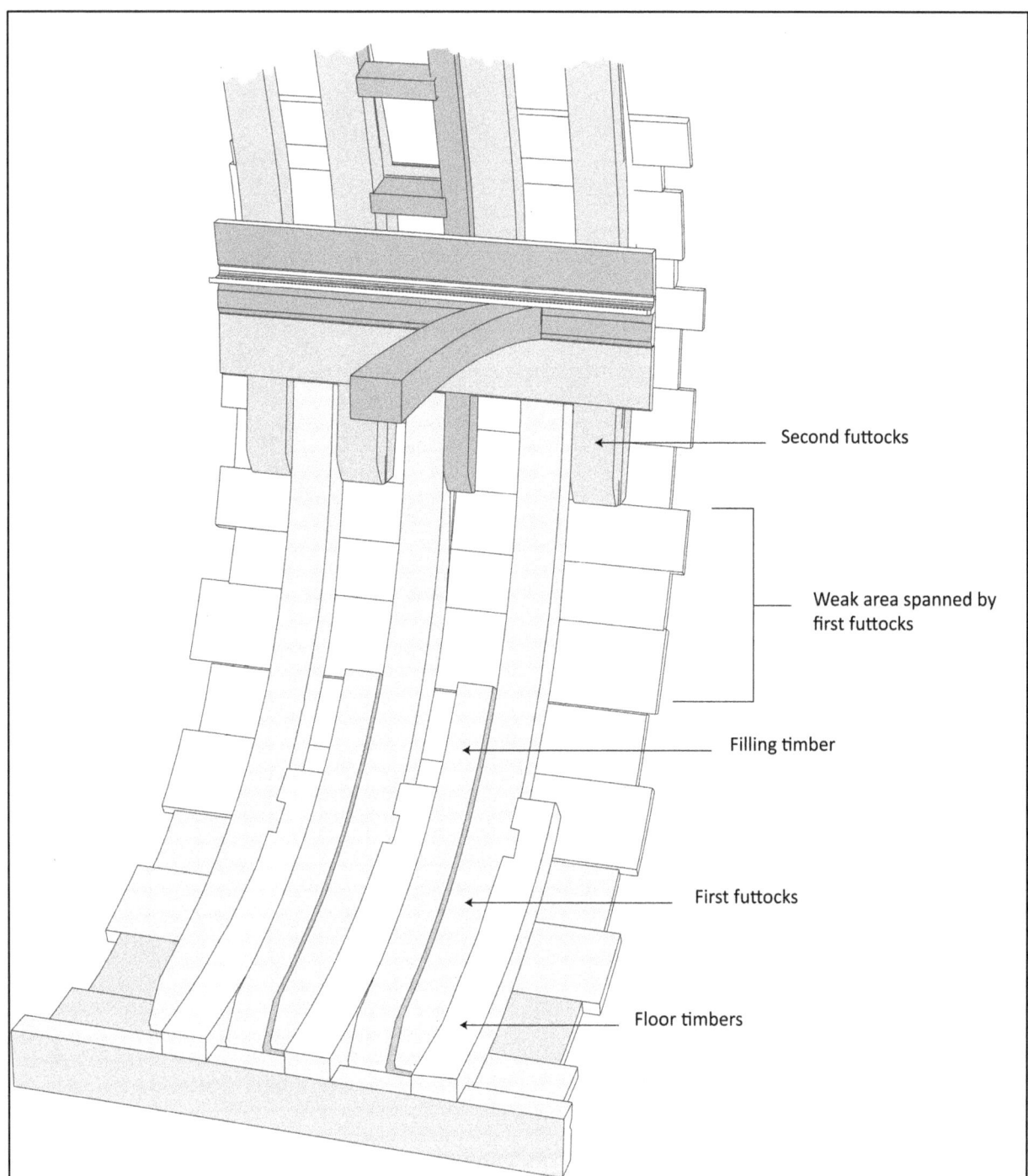

Figure 3-22: Diagram of the frame layout showing the weak area between the floor and bilge and the level of the deck (M. Ditta)

several strakes of planks, which run from bow to stern. Each strake is in turn made up of several individual planks. At different heights in the hull, assemblages of stronger or thicker planks, so-called wales, provide additional longitudinal strength. Inside the hull, the ceiling or inner planking completes the structure and prevents parts of the cargo from falling in between the frames.

On the four hull sections which represent the port side of the Princes Channel Wreck, the remains of 17 strakes of outer planking are preserved. On the bow section, the ends of six eroded outer planks remain connected on the starboard side and seven planks are visible on the port side. Based on the reconstruction of the ship (see Chapters 5 and 6), it is assumed that the last preserved plank on section 3a originally joined up with the third plank from the bottom on section 4. This would mean that the remains of a total of 19 strakes are preserved on the port side, while only the ends of six eroded outer planks are left on the starboard side. The 19 strakes on the port side are made up of 42 outer planks or plank fragments. On the height of the lowest continuous deck, three strakes of planking (strakes 14–16) form a wale (Figure 3-23).

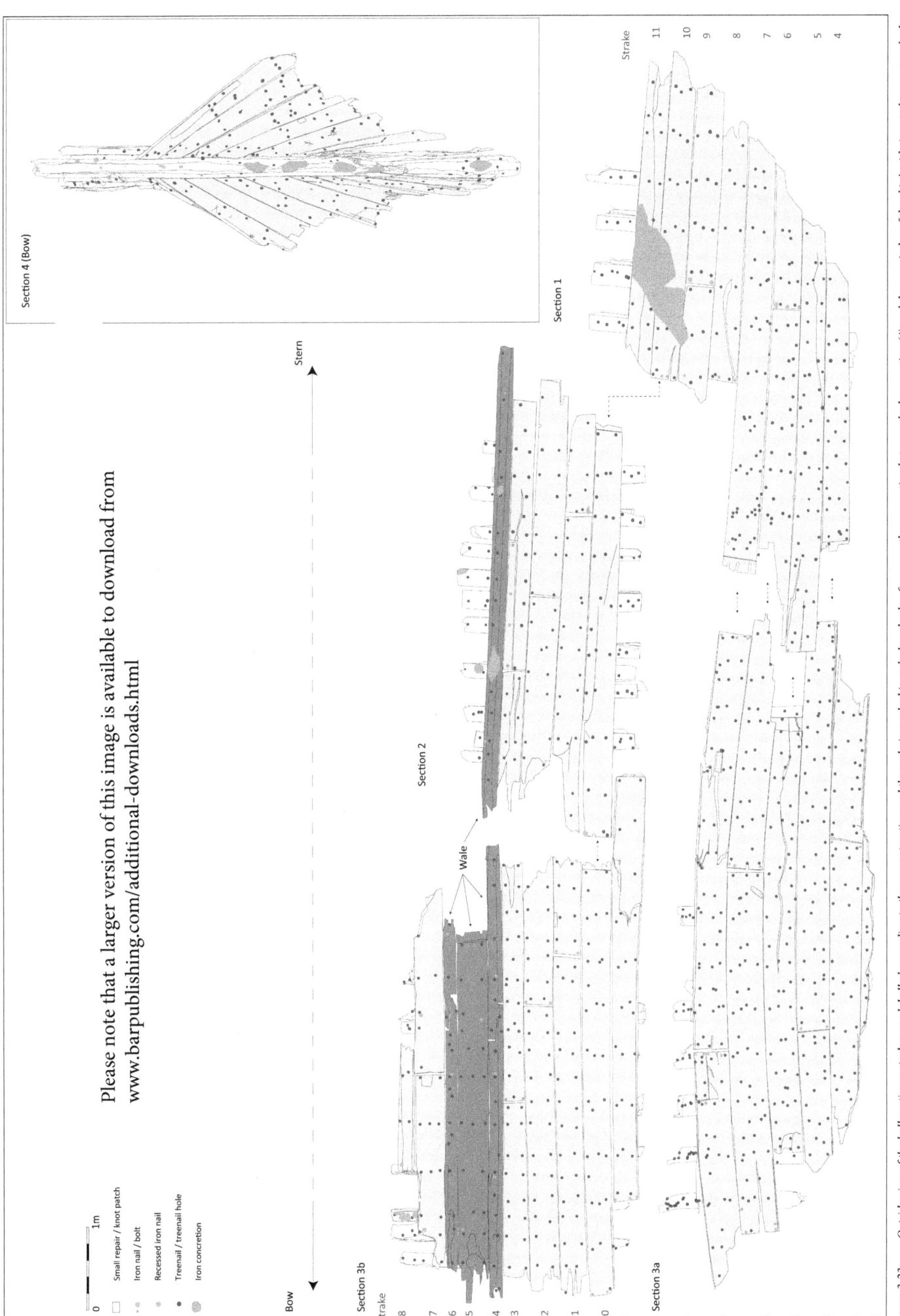

Figure 3-23: Outside view of the hull sections: strakes are labelled according to the reconstruction and the wale is marked in a darker shade of grey; as the connection between the bow section (4) and the remainder of the ship's side is not clear, outer planks are not labelled (J. Auer based on the original recording results and illustrations by Wessex Archaeology)

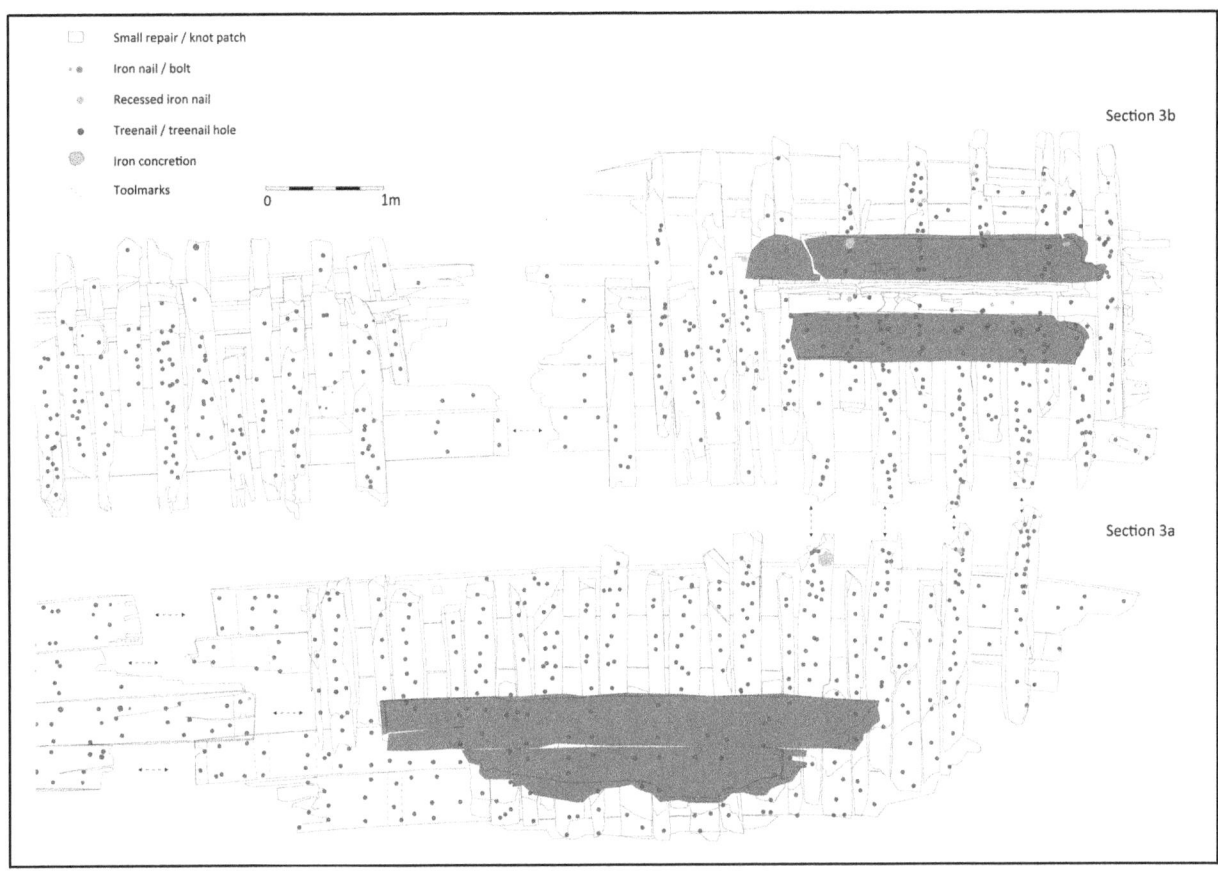

Figure 3-24: Inside view of the hull sections with the ceiling planks marked in grey (J. Auer based on the original recording results and illustrations by Wessex Archaeology)

On the inside of the hull, the fragments of four ceiling planks remain in place. Two of these are associated with the construction of the deck. Originally, the whole inside hull was covered by ceiling, but a number of planks were lost during clearance attempts and during the recovery (Figure 3-24).

Outer Planking

The outer hull planking was cut from moderately large and moderately straight oak trees of medium growth rate (Goodburn, 2004). The planks were tangentially faced, presumably with the help of a pit-saw, and then carefully dubbed with an adze. There is generally no sapwood left on the hull planks which are up to 48 cm wide. This suggests the use of oak logs of around 65 cm at their mid length (Goodburn, 2004). The closeness of plank seams, as well as the occasional use of Dutchmen over natural fissures in the timber, suggests that the planking used was seasoned or at least half seasoned (Goodburn, 2004).

Plank length varies from 4.2 m to 5.27 m with the majority of the planks being around 5 m long. The average plank thickness is 7 cm. The width of the outer planks varies throughout the port side and planks taper slightly towards bow and stern. Generally the outer planking can be divided into two groups: planks below the line of furring with a maximum width of between 43 cm and 48 cm and planks above the line of furring which have a maximum width of 36 cm to 38 cm. The fore-and-aft taper is particularly noticeable in the lower strakes, which are preserved across sections 3a and 1. The width of planks in strake 4 tapers from 38 cm near the bow to 43 cm and back to 30 cm towards the stern on section 1. In strake 7, planks taper from 45 cm near the bow on piece 3a to 36 cm towards the stern on section 1.

Remarkable is the joining of strake planks in vertical scarf joints. This is an unusual phenomenon in carvel shipbuilding. All the outer planks in the Princes Channel Wreck are connected with vertical scarf joints 15 cm to 22 cm long and 4 cm to 5 cm deep. The orientation of scarfs varies throughout the hull. The joints are secured with trenails, as well as up to four iron nails. They are staggered and spaced at least 2 m apart in neighbouring strakes in order to avoid weaknesses in the hull structure (Figure 3-25 and 3-26).

The waterproofing of the outer hull planks in the Princes Channel Wreck is another interesting deviation from common carvel building techniques. The hull was not caulked, a process which involves driving waterproofing material into plank seams, but instead furnished with a type of inlaid waterproofing. V-shaped or u-shaped recesses up to 1 cm deep, filled with three strands of tarred animal hair, had been carved into the lower edges of all outer hull planks (Figures 3-27 and 3-28). As a result, plank seams are extremely narrow. As small bumps in the seam edge are replicated from one plank to another, it can be assumed that a two stage-hanging process was used: The spiled planks were offered up,

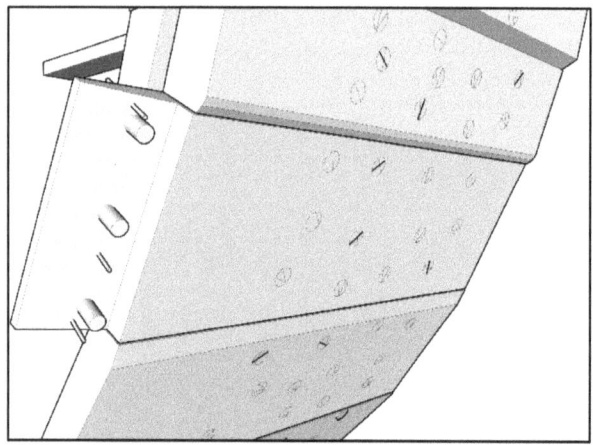

Figure 3-25: Isometric drawing of scarf joint between outer planks (J. Auer)

Figure 3-26: Vertical scarf joint between two outer planks on section 3a (J. Auer)

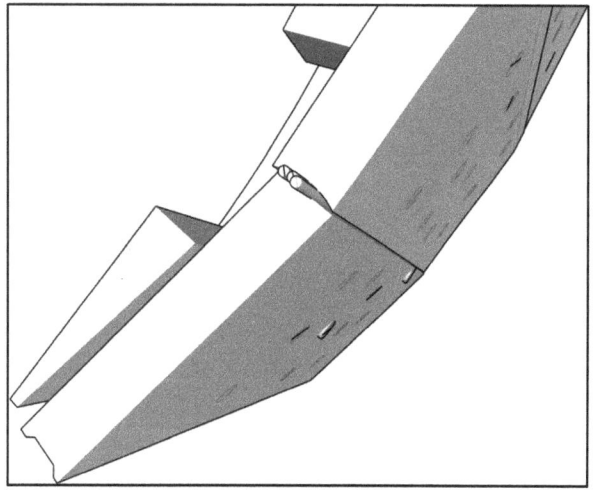

Figure 3-27: Illustration of the inlaid waterproofing between outer planks (drawing J. Auer)

clamped tight and then close scribed to their neighbours. They were then removed, trimmed and furnished with a waterproofing groove before final hanging (Goodburn, 2004).

Caulking in the traditional sense was only observed around the wales, which must have been in place prior to the surrounding planking and in connection with repairs.

As the wales were left in place, the waterproofing material used for caulking could not be analysed. Visible

Figure 3-28: Waterproofing recess on the lower edge of a garboard plank (photo J. Auer)

Figure 3-29: The wale arrangement on the outside of section 3b (photo J. Auer)

remains in larger gaps do, however, suggest the use of moss.

On the inside face of some outer planks on section 3a, series of roughly hacked or cut marks were observed. These seem to indicate the position of filling timbers. The position of other framing components was not marked out on the outer planking.

Wale

The preserved main wale assembly is located at the level of the lowest continuous deck and consists of strakes 14, 15 and 16 (Figure 3-23). A central strake 41 cm wide and 8.5 cm thick is framed by two narrower and thicker strakes above and below. The lower strake has a chamfered lower edge and is 18 cm wide and 16 cm thick. The upper strake has a width of 14 cm and a thickness of 15 cm (Figure 3-29). The wale planks are of oak and were shaped in the same way as the outer hull planking.

While planks in the central strake were joined in the same way as other outer hull planks, planks in the thicker wale strakes were connected with flat horizontal scarf joints up to 47 cm long. The joints are secured by a combination of vertically driven trenails and iron nails as well as trenails, which fasten the wale strakes to the underlying framing. A number of redundant trenails

Figure 3-30: Knot patch in one of the loose planks seen from the inside (left) and outside (right); small wedged trenail heads are visible around the patch (J. Auer)

Figure 3-31: The position of a knot patch marked on one of the outer planks (J. Auer)

observed in the wale might be associated with nogging shores used during the construction process (Goodburn, 2004).

The seams between the individual components of the wale and the outer planking below and above seem to have been caulked, presumably with moss.

Ceiling

After recovery the remains of four ceiling planks were left connected on the inside of section 3a and 3b. Further planks were observed during the excavation, but were lost during recovery.

Two of the preserved ceiling planks are adjacent to the deck construction on section 3b and will be described in the related chapter. The other two are located near the keel at the lower edge of section 3a. Ceiling planks are also of oak and were shaped in the same way as the outer hull planks. They have a width of up to 45 cm and are approximately 6 cm thick. Although the ends are eroded, it would seem that ceiling planks were joined with vertical scarf joints, similar to those found between outer planks.

Repairs

There are numerous signs of repairs to the outer planking on all preserved hull sections. While some repairs were probably preventive measures, carried out during the construction process, others are associated with the maintenance of the vessel in use. Generally, the frequency of all types of repairs seems to be higher in the lower part of the vessel, below the line of furring.

A typical type of repair of the first category is the treatment of knots in the planks. Larger knots were removed by cutting out a rectangular area of wood around the knot and filling it with a small wooden patch. Such knot patches sometimes penetrate the full thickness of a plank and are nailed on with iron nails, but in the majority of cases only half the thickness of a plank was removed. The resulting recess was lined with waterproofing material and then carefully filled with a wooden patch, which was secured by small wedged trenails. Such patches were applied both to the inside and outside face of hull planks and are only visible from one side (Figure 3-30). In some cases their position was carefully indicated with incised lines on the plank (Figure 3-31).

Larger graving pieces are also present throughout the hull. These rectangular wooden patches were used to replace damaged parts of a plank with sound wood. Graving pieces vary in length from 10 cm to well above a metre. They are attached with either iron nails or trenails. While some graving pieces might have been applied during the construction process, others are definitely associated with later maintenance. On strake 7, the upper portion of a damaged outer plank was replaced with a graving piece 58 cm long at the vertical scarf joint to a neighbouring plank. The damaged area was cut out so that the wooden patch would be supported by underlying frames and old trenails were cut flush with the outer sided face of the framing timbers. The graving piece was furnished with a vertical scarf joint on one side and fastened with a new set of trenails. The seams around the graving piece were carefully caulked with animal hair dipped in tar.

Figure 3-32: Graving piece near a scarf joint in a plank on section 3a; underneath the graving piece (above in the photograph), a splinter was re-attached with small iron nails (J. Auer)

Underneath the patch, a large superficial splinter was reattached with a series of small, square-shafted iron nails, measuring 5 mm in section. The edges around the splinter were then cleaned and caulked (Figure 3-32).

This method of reattaching superficial splinters could also be observed on other hull planks, as well as on a number of loose outer planks found in association with the wreck.

Many of the hull planks below the furring line had long splits or cracks, caused either by auger holes for the trenails or possibly by bending the planks into shape. Above the furring line, such cracks are less numerous and relatively short. All splits were cleaned and caulked or filled with waterproofing material to prevent further damage. As an additional measure, some cracks were stopped with incisions across the grain.

Hull fasteners

As the hull sections of the Princes Channel Wreck were left assembled, it is difficult to conduct a full analysis of all hull fasteners. The description in Table 3-1 is therefore based on outside observations made in the process of timber recording and only includes measurements that could be obtained with the fasteners remaining in situ.

Trenails

Wooden nails are the most common type of fastening used during the construction of the Princes Channel Wreck. These are cleft oak trenails, which were shaved but not mooted (Goodburn, 2004). The outboard ends were split with two blows to form a 'V' or an 'X' and then caulked (Figure 3-33).

Most inboard ends were split and wedged with small oak wedges, although some trenails on the ceiling planking on section 3b were caulked. Some of the trenail holes were enlarged inboard, either to provide an auger starting hole or to allow the ends to expand more (Goodburn, 2004). Trenails have a diameter of between 30 mm and 32 mm. The length varies, depending on the elements that are fastened, but the longest trenails, which connect

Figure 3-33: Caulked oak trenail in the outer hull planking (J. Auer)

outer planking, furring timbers, framing timbers and ceiling plank, have a length of up to 70 cm.

Most trenails associated with the hull planks fasten the outer planks only to the framing timbers, while a smaller proportion also extends through the ceiling plank. The furring timbers were fastened to the existing frames with separate trenails and further trenails were used to reattach new planking after the furring process. As a result, the number of trenails recorded on the inboard side of the wreck sections above the furring line varies considerably from the number recorded on the outside. For example, a plank in the ninth strake was connected to the underlying futtock and furring timbers with three trenails. However, eight trenails were counted on the inner sided face of the same futtock.

It is interesting to note that the distribution of trenails is different below and above the line of furring. Below the furring timbers, trenails are distributed in a seemingly random or even chaotic way. There is a substantial number of trenails per plank, up to 59 on a plank 5 m long, but it is not possible to recognize a pattern or system in their distribution and spacing.

In the furred section, each joint between plank and frame is secured by either two or three trenails. Trenails are either spaced so that they form a vertical line or are slightly offset. The distribution of trenails in the upper part of the hull of the Princes Channel Wreck gives a clear indication of the underlying framing pattern. This results in 35 trenails on a plank 5 m long (Figure 3-23).

Trenails of 25 mm to 30 mm diameter were also used as additional fastenings for more solid structural elements, such as the stempost and the apron, and to secure joints. A number of redundant trenails, which were observed in the wale and the keel, might be associated with the construction process.

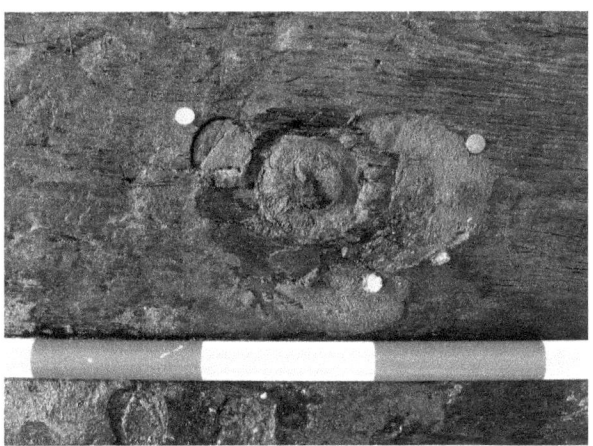

Figure 3-34: Head of an iron bolt next to a caulked oak trenail in the wale on section 3b (J. Auer)

Figure 3-35: Two countersunk iron nails and four trenails in a repair at a scarf joint between two outer hull planks on section 3a; the nails have corroded and the resinous material in the holes has been removed (J. Auer).

Small oak trenails of 15 mm diameter were used to fasten knot patches. These trenails were secured with rectangular oak wedges on the side on which the patch was applied (Figure 3-30).

Iron bolts

Iron bolts were the main method of fastening the larger structural components. They were observed in stempost, keel and apron, and in the wale. The iron bolts in the bow section were heavily eroded and could not be measured. In the wale, bolt head impressions were preserved in some places and the bolt diameter could be measured. It is, however, not clear how the bolts were secured on the inside.

The iron bolts had a diameter of 25 mm to 30 mm. Bolt heads were circular and measured 50 mm to 55 mm in diameter. In the wale, bolts were spaced between 1.2 m and 1.5 m apart (Figure 3-34).

Iron nails

Iron nails are used for a variety of purposes in the construction of the Princes Channel Wreck. They are regularly employed to fasten the hood-ends of outer planks and vertical scarf joints between planks. They also appear in association with repairs and seem to have been used as temporary fasteners of hull components such as ceiling planks.

Two sizes of iron nails occur. Square shafted nails measuring 5 mm in section are used only to fasten superficial splinters on outer hull planking. Larger, square shafted nails with a section measuring 10 mm to a side are more common.

It is unclear whether the nails were driven through previously drilled pilot holes. However, at the hood-ends and in the scarf joints between the outer hull planks, the nails are located in round, seemingly augered countersunk holes of 1 cm depth. These holes have a diameter of 30 mm and were filled with a resinous material, probably pitch, which protected the nail heads (Figure 3-35).

Fastener	Section	Description	Function
Trenail	30–32 mm	Round, caulked or wedged	Hull planks to frames, floor-timbers to first futtocks, ceiling planks, joints between keel and post, apron, furring timbers
Trenail	15 mm	Round, wedged	Knot patches
Iron bolts	25–30 mm	Round, with 55 mm round heads	Fasten components of wale as well as floor-timbers in bow, apron and stempost/keel
Iron nails	10 mm	Square section, often countersunk, head?	Scarf joints between planks, hood-ends, additional or temporary fastening, repairs
Iron nails	5 mm	Square section, head?	Repairs

Table 3-1

The Ship

Above the line of furring, two iron nails and two trenails were used to secure each scarf joint. In the wider planks in the lower part of the hull, up to four iron nails connect each joint.

The hood-ends of the outer planks in the stempost were fastened with trenails and up to two countersunk iron nails.

Surface treatment

Remains of a white or cream-coloured surface covering were observed on the stempost as well as on the better preserved outer planks on the port side of the bow section. This covering, up to 2 mm thick, had series of fine parallel grooves running through it at different angles. These are currently interpreted as strokes of a hard brush (Figure 3-36). It would seem that the surface covering is the remains of a viscous paint or substance, which was applied to the underwater hull with brushes, possibly as protection against marine growth or shipworm. A sample analysis showed that the main components were iron (163.07 g/l) and calcium (22.55 g/l).

This suggests that despite the light (perhaps bleached) colour, a compound containing iron oxides and chalky clay was used, perhaps as primer. Paints containing iron oxides and clay were used mostly for priming or as antifouling protection and were called 'minio de hierro' in Spanish or 'ijzermenie' in Dutch (iron minion), to distinguish them from red lead. The colour is also referred to as 'English Red'. Such colours continue to be used mostly as anticorrosive treatment in present day Netherlands, Belgium and France.

Deck construction

The remains of the deck construction are preserved on the upper ends of section 2 and 3b (Figures 3-37 and 3-38). As there is no evidence for another deck below this point, this was probably the lowest deck in the vessel. The deck was situated above the waterline and coincides in height with the wale on the outside of the hull. Based on the reconstruction evidence, the deck would have been located approximately 3.24 m above the upper face of the keel (see Chapter 5.8, page 65). Gunports located above the deck indicate that it was used as a platform for artillery (see Chapter 4). Based on the reconstructed size of the Princes Channel Wreck, it is very possible that the preserved deck construction represents what remains of the main, possibly only, deck of the ship.

Deck beams

The deck was supported by oak beams spaced 2.6 m apart (Figure 3-39). On section 2, the heavily eroded end of a deck beam was preserved, while on section 3b beam positions are only indicated by recesses in beam shelf and framing. The preserved beam end measured 23 cm x 24.5 cm in section, while recesses measure approximately 25 cm by 25 cm. The preserved beam end was rebated to interlock with a neighbouring second futtock into which another rebate was cut. Beam recesses

Figure 3-36: Detail of the surface covering on the outside of the bow, section 4 (J. Auer)

on section 3b indicate chamfers on the lower edges of the beams, these were, however, not observed on the beam end on section 2.

The beams were supported by a beam shelf, but also by framing timbers, which were either rebated to fit around the beam, or end underneath the beam. This means that beam ends originally butted against the outer planking, or more specifically against the former wale, which, in the process of furring, became no more than a longitudinal reinforcement, sandwiched between original frames and furring timbers. The beam ends were held in place by trenails driven through the outer planking, as well as nails driven vertically into neighbouring frames.

Beam shelf

On section 3b, a section of the beam shelf 2.5 m long is preserved (Figure 3-39). This is an oak plank 39 cm wide and 7 cm thick, which is chamfered along the bottom edge. The plank is recessed at the top edge to fit around the beams. It is held in place by trenails, the ends of which were expanded with small oak wedges.

Half beam clamp

Above the beam shelf and between the beam recesses, a heavily eroded half beam clamp remains in situ on section 3b (Figure 3-39). The beam clamp consists of two rectangular oak timbers, 80 cm and 1.54 m in length respectively, which are connected with a scarf joint. The ends on both sides are sawn off and would have butted against the deck beams. The clamp is 16.5 cm wide and has a thickness of 14 cm. The bottom edge is chamfered. It was fastened with a combination of iron bolts and trenails. Along the top edge of the timber, a series of mortises indicate the position of half beams or ledges. The mortises are spaced 34 to 37 cm apart and vary in size and shape. The foremost mortise is 16 cm wide and 4 to 5 cm deep. This is followed by a mortise 6 cm deep, which measures 10 cm along the bottom edge and 14 cm along the top edge. The last visible mortise is 10.4 cm long and 4 cm deep.

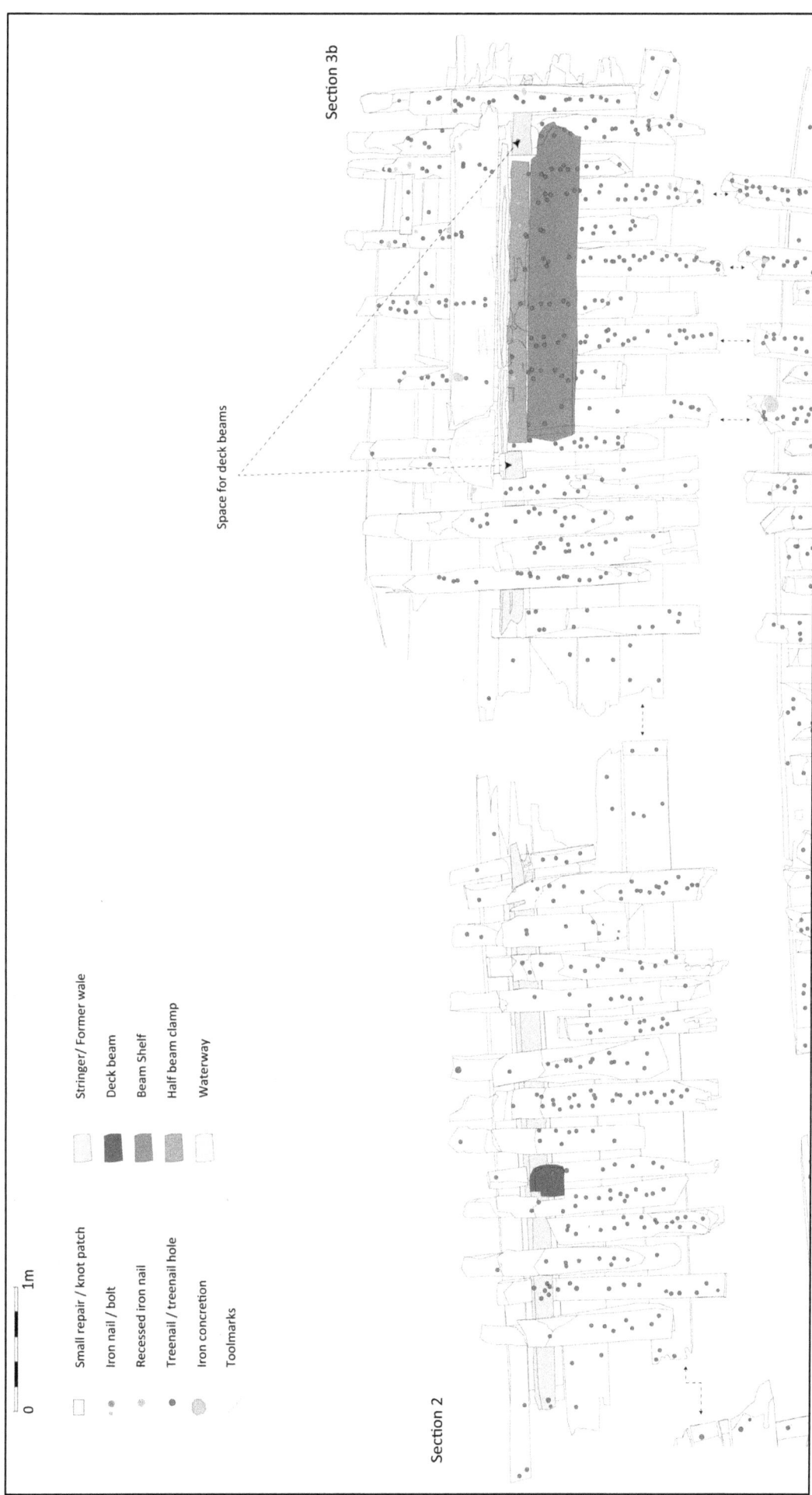

Figure 3-37: Inside view of the hull sections with the elements relating to the deck construction marked in different shades of grey (J. Auer based on the original recording results and illustrations by Wessex Archaeology)

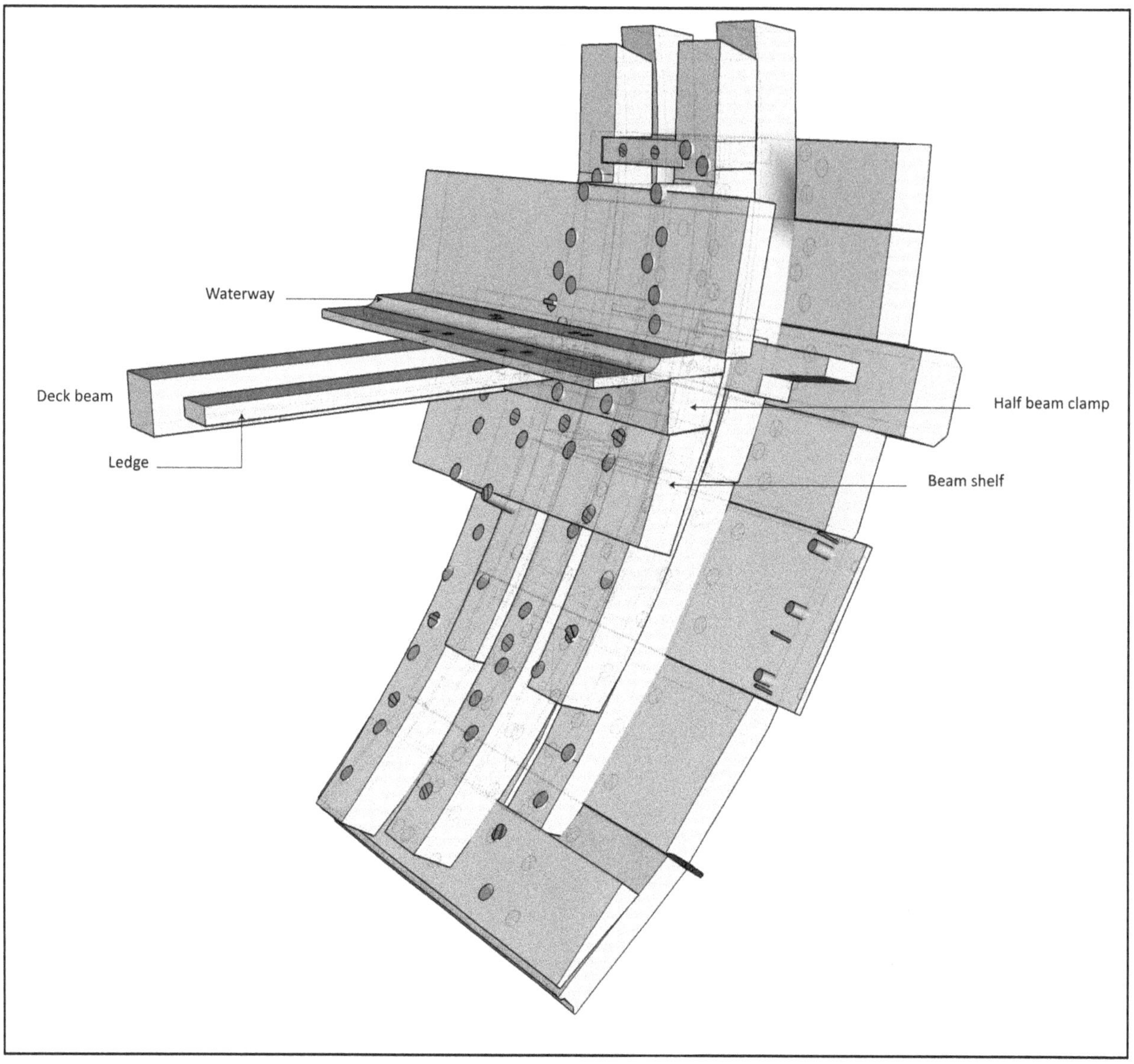

THE SHIP

Figure 3-38: Isometric view of the reconstructed deck construction; the knee has been omitted for clarity (J. Auer)

Figure 3-39: Space for a deck beam on section 3b; the frames on either side of the beam are recessed to make space for the beam; on the right hand side the eroded ends of (from the top) overlying ceiling plank, waterway, half beam clamp and beam shelf can be seen (J. Auer)

Waterway

Above the half beam clamp, the eroded remains of the outermost deck plank, the waterway, were observed (Figure 3-39). This is an L-shaped oak timber, which was fastened to deck beams, half beams and ledges, presumably with iron nails. The vertical height of the timber is 9 cm and the thickness of the horizontal part was 4 cm. As only about 2 to 3 cm of the horizontal part are preserved, the width of the waterway is unclear. The waterway was part of the water management system of the ship and would have allowed water to flow along the sides of the vessel to a point where it could be led down to the bilge and the pumps.

Ceiling above deck level and evidence for possible knees

The uppermost preserved component of the deck assembly is an oak ceiling plank 37 cm wide and 8 cm thick, which was fastened on top of the waterway (Figure 3-39). The top edge of the plank is chamfered. The plank is fastened with a combination of caulked and wedged trenails and iron nails. On both ends of the ceiling plank,

Figure 3-40: Gunport on section 3b. The doubled up lower sill is still in place, but the upper part of the gunport is eroded (J. Auer)

Figure 3-41: A trenail, which connects floor timber and first futtock is cut by a nail attaching the outer planking on section 3a (J. Auer)

and just above the deck beam recesses, broken trenails and concreted iron bolts, as well as pressure impressions indicate that further timbers, approximately 22 cm wide were fastened against the plank. These could well have been standing knees. These would have been fastened to the deck beams and to the side of the vessel to provide rigidity. The location of these possible knees coincides with a change in the framing pattern. While the head of each first futtock is generally framed by the foot of two second futtocks, leaving a gap of around 40 cm between the second futtocks extending upwards, further futtocks were inserted above deck beams. These are located besides existing futtocks, effectively reducing the spacing between second futtocks in this area to between 10 cm and 20 cm. The standing knees would have been fastened to these additional framing components with the help of iron bolts and trenails.

Gunport

In the forward end of the vessel, above the deck, the lower part of a gunport is preserved. Another gunport was probably located 2.5 m further aft. However, its position is only indicated by an eroded mortise in a second futtock. The surviving gunport was located approximately 75 cm above deck level. It spans the width between two second futtocks, about 40 cm. Due to the state of preservation, the height could not be established. As the area around the gunport is still affected by furring, the port has twice the depth it would have had prior to the furring process. The lower gunport sill consists of two timbers, one the original and one added when the ship was furred, respectively 48 cm wide and 10 cm thick, slotted into mortises 5 cm deep in the second futtocks and their furring timbers. These two sill components, 27 cm and 17 cm deep, were connected with trenails and fastened with a single trenail through an outer plank, which was recessed to accommodate the gunport. The extreme depth of the gunport, as well as the location of a possible standing knee only 20 cm forward of the port, would have restricted the firing arc of any gun positioned here.

3.4 Some thoughts on the sequence of construction

The complex nature of the preserved hull sections and the fact that the sections were left assembled makes an analysis of the construction sequence a difficult task. Many details are concealed by overlying timbers and could not be recorded in detail.

There are, however, a number of clues, which give an indication as to the sequence in which the ship was put together. In this section, an attempt is made to reconstruct the process of construction and rebuilding of the Princes Channel Wreck (Figures 3-42 to 3-46).

Building the original ship

The construction of the ship from the Princes Channel probably started with laying down the keel. This might have been a single oak timber, but could also have been made up of a number of components, which were connected by scarf joints. Stempost and sternpost were then raised and connected to the keel, in the case of the stempost with a vertical scarf joint, which was secured with trenails and iron nails. Next the apron was fastened to the inside of the bow to provide additional strength.

All visible floor timbers and first futtocks are connected with interlocking joints, which are secured with vertically driven trenails. As the space between frames is insufficient to drive these trenails with neighbouring frames in place, the floor timbers and first futtocks were either erected as pre-assembled units, or assembled in sequence. The only visible exceptions are the crotches in the bow, where first futtocks were not fastened to floors, but only overlapped. Futtocks in this area must have been added once some of the outer planking was in place. In a number of cases elsewhere, trenails which connect joints between floors and first futtocks are cut by those which attach the outer planking to the frames, a clear indication that the pre-assembled frames were in place prior to the application of planks (Figure 3-41).

The pre-assembled frames reached up to a level just above the lowest and possibly only deck and would almost certainly have been connected by temporary ribbands, flexible battens, which provided rigidity and helped with the process of fairing.

After the outer sided faces of the pre-erected frames were adzed to the desired shape, some of the outer planking could be put in place, starting with the garboard strake. This would have been a laborious process, which was probably conducted in two stages. The scarf joints between planks had to be evenly distributed to avoid weaknesses in the hull and the chosen method of waterproofing also required extremely tight plank seams.

The spiled planks were probably offered up, clamped tight, close scribed to their neighbours and then unclamped. Now the joint could be made and the plank could be trimmed for a perfect fit. The lower edge of each plank was hollowed out in order to make space for the waterproofing material. During the final hanging process, three strands of rolled and tarred animal hair were laid between strake planks and the planks were

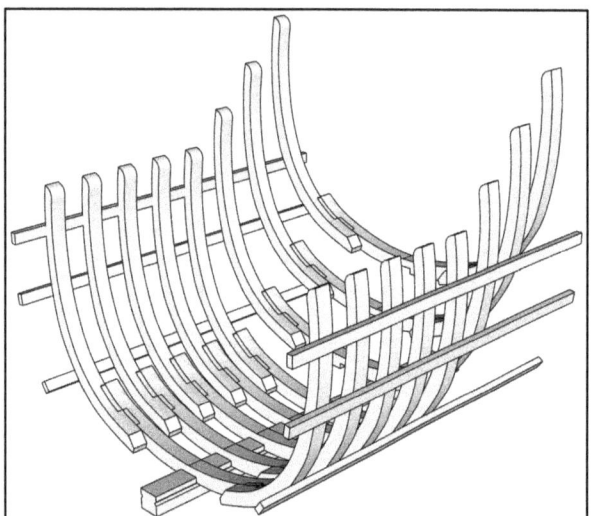

Figure 3-42: The pre-assembled floor timbers and first futtocks have been erected on the keel and connected by ribbands (M. Ditta)

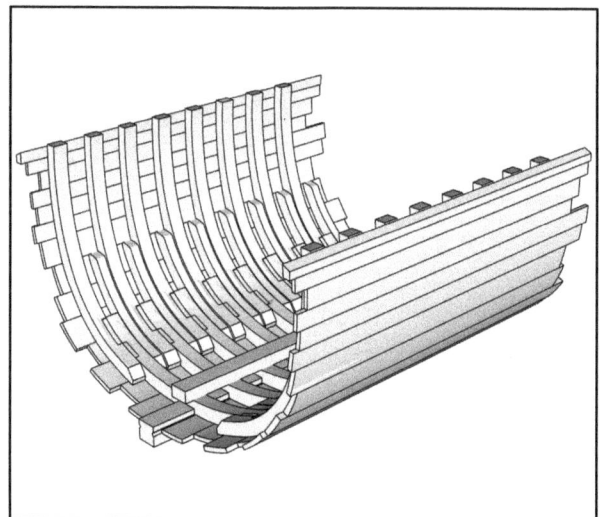

Figure 3-43: The outer planking has reached a level near the head of first futtocks. The filling frames might have been inserted at this point (M. Ditta)

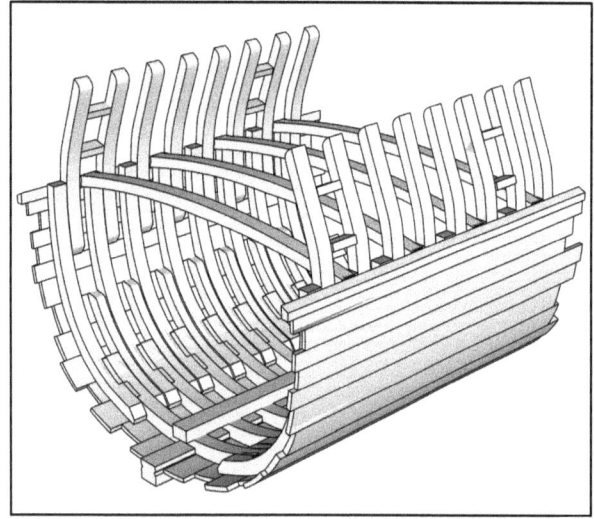

Figure 3-44: Second futtocks and deck beams are added in a sequential procedure (M. Ditta)

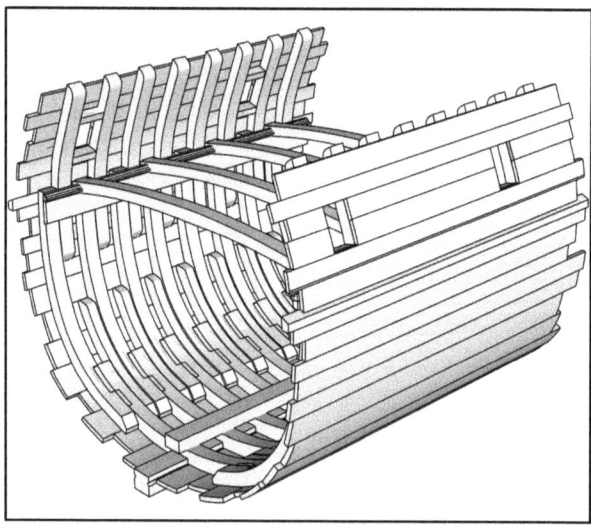

Figure 3-45: Outer planking and framing advance alternately. The remaining deck construction, including the beam shelf, could also be added at this point (M. Ditta)

fastened with trenails, which were caulked on the outside and secured with wedges on the inside. Joints and hoodends were additionally secured with countersunk iron nails. Prior to hanging, smaller defects in the planks were addressed. Some of the knot patches in particular are located in areas which would have been inaccessible after hanging. After hanging, damage related to the hanging process, such as smaller splinters and cracks, could be repaired.

A puzzling feature in the construction of the Princes Channel Wreck are the filling timbers, which fill the space between the pairs of floors and first futtocks in the area around the bilge. As only the upper parts of these timbers are preserved, we do not know whether they extended all the way to, or even across, the keel, although this would be logical. They were certainly put in place after the lowest outer planking was attached, as they are not fastened to the other frames. On the inside of some outer planks on section 3a, some roughly hacked lines indicating the position of filling timbers were seen. This is interesting, as none of the other, pre-assembled framing timbers were marked out in this way.

It seems unlikely that the filling timbers were marked on the outer planks prior to hanging, especially if they were fastened after the planking was in place. But why would the position of filling timbers be marked out on the attached outer planking? Wouldn't the gaps between pre-

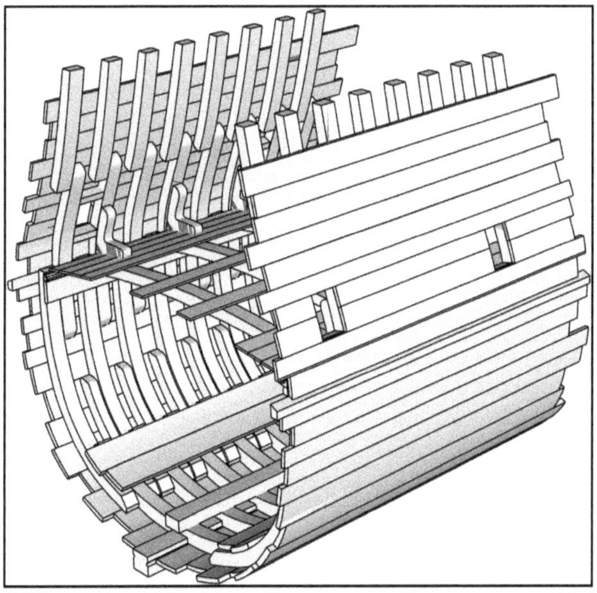

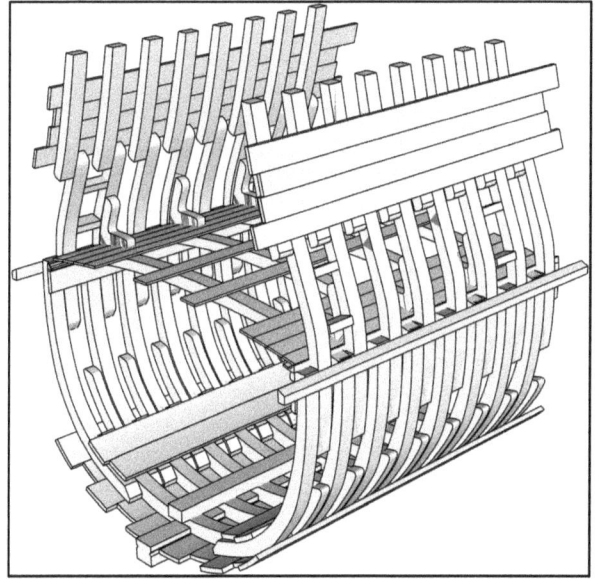

Figure 3-46: The finished hull section, with ceiling, deck and standing knees in place (M. Ditta)

Figure 3-47: The furring process begins: original outer planking has been removed; however, a wale has been left in place and serves as ribband (M. Ditta)

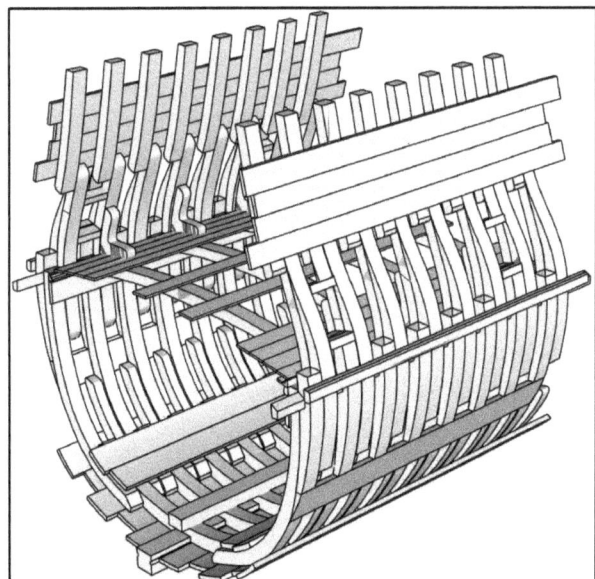

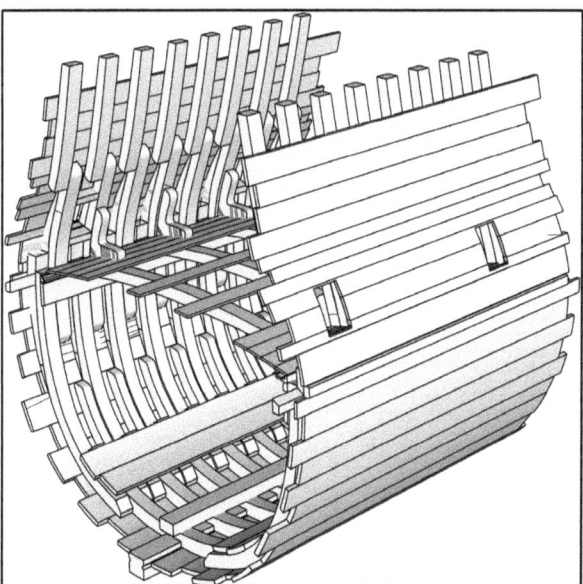

Figure 3-48: The furring timbers have been attached and rest on a plank with a triangular section. The new wale has been put in place. The hull is now ready for re-planking (M. Ditta)

Figure 3-49: The ship after the furring process (M. Ditta)

assembled frames be sufficient guidance as to the size of filling timbers?

Or could the filling timbers be a later addition, possibly associated with the process of furring? With the current set of dendrochronological samples not providing any clues, this question must remain unanswered. But even if this were the case, the purpose of marking would not be obvious. It might, however, be related to the distribution of work in the dockyard. The only features which are clearly marked out on the hull planks are the locations of some knot patches and graving pieces. It can be imagined that the master shipwright or a skilled carpenter marked these features, while the actual work was undertaken by less skilled labourers.

As no evidence of the keelson is preserved, we do not know what this timber looked like or when it was put in place. It would, however, be logical for this to happen at this point.

Once the outer planking reached up to a point near the head of the first futtocks, the second futtocks could be put in place. These are connected only to the outer planking and would probably have been shored from the outside and connected across the ship with so-called cross-palls for stability. As the deck beams were connected to second futtocks with vertically driven trenails, these must also have been added at this stage. Once all second futtocks were in place, there would not have been sufficient space to drive the nails. Here, a sequential procedure can be imagined.

As the majority of trenails securing the outer planking to the frames do not extend into the ceiling planks, these must have been added at a later stage, possibly after the second futtocks and beams were in place. If the beams were resting only on the beam shelf, this should have been in place prior to attaching them. However, the beams of the Princes Channel Wreck butt against the outer planking and are supported by first and second futtocks. This makes a later addition of the beam shelf together with the ceiling planking more likely.

Now outer planking and framing could advance alternately. The gunports were probably installed while the outer planking progressed and the remaining deck construction could be added, including the standing knees, which were fastened to additional futtocks.

As we have now reached the uppermost preserved timbers on the Princes Channel Wreck, any further reconstruction of the construction sequence would solely be based on conjecture. It is unclear how construction progressed from this point or indeed what the upper works of the ship looked like.

Furring or rebuilding the ship

One of the first questions that comes to mind when looking at the complex hull structure of the Princes Channel Wreck is related to the process of furring or rebuilding. The reasons for this modification are clearly stated by Mainwaring:

> The occasion of it is to make a ship bear a better sail, for when a ship is too narrow and her bearing either not laid out enough or too low, then they must make her broader and lay her bearing higher (Perrin and Manwaring, 1922, 153).

But when was this carried out and by whom?

The exact gap in time between the original construction and the furring could not be established using dendrochronology, partly because, while most planks did have enough rings to give a dendrochronological date sequence, the few furring timbers sampled did not offer the clear bark edge needed to determine the date of felling, but also because the phenomenon of furring was not recognized until after the first dendrochronological samples had been obtained. The sampling strategy at the time was guided by the quality of timber for dating rather than analytical questions (see Section 3.5, pages 43–6).

There are, however, a number of indicators that point to some lapse in time between the original construction and the furring.

As trenails cut flush with the outer sided face of first and second futtocks were observed on all wreck sections, it is clear that the hull had already been planked, at least up to the first deck, prior to furring. The outer planks below applied in an irregular and seemingly chaotic pattern, fewer fastenings were used in the planks associated with the line of furring also differ from those above. The latter are an average 10 cm narrower and show substantially fewer signs of repair and wear. There is also a considerable difference in the number and pattern of fastenings. While trenails below the line of furring are the furring and a clearly defined, regular pattern is recognizable.

It would therefore seem that the planking below the line of furring represents the original outer planking associated with the construction of the vessel. The seemingly newer outer planks above the line of furring were replacements added during the furring process. This indicates that the ship was in use for a while prior to being rebuilt in order to improve stability and seaworthiness.

If this is the case, the rebuilding could have been undertaken in a different shipyard and by different shipwrights from the original construction. However, both furring timbers and original framing timbers seem to have been sourced in Eastern England (see Section 3.5). Furthermore, the new outer planking was joined and waterproofed in exactly the same way as the original planking.

Consequently it is likely that the ship was furred in the same shipyard as was responsible for its original construction.

The sequence of furring

How and in what sequence was the furring carried out? Again the preserved hull sections offer a number of clues (Figures 3-47 to 3-49).

Generally, the process seems to have followed the description provided by Mainwaring:

> to rip off the first planks and to put other timbers upon the first, and so to put on the planks upon these timbers (Perrin and Manwaring, 1922, 153).

From the eighth strake upwards, the original outer planking was removed and trenails were cut flush with the outer sided surface of the framing timbers. The original wale was, however, left in place, probably to serve as a ribband during the rebuilding process and to provide additional longitudinal strength in the converted ship.

In a next step, the furring timbers were attached starting with the wedge-shaped plank on strake 8. This plank was secured to the existing frames with trenails. While its main function was to serve as a support for the heel of the lowermost furring timbers, it also provided additional longitudinal strength. Following this, the remaining furring timbers were fastened to the existing frames. They were carefully rebated to fit around the old wale in situ. Wherever the right thickness could not be achieved with a single timber, additional filling pieces and wedges were used. The quality of the furring timbers was generally not very good, with some timbers even being affected by heart rot before they were used.

With all furring timbers securely fastened, the wale was put in place next, either to serve as a guide for fairing or to enhance the rigidity of the structure. The gunports were extended through the furring timbers. Then re-planking could begin, probably from the bottom up and in the same manner in which the original planks were attached.

With the new outer planks ending in the stempost rabbet in a different angle, the rabbet had to be modified to accommodate the new, fuller shape of the ship. This was achieved with smaller wedges and filling pieces. Once the outer planking reached up to the level of the wale, a narrower, fitting strake was inserted to fill the gap between the other outer planks and the wale. As this strake could not be waterproofed in the same way as the remainder of the hull, the seam between wale and uppermost outer plank was caulked.

Above the wale re-planking continued in the same way as below. Once the furring was completed, the ship had gained a good 60 cm in beam while the internal structure and volume had not been altered.

3.5 Oak dendrochronology (Nigel Nayling)

This section provides an overview of the dendrochronological analysis undertaken on timbers from the Gresham Ship following the initial evaluation of the first two sections of ship to be recovered and again after the recovery of three further main sections when additional samples were taken. The first phase of analysis was commissioned by Wessex Archaeology as part of a Princes Channel Wreck evaluation (Project No: 56470). The aim of the study was to determine the date of the construction of the vessel and the geographical origin of the timbers used in its construction. Additional sampling of the sections subsequently recovered from the Princes Channel aimed to confirm the precise dating of the ship by targeting samples with well-preserved bark edge and also to address the date of the furring of the ship, evidence for which had become apparent during detailed recording of the articulated sections of the hull.

The data presented here is guided by English Heritage recommendations on the format and content of dendrochronological reports (English Heritage, 1998).

Methodology

Methods employed at the Lampeter Dendrochronology Laboratory in general follow those described by English Heritage. Details of the methods used in the investigation of this vessel are described below.

A detailed examination of the timbers in store was carried out in 2004 in the company of Hanna Steyne from Wessex Archaeology, one of the team employed to record and subsequently to evaluate the wreck. The primary objective was the recovery of tree-ring samples from oak timbers with suitable ring sequences for analysis. Those with more than 50 annual rings and some survival of the original sapwood and bark edge were sought. As the timbers were still damp, coring was not possible and slices were recovered using a chainsaw following standard practice for waterlogged timbers.

Following the recovery of additional sections of the hull by a Wessex Archaeology dive team (including the author of this chapter), further timbers were selected for sampling based on the presence of sufficient rings and bark edge, which included framing timbers applied to broaden the vessel through the process known as furring. Analysis of timbers with complete sapwood aimed to confirm the original date of construction and that of the alterations to the beam of the vessel.

The slice samples were cleaned by paring the surface with traditional razor blades to define each successive annual ring. The complete sequences of growth rings in the samples were measured to an accuracy of 0.01 mm using a micro-computer-based travelling stage (Tyers, 1999). Cross-correlation algorithms (Baillie and Pilcher, 1973; Munro, 1984) were employed to search for positions where the ring sequences were highly correlated. The ring sequences were plotted electronically and exported to a computer graphics software package (Coreldraw™ v.8) to enable visual comparisons to be made between sequences at the positions indicated and, where these were satisfactory, new mean sequences were constructed from the synchronized sequences. The *t*-values reported below are derived from the original CROS algorithm (Baillie and Pilcher 1973). A *t*-value of 3.5 or over is usually indicative of a good match, although this is with the proviso that high *t*-values at the same relative or absolute position must be obtained from a range of independent sequences and that satisfactory visual matching supports these positions.

All the measured sequences from this assemblage were compared with each other and those found to cross-match were combined to form a site master curve. These and any remaining unmatched ring sequences were tested against a range of reference chronologies, using the same matching criteria: high *t*-values, replicated values against a range of chronologies at the same position and satisfactory visual matching. Where such positions are found these provide calendar dates for the ring-sequence.

The tree-ring dates produced by this process initially date only the rings present in the timber. The interpretation of these dates relies upon the nature of the final rings in the sequence. If the sample ends in the heartwood of the original tree, a *terminus post quem (tpq)* for the felling of the tree is indicated by the date of the last ring plus the addition of the minimum expected number of sapwood rings, which are missing. This *tpq* may be many decades before the real felling date. Where some of the outer sapwood or the heartwood/sapwood boundary survives on the sample, a felling date range can be calculated using the maximum and minimum number of sapwood rings likely to have been present. The sapwood estimates applied throughout this report are a minimum of 10 and maximum of 46 annual rings, where these figures indicate the 95% confidence limits of the range. These figures are applicable to oaks from the British Isles (Tyers, 1998). Alternatively, if bark-edge survives, then a felling date can be directly utilised from the date of the last surviving ring. The dates obtained by this technique do not by themselves necessarily indicate the date of the structure from which they are derived. It is necessary to incorporate other specialist evidence concerning the re-use of timbers and the repairs of structures before the dendrochronological dates given here can be reliably interpreted as reflecting the construction date of phases within the structure.

Results

All of the twelve samples taken during the first phase of sampling (labelled PCW01 to PCW12) had sufficient rings to merit analysis and were cleaned to reveal the tree-ring sequences (see Appendix Table A-1 for details, Figures 3-50 and 3-51 for location of samples). All these samples were measured and the resultant ring sequences compared. Ten of the sequences were cross-matched with significant computer correlations and satisfactory visual matching. A ten-timber mean was calculated and then compared with dated reference chronologies from throughout the British Isles and northern Europe and dated against British chronologies and site mean sequences at the dating position of AD 1296–AD 1574 (Nayling, 2004).

Samples	PCW21
PCW01	13.28

Samples	PCW18
PCW16	13.11

Table 3-2. Correlations between individual samples indicating timbers derived from the same parent trees

A further thirteen samples (labelled PCW13 to PCW25) were provided following the second phase of sampling. Two of these samples were unsuitable for analysis, having fewer than 50 rings, and were not measured (PCW24 and PCW25). The remainder were prepared and analysed in the same way as the first tranche of samples. Very high correlations and close visual matching of the ring-width sequences between two pairs of samples (PCW01 and PCW21, and PCW16 and PCW18, see Table 3-2) indicate that these samples came from common parent trees – samples PCW16 and PCW18 come from fragments of the same first futtock found on sections 3a and 3b. In each case, combined raw ring-width sequences (PCW01_21 and PCW16_18) were calculated for comparison with remaining individual timber ring-width sequences. A total of twenty ring-width sequences correlated well against each other and a new 21-timber, 306-year site mean 'GreshamS' was calculated. Appendix Table A-2 shows the computer correlations between the synchronized tree-ring sequences.

This mean sequence was cross-matched against numerous British regional chronologies and site means (Table 3-3) at the dating position of AD 1296–AD 1574. The consequent dating and the chronological positions of the sequences from individual timbers are shown in Figure 3-51.

Discussion

Although the dating of the first set of samples, reported in 2004, was successful in providing both dating and a likely provenance for the timbers used in the ship's construction (Nayling 2004), the relatively poor condition of the sapwood on the samples, caused by drying out following recovery of the first two hull sections from the seabed limited confidence in the identification of the bark edge and hence identification

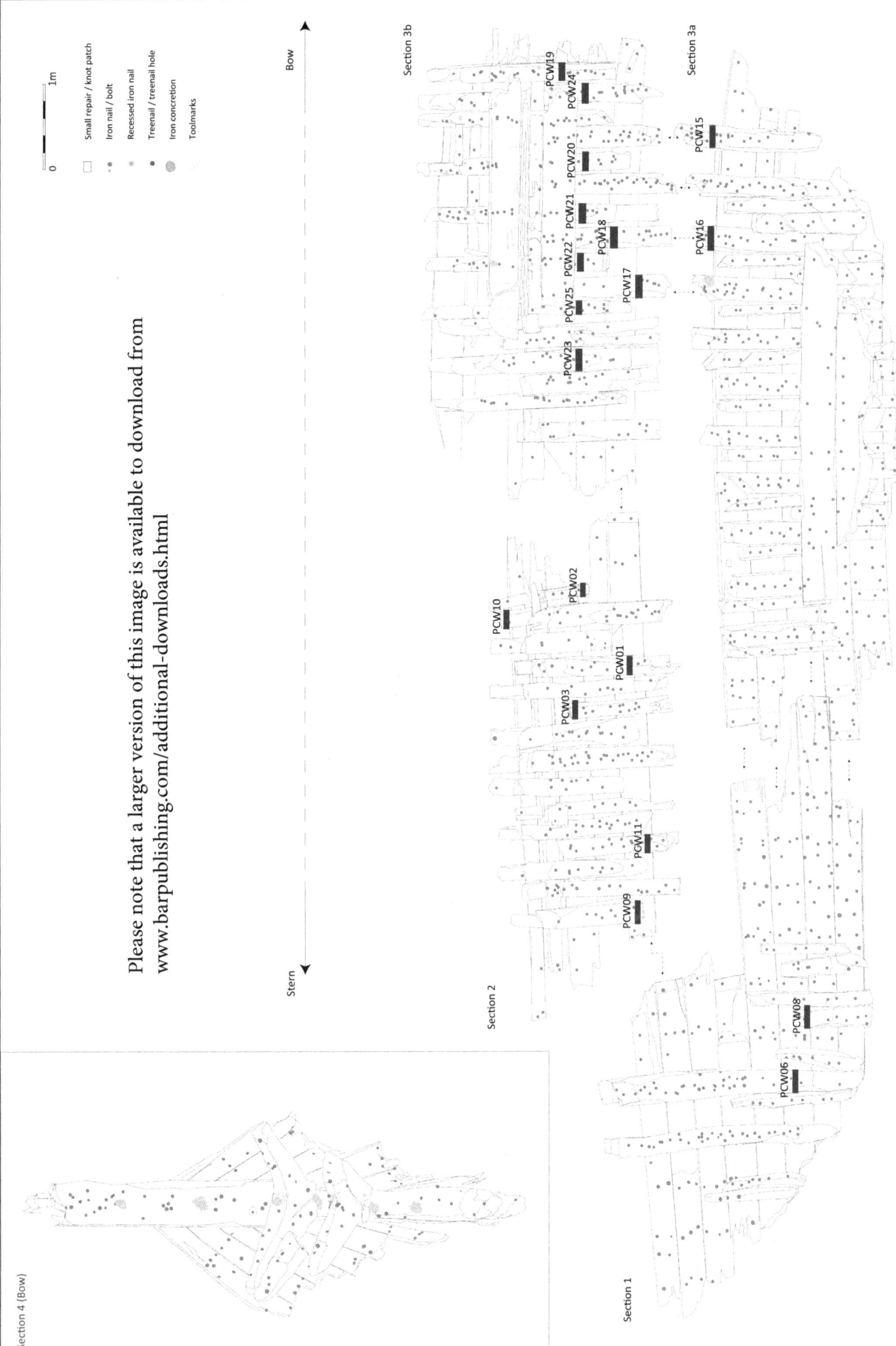

Figure 3-50: Inside view of the hull sections with the positions of dendrochronological samples marked (J. Auer, based on the original recording results and illustrations by Wessex Archaeology); section 4 (inset) was originally located forward of sections 3a and 3b

Area	Reference chronology	t-value
England	East Midlands (Laxton and Litton, 1988)	7.64
England	East Anglia 121 chronology mean (Ian Tyers, pers. comm.)	15.76
England	London region 86 chronology/1475 timber mean (Ian Tyers, pers. comm.)	11.28
England	West Midlands 89 chronology mean (Ian Tyers, pers. comm.)	7.8
England	South East 75 chron/566 timber mean (Ian Tyers, pers. comm.)	11.56
England	South West 101 chronology mean (Ian Tyers, pers. comm.)	9.22
East Anglia	Chicksands Priory, Bedfordshire (Howard *et al.*, 1998)	10.75
East Anglia	Croxley Hall Farm Barn, Rickmansworth, Hertfordshire (Bridge, 2000)	5.63
East Anglia	Ely, Cambridgeshire (Groves, pers. comm.)	10.43
Essex	Gosfield Hall, nr Halstead (Bridge, 1998)	11.26
Essex	Netteswellbury Barn, Harlow (Tyers, 1997)	10.19
London	Hays Wharf, Southwark (Tyers, 1996; Tyers, 1996)	11.54
South East England	Mary Rose Original build/Hampshire timber (Bridge and Dobbs, 1994)	7.65
South East England	Mary Rose refit/Kent timber (Bridge and Dobbs, 1994)	6.04

Table 3-3   Dating the mean sequence GreshamS, AD 1296–1574 inclusive; t-values with independent reference chronologies (regional chronologies and site masters)

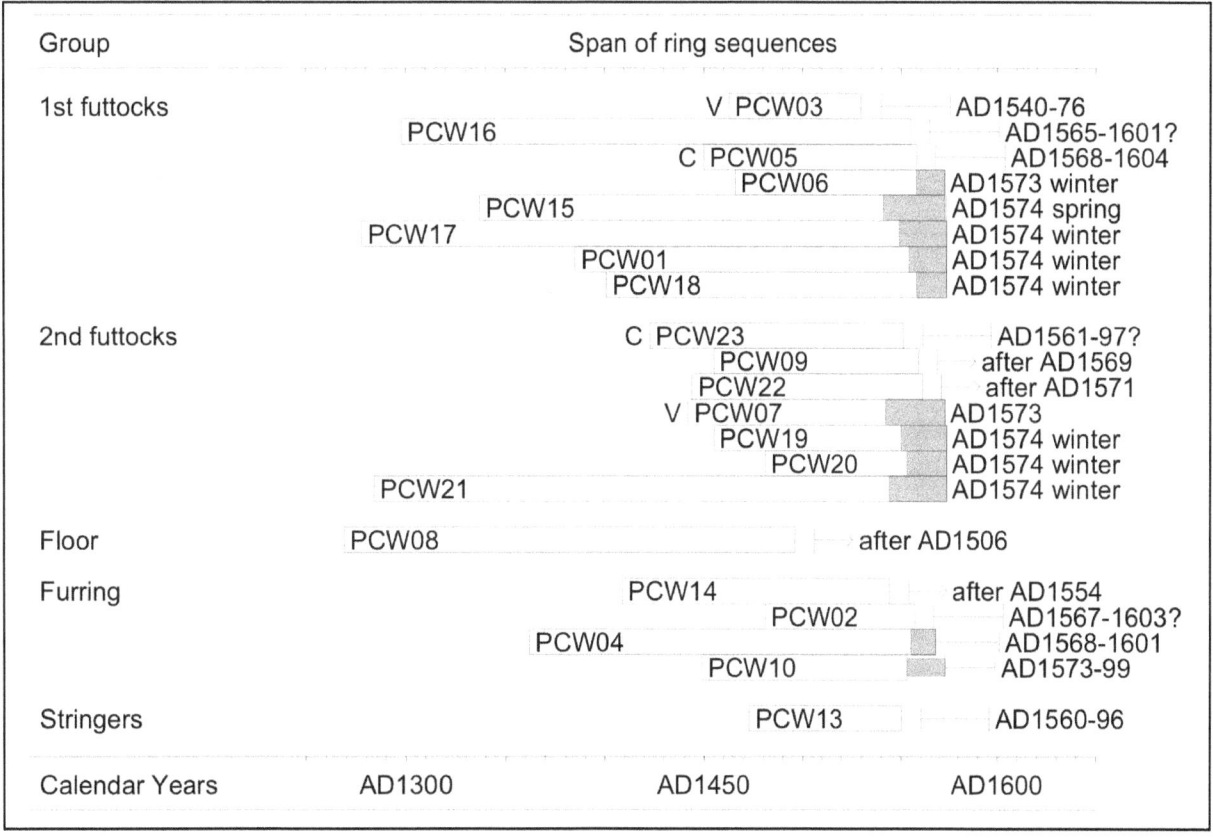

Figure 3-51:   Bar diagram showing the chronological positions of the dated timbers from the Gresham Ship; sapwood is shaded and the estimated felling period for each sequence is also shown (N. Nayling)

of a definitive date for construction. Recovery of further samples from sections 3a and 3b soon after the lifting and the recording of these sections sought to address this problem. Observation of the alteration to the hull through the addition of framing timbers (furring) to increase the beam of the vessel also encouraged recovery and analysis of additional samples.

Eight timbers from the primary construction of the ship with an observed bark edge were absolutely dated (Figure 3-51). One timber came from a tree felled in the winter of AD 1573/4 (PCW06), one timber (PCW15) was derived from a parent tree felled in the spring of AD 1574 and six from trees felled in the winter of AD 1574/5. The ship could not therefore have been constructed before September AD 1574. This result also suggests that some of the timbers used in the original construction were stockpiled.

Four timbers associated with the furring of the ship were absolutely dated, but none had a definite bark edge. The provenance of the sampled timbers is suggested by varying computer correlations with contemporary regional chronologies (Table 3-3). There appears to be a clear bias towards eastern England, particularly East Anglia and Essex.

3.6 The ship's anchor

The only part of the ship's fittings and equipment to survive is a single anchor. The anchor was amongst the material recovered during clearance attempts and was recorded by Wessex Archaeology in August 2003 (Thomsen, 2003). It is now located besides the preserved wreck sections in Stoney Cove. The following description is based on the results of the remedial archaeological recording in 2003 (Thomsen, 2003).

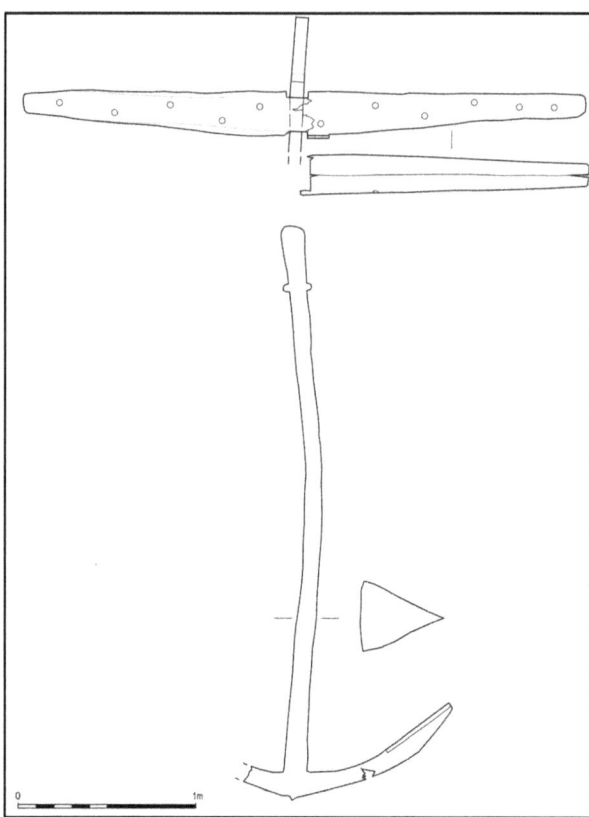

Figure 3-52: The anchor found on the Princes Channel Wreck (K. Brandon, Wessex Archaeology)

The anchor is made of iron and has a total length of 3.13 m. The original width measured between fluke tips was 1.72 m. The ring is missing and one arm is broken off 0.18 m from the shank, which is slightly bent. When raised, the anchor was still fitted with its 3.11 m long double-tapered wooden stock. This was made from two symmetrical halves, which were trenailed together around the anchor shank.

Chapter 4: The Armament
by Delia Ní Chíobháin

When the Princes Channel Wreck was first identified in April 2003, a grab barge was used to remove the obstruction and this lifted a number of ship timbers, an anchor and two guns; one of wrought iron and one of cast iron. While one of the guns was initially mistakenly identified as being from the late 18th century/early 19th century, the other was dated to the early 16th century (see Chapter 1.3, page 2). This early date, combined with the ship timber evidence, warranted an archaeological investigation. The five coherent sections of the wreck that were raised in the process have been described in the previous chapters. One of the sections contained components of one gunport and evidence of another (see Chapter 3.3, pages 38–9). In all four pieces of ordnance were excavated, three of cast iron and one of wrought iron, in addition to the chamber of the latter. Moreover, a fragment of an elm carriage was excavated and the wrought-iron gun also had fragments of its carriage attached. The reason for analysing the armament in the context of this volume is that, more than the cargo that the ship carried on its last journey, the armament stands in close relation to the ship's construction and what the archaeology allowed us to learn from it. It is also for that reason that we shall start with some structural evidence.

4.1 The Structural Evidence

Section 3b contained the remains of two gunports along its upper edge. The ports were at a height of 70 cm above the orlop deck construction and are spaced 2.5 m apart. The forward gunport (Figure 3-40, page 39) is in much better condition and measures 40 cm wide at the sill, while the original height is unknown as the lintel is missing due to erosion. The second gunport is known only from a mortise cut into a futtock for the shelf construction. Based on the gunport remains, the reconstruction suggests that, if all gunports were evenly distributed along the ship's sides, a total of six to eight guns might have been located along each side. While the height of the gunports is unobtainable, it is possible that they were higher than they were wide. William Bourne's 1587 *The Arte of Shooting in Great Ordnance* advises that, 'when the carpenters dothe cutte out anye portes in a shippe, then lette them cutte out deep ynough uppe and donne', so that the face of the gun will have sufficient room to manoeuvre when being aimed (Bourne, 1587, 57). The *Warwick*, wrecked in Bermuda in 1619, was a Virginia Company armed supply ship. A rectangular gunport lid recovered from the site in 1979 measured 432 mm wide and 546 mm high. It was 60 mm thick, which corresponded with the thickness of the first layer of the ship's outer planking. The lid was constructed of a single piece of wood with two steps, the outboard step 33 mm thick, and that inboard 27 mm thick with a 31-mm rebate. These steps ensured a tight fit between the lid and the gunport. A large iron ring on the inboard face was used to open and

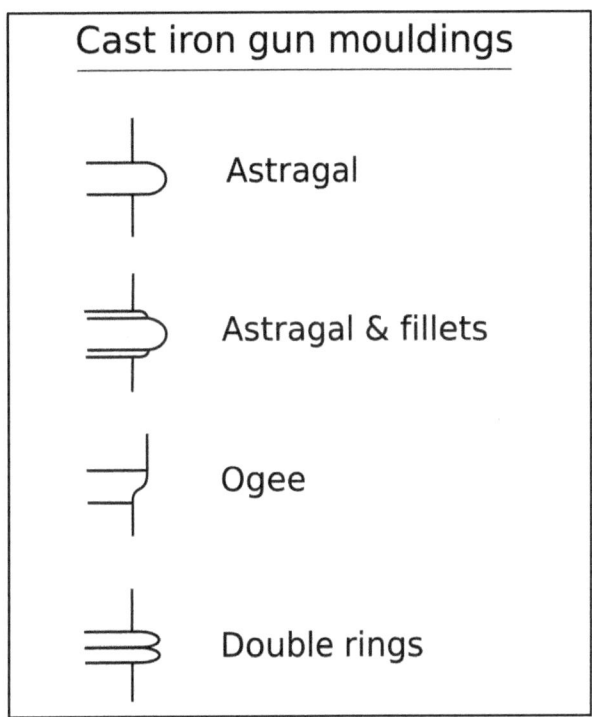

Figure 4-1: Cast iron gun decorative mouldings (drawing D. Ní Chíobháin)

close the lid and it hung on two vertical hinges. The excavation report also notes evidence of a fitting for a rope on the outboard face, perhaps to secure the lid whilst open (Bojakowski and Custer-Bojakowski, 2010, 25).

The 16th-century wreck off Alderney also revealed a gunport lid measuring 371 mm wide and 462 mm long. Its thickness decreased from 63 mm at the top to 48 mm at the bottom. Its sides were bevelled for sealing to the ship's side and it had a rebate cut along its top edge. Two hinges were present when it was first found and a hole 21 mm in diameter was located 102 mm from its lower edge. The hole revealed the presence of a bolt, thought to have taken a rope that raised and lowered the lid (Bound, 1998, 66). While no evidence exists for the height of the gunports, the rectangular shape of both the *Warwick* and the Alderney example would suggest that the gunports on the Princes Channel Wreck were likely to have measured over 40 cm in height.

Much research has been conducted on the production of English cast-iron ordnance when compared with the study of wrought-iron pieces. For the identification and dating of the cast-iron guns there is the work of Charles Trollope (2002), which outlines the various series of guns that were produced in England according to their design and proportions.

Each artefact excavated by Wessex Archaeology was assigned a find number. For the purposes of the

The Armament

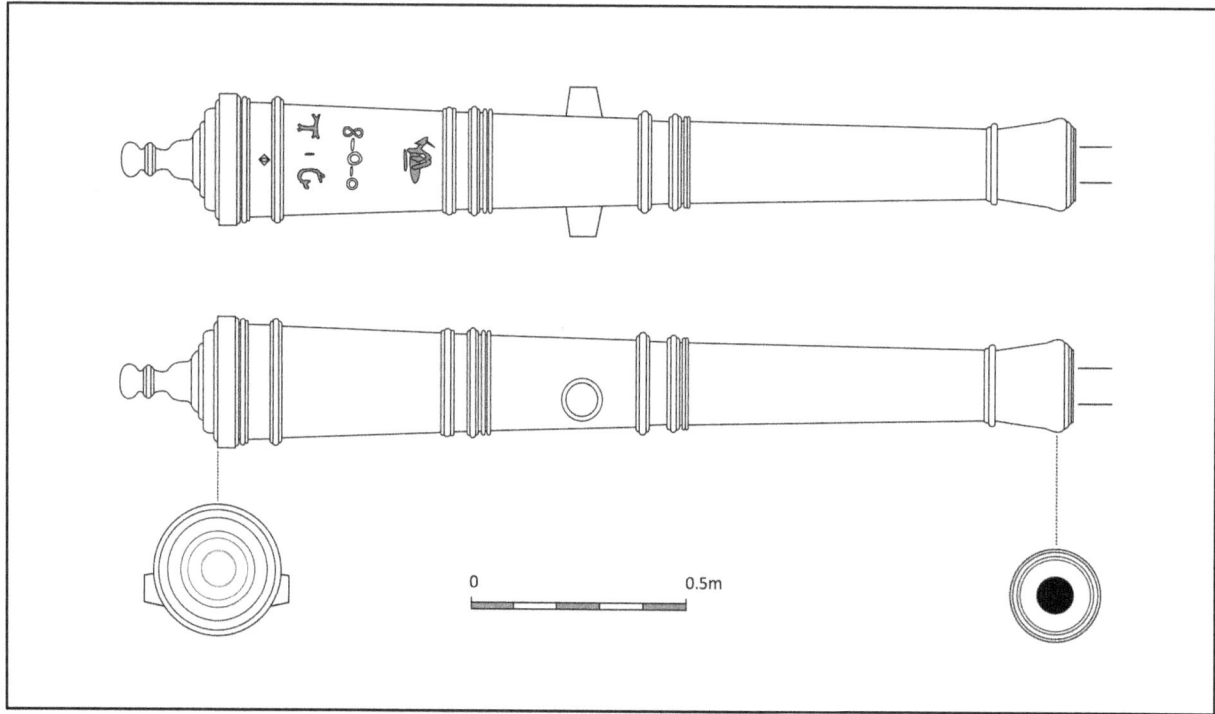

Figure 4-2: Drawing of PC1 (D. Ní Chíobháin)

ordnance study each piece of ordnance from the Princes Channel was provided with a new code, in order to ease comparison specifically with the Wittenbergen wreck (Ní Chíobháin, 2011; Stanek, 2011). These numbers correspond to the recording sequence, the first being PC1. Figure 4-1 shows the mouldings, or decorative features, common to the cast-iron guns.

4.2 PC1: A Cast-Iron Falcon

PC1 is a cast-iron muzzle-loading gun-barrel that was recovered from the Princes Channel Wreck site during the 2004 excavation by Wessex Archaeology (Figure 4-2). This gun was within a concretion when it was found, which was removed by archaeologists shortly after its discovery. The piece has a length of 1.99 m (6′ 6″); with a 235 mm breech cascable, a 615 mm first ose on the a 475 mm second reinforce, a 725 mm chase and the muzzle measures 180 mm with a 195 mm swell.

In total the piece is 2.23 m long. It has a 76 mm bore (3″), a diameter at the vent of 265 mm and a minimum diameter in front of the muzzle reinforce of 156 mm. The trunnions are 65 mm long and measure between 90 and 70 mm in diameter. The touch hole measures 9 mm in diameter and has a circular shaped rebate surrounding it, although corrosion may have obscured its original shape. Between the astragal at the vent and the first reinforce are a moulded grasshopper motif (Figure 4-3) and the weight of the gun in hundredweight, '8-0-0' incised. The initials 'TG' are moulded below the weight. There are no visible markings on the trunnions. The cascable mouldings consist of a flattened, rounded button joined to the neck by an astragal and fillets. The breech mouldings are a

Figure 4-3: Detail of the grasshopper motif on PC1 shortly after de-concretion (J. Auer, Wessex Archaeology

neck fillet, a breech fillet, breech ogee and a breech fillet. The first reinforce begins with the base mouldings which include the base ring, measuring 300 mm in diameter, followed by an ogee and an astragal with one fillet. The vent field is terminated with an astragal and fillets. The first reinforce mouldings consist of two sets of astragals and fillets. The second reinforce begins with double rings and contains the trunnions. It is terminated with two sets of astragals and fillets. The chase girdle measures 185 mm in diameter and its mouldings consist of double rings. The muzzle astragal has one fillet aft and the muzzle face mouldings consist of an ogee, a fillet and a ring.

The markings on the first reinforce tell us a great deal about the gun and its origins. The numbers '8-0-0' marked on the piece indicate its weight in hundredweight, 8 cwt (406 kg). According to Schubert's list (1957, 251), reproduced in Teesdale's table (1991, 21) the bore diameter of 76 mm (3″) combined with the weight in pounds, 896 lb, would classify this gun as a falcon. According to the calibre table created by Roth through comparison of examples from various countries, the size of the bore also indicates that this piece fired 3-pound shot (Roth, 1989, 193). The grasshopper motif and the initials TG were discovered early on to belong to Sir Thomas Gresham, a prominent English merchant and financier, who owned a gun foundry in the Weald in south east England from 1567/8 to 1582 (Teesdale, 1991, 128). The grasshopper was the symbol on the crest above the coat of arms of his family and is known from another example of his guns now located in the Royal Armouries in Copenhagen. There are very few known examples of guns from Gresham's foundry. The Copenhagen gun, a saker, bears the grasshopper motif and the TG initials; it is 2.4 m long (8′) and has a bore diameter of 95 mm (3¾″). A third example stems from the Wittenbergen wreck (Ní Chíobháin, 2011; Stanek, 2011). Another gun marked with Gresham's initials is located on Nevis in the West Indies (Trollope, 2002, 54), but specific details are lacking. A falconet with the TG initials and a possible grasshopper motif has been excavated in Bergen op Zoom in the Netherlands and measures 1.85m (6′) long with a bore diameter of 55 mm (2⅛″) (Vermunt, 1999, 3).

Sir Thomas Gresham (1519–1579) is remembered as a skilful and important financier and merchant, but he also owned his gun foundry at a time that saw growth in production and export of cast-iron ordnance from England. His foundry was located in Mayfield in the Weald, at the time England's main gun founding region. The area was naturally suited for this type of industry. It had a natural source of iron ore. A sufficient water supply to power furnace bellows and forests and woodlands for the production of charcoal were readily available (Cleere, 1985, 133). While figures vary, the number of gun founders in operation in the area in the 1570s was around ten, while the number of blast furnaces totalled 51 (Hodgkinson, 2000, 34), compared to just one gun founder in 1546 (Brown, 2011, 98). The Mayfield furnace was in operation under Gresham from 1567 or 1568 until 1582, despite Gresham's death in 1579. It is thought that his wife continued the foundry and the export of guns after his death. After 1582 the foundry was taken over by his niece's husband, Sir Henry Neville (Teesdale, 1991, 129).

Trollope's classification places Gresham's guns in what he refers to as the alternative commercial series from about 1570. This ran parallel with Sir William Wynter's series of the same period which was made primarily for the Navy. The commercial series was produced with the merchant ship market in mind and the locations of the decorative rings conform to those of PC1. These dates also correspond to the time that Gresham's foundry was in operation. Four bands of decoration adorn the piece, two half way between the vent and the trunnions and two more just behind them. Among other founders, Trollope specifically names Thomas Gresham as being associated with this gun type. This gun design is also significant in that it formed the basis of the Swedish Finbanker design, guns which became popular during the 17th century (Trollope, 2002, 54).

4.3 PC2: A Cast-Iron Minion

PC2 is a cast-iron gun-barrel (Figure 4-4). The gun was within a concretion when it was found; this was later removed by staff at Fort Nelson where it has been undergoing conservation since. The concretion enclosed a copper-alloy plate (Figure 4-5) and a ceramic jar (Figure 4-6). The condition of the metal is fair with some concretion remaining around the cascable and some erosion on the surface layer of iron.

The piece has a length of 1.92 m (6′ 4″), with a 250 mm breech cascable which is damaged, a 565 mm first reinforce, a 460 mm second reinforce, a 730 mm chase and the muzzle measures 165 mm long with a 194 mm swell. In total the piece measures 2.175 m long. It has an 86 mm bore (3⅓″), a diameter at the vent of 275 mm and a minimum diameter in front of the muzzle reinforce of 153 mm. The trunnions are 70 mm long; they have a tapering plan and measure between 85 and 79 mm in diameter. The touch hole is rectangular in shape and measures 25 by 10 mm. There are no markings on the first reinforce, the base ring or on the trunnions.

The cascable mouldings consist of a small rounded button on a large flat rounded button, separated from the neck with an astragal and fillet. The breech mouldings are a neck fillet, a breech ogee, two breech fillets, a breech ogee and a breech fillet. The first reinforce begins with the base mouldings which include the base ring, measuring 300 mm in diameter, followed by two sets of fillets. The vent field is terminated with an astragal and fillets. The first reinforce mouldings consist of an astragal with double fillets. The second reinforce begins with double rings and contains the trunnions. It is terminated with double rings followed by an astragal with two forward fillets. The chase mouldings consist of double rings on either end. The muzzle mouldings consist of an astragal and fillets and the muzzle face mouldings consists of a muzzle ring just after the muzzle swell.

In trying to identify what kind of gun this is, we lack some relevant pieces of information. There are no gun founder's marks on the gun and so we do not know by whom or where it was made. The weight of the piece is not marked as in PC1 and due to various circumstances it has not been possible to weigh any of the guns and in any event we would not know what mass was lost to corrosion. This is regrettable as

The Armament

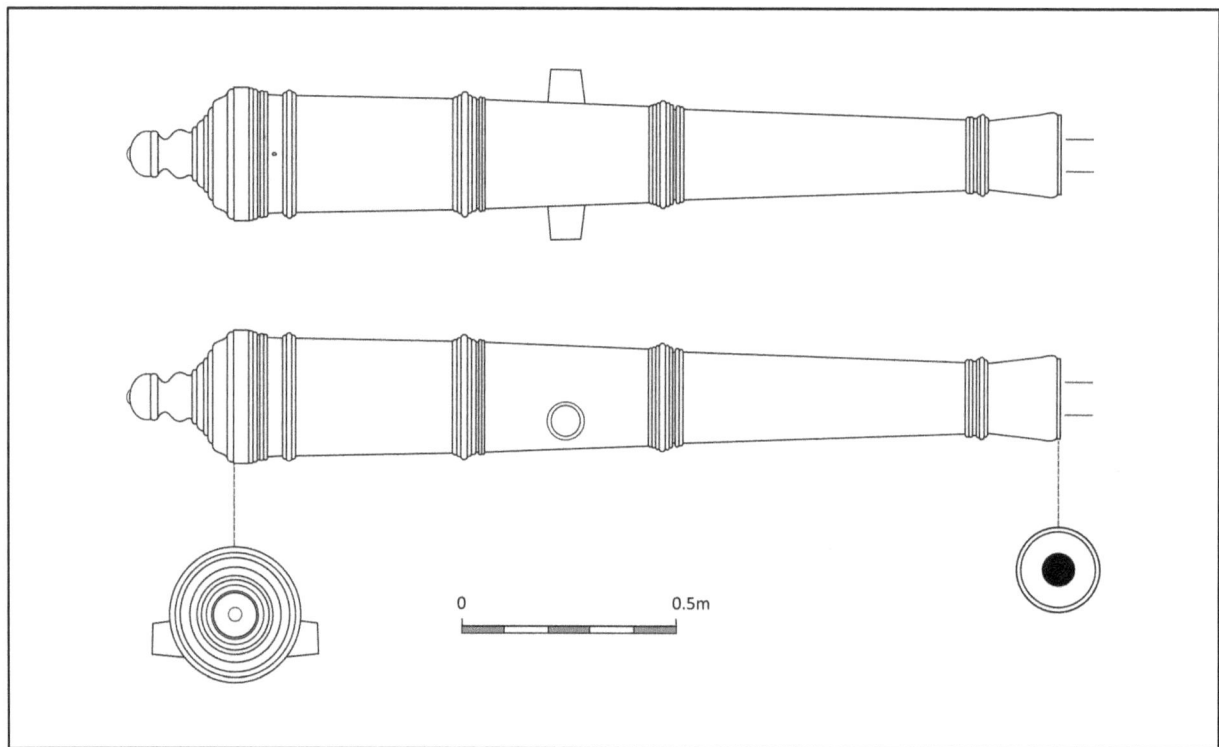

Figure 4-4: Drawing of PC2 (D. Ní Chíobháin)

Figure 4-5: Copper alloy plate concreted to PC2 (Royal Armouries, Fort Nelson)

Figure 4-6: Ceramic jar uncovered during the de-concretion of PC2 (Royal Armouries, Fort Nelson)

contemporary gun classification was partly based on the weight of any given piece.

The calibre and the overall design, however, are known. The bore of 86 mm (3⅓″) would have made this a 4- to 6-pounder gun (Roth, 1989, 193) and, although the weight of the piece is unknown, the bore and vent dimensions can be used to determine whether the gun's proportions relate to any known gun types. Dividing the diameter at the vent, in this case 275 mm, by the diameter of the bore design, 86 mm, gives a the ratio of 3.2. According to Roth cast-iron guns have proportions from 2.9 to 3.7 (Roth, 1989, 193). In Teesdale's table a bore size of 3⅓″ is given for English minions from the 1580s and 1590s; accordingly this gun is likely to have been cast as a minion (Teesdale, 1991, 21).

Additionally, the design of the cascable decorations can give approximate dates for the casting of iron ordnance. The neck of the cascable was usually separated from the button with an astragal and fillets on earlier guns. This gradually changed to an astragal and one fillet, and by 1700 the neck had been taken out of the cascable design (Caruana, 1985, 13). The number of reinforces can also help to date the pieces. Earlier cast-iron guns, pre-1550s, were constructed with one reinforce. The additional reinforce was added to further reduce the amount of metal toward the muzzle. The walls of the guns were required to be thickest by the vent where the powder ignited. The powder used at this time was shifting from serpentine powder to corned powder and it is during the time that serpentine powder was improving in reliability that the changes in gun reinforces appear (Trollope, 2002, 51). Therefore the presence of an astragal and fillet as the neck moulding along with the presence of two reinforces suggest that the gun was most probably cast during the late 16th century, at a similar time to PC1 which shares these design characteristics.

The proportions of PC2 appear to fit into a series of guns described by Trollope (2002, 53) as Sir William Wynter's series that ran from about 1569 to 1586. While the actual mouldings of the reinforcing rings do not precisely match the examples given by Trollope, the dimensions correspond to suggest the gun was cast according to this design and at this time.

William Wynter was Master of Ordnance from 1569 to 1598 and he established the Proportion of 1569, specific ordnance requirements for fitting out the Royal Navy. The guns have a standard rule where the circumference at the vent is ten times the diameter of the shot. This general rule was taken from earlier cast-bronze guns that were known to have fired successfully. In the case of PC2 the ratio works out at 864 mm: 86 mm, which corresponds closely when taking corrosion of metal into account. The rule also includes the design feature where the first reinforce is at a quarter of the gun's length and a defining step down is apparent at the beginning of the second reinforce. This step down is present on PC2 and the first reinforce measures 564 mm and the gun measures 1920 mm, 84 mm longer than one quarter of the gun's length. Furthermore the rule states that the trunnions are to be located at $^{2}/_{5}$ along the length of the gun and on PC2 the centre of the trunnions is located at this point. The recommended sequence of decorative rings also corresponds to that of PC2 with one set at the end of the first reinforce and one or two sets following the trunnions. While the individual moulded rings on PC2 are more numerous than the examples in Trollope's paper, their function of delineating the reinforces remains the same. The English Royal Navy's preference for brass ordnance meant that very few of these cast-iron guns were used on naval vessels. An example of this is shown when in 1571 the Board of Ordnance acquired 80 brass guns and 29 cast-iron guns, despite the high cost of the brass kinds. On the other hand, the cast-iron guns were extensively produced for English merchant ships and were also sold abroad, by legal and illegal means (Trollope, 2002, 51f.).

4.4 PC3: A Cast-Iron Falcon

This cast-iron gun barrel was within a concretion when it was found. However, this was removed by Port of London Authority personnel shortly after its discovery in the grab. The gun was among the first material recovered from the site during the initial attempts to disperse the wreck. It has a length of 2.24 m (7' 4"); with a 110 mm breech cascable which is damaged at the neck, a 660 mm first reinforce, a 550 mm second reinforce, an 800 mm chase and the muzzle measures 230 mm with a 210 mm swell. In total the piece measures 2350 mm long. It has a 77 mm bore (3"), a diameter at the vent of 288 mm and a minimum diameter just aft of the muzzle reinforce of 176 mm (Figure 4-7). The trunnions are 77 mm long; they have a tapering plan and measure between 92 and 84 mm in diameter. The touchhole measures 9 mm in diameter, but corrosion may have obscured its original size. There are no markings on the first reinforce, the base ring or on the trunnions. The condition of the gun is quite poor, with the end of the cascable missing what may have been a neck and button, as well as layers of iron having peeled from its surface. While no evidence of markings were detected, it cannot be ruled out that there may have been some originally. Due to its poor condition the recorded bore diameter of the piece is questionable as having been the original size. The cascable mouldings are broken at the base of the neck; the remaining breech mouldings consist of three fillets and two intermitting ogees. The first reinforce begins with the base mouldings which include the base ring, measuring 320 mm in diameter, followed by an ogee and a fillet. The vent field is terminated with an astragal and fillets. The first reinforce mouldings consist of a reinforce ring flanked by two fillets. The second reinforce begins with double rings and also contains the trunnions. It is terminated with two sets of astragals and fillets. The chase mouldings begin with double rings while the muzzle mouldings consist of double rings and an astragal with fillets. The muzzle face mouldings consist of an ogee, a fillet and a ring.

As this gun, like PC2, is without markings of its weight or founder, any attempt in classifying its type, origin or date are dependent on its mouldings and design. While not certain to have been the original size, the muzzle bore of 77 mm (3") would, according to Roth's table, classify this gun an English 3- or 4-pounder (Roth, 1989, 193). When related to Teesdale's table (Teesdale, 1991, 21), despite the absence of the gun's weight, a calibre of this size would make this piece either a minion or a falcon. William Bourne describes falcons as having a bore of 3¾", of firing an iron shot of 2⅛ lb and measuring 'seven foot more or less' (Bourne, 1587, 70). The length and bore diameter of PC3 accord best with the dimensions of a falcon. However, interpretation of specific gun types can be uncertain as some ordnance sold for commercial use was sold as one type and bored out later as another, as a way to evade the English crown's export laws (Trollope, 2002, 51).

The mouldings and overall design of this piece relate to a gun type described by Trollope as having been produced during the Transitional Period 1549–69 (Trollope, 2002, 52). The term transition is in relation to the change from making cast-iron guns with one long reinforce to two shorter reinforces, as detailed above, and Trollope suggests this first began in English gun founding around 1549. Only two examples are given of

The Armament

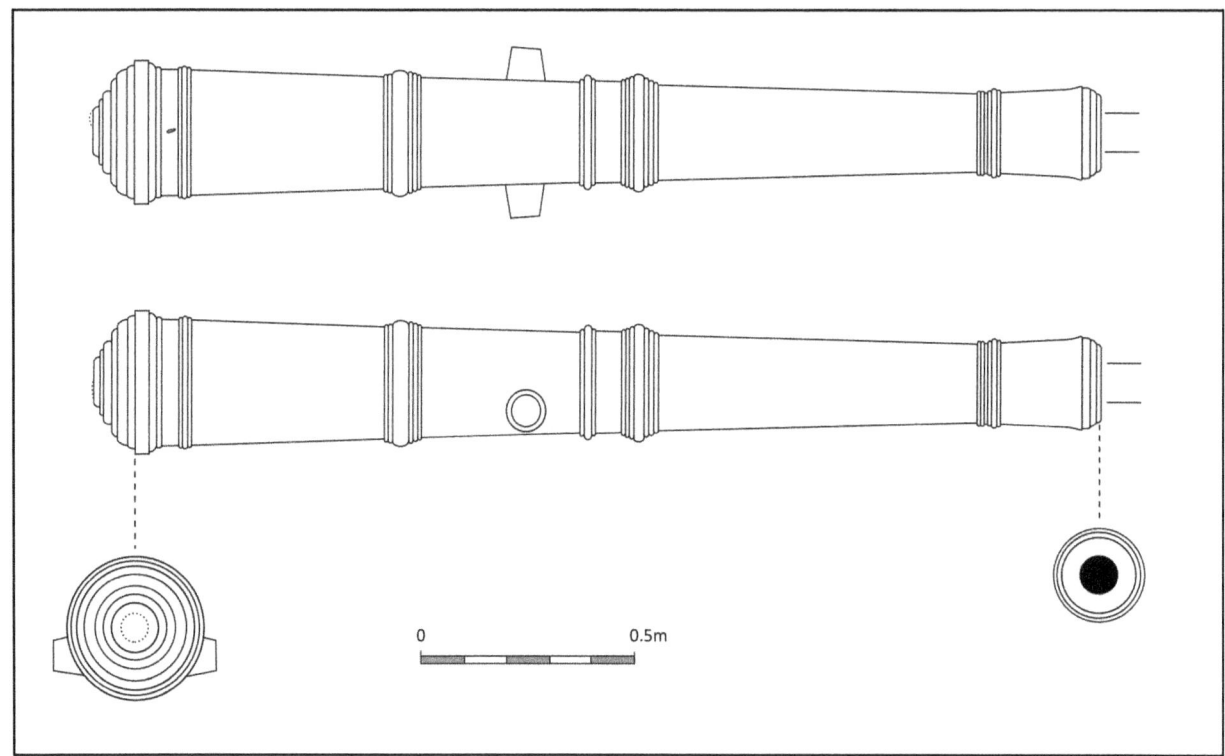

Figure 4-7:   *Drawing of PC3 (D. Ní Chíobháin)*

this type by the author, as so few of them survive. Examples of earlier guns are scarce since the metal from older guns was often recycled. The end of the first reinforce is from this time marked with one or two outer ring mouldings, typically an astragal and fillets; however, their purpose is not clear. Trollope (2002, 52) suggests the mouldings may have been used as an aid in loading the pieces, but due to the few examples in existence this is difficult to determine definitely.

This gun type has design characteristics similar to those described for the later PC2 where the circumference at the vent is ten times the diameter of the shot. In the case of PC3 the ratio is 905 mm: 80 mm, which fairly approximately follows the rule. The design of PC2, where the trunnions were situated at $^2/_5$ the gun's length, is similar to that of PC3 (Trollope, 2002, 51).

The muzzle swell is a characteristic present on all cast-iron guns from the Princes Channel Wreck, but was being introduced only at the time of the design of PC2 (Trollope, 2002, 52). Caruana dates the arrival of the muzzle swell on ships' guns to the reign of Elizabeth which is somewhat later than Trollope's classification;

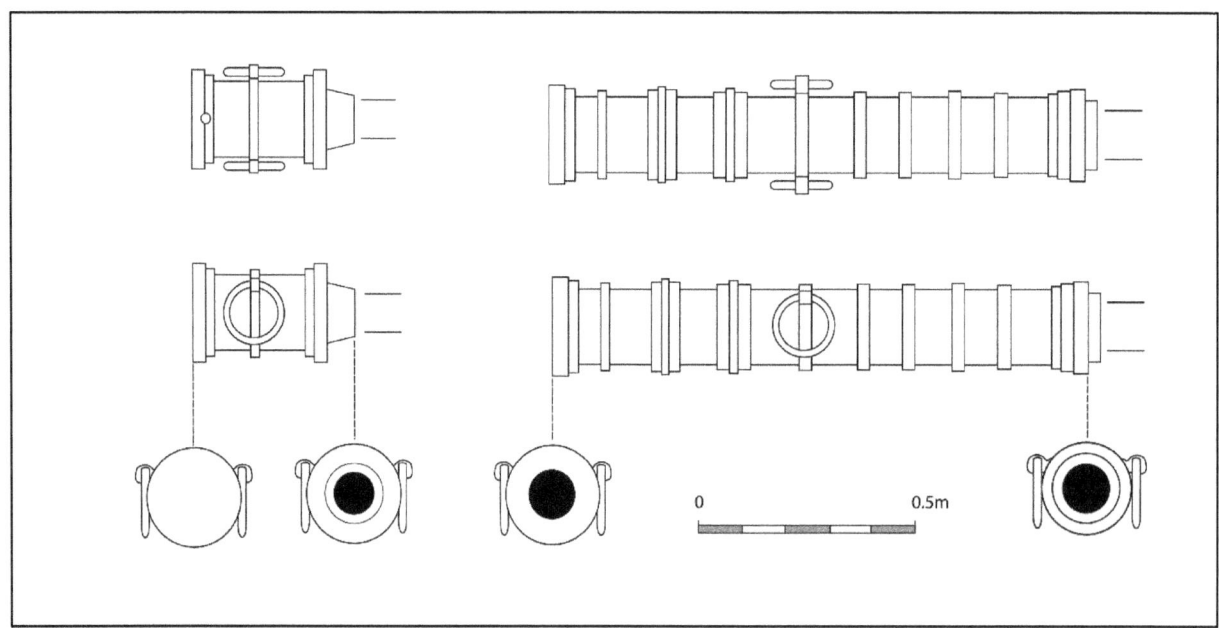

Figure 4-8:   *Drawing of PC4 (D. Ní Chíobháin)*

however, Caruana's study deals primarily with naval ordnance. Prior to the introduction of the muzzle swell guns were reinforced at their muzzles with a series of rings, as evident on contemporary guns used on land. However, these rings could have caused damage to the sides of a ship's gunports when fired. The introduction of the muzzle swell placed the narrowest point of the gun in the area of the gunport, thereby reducing the risk of the gun hitting the gunport when fired (Caruana, 1994, 29). The final characteristic of this gun design series is the introduction of the long cascable design. However, as the end of the cascable of PC3 is missing no analysis can be made (Trollope, 2002, 51).

4.5 PC4: A Wrought-Iron Perrier

This wrought-iron piece was also identified in the grab material lifted off the site in 2003. It was encased within a layer of concretion, as was its chamber, which was found separately. Both pieces were de-concreted by Wessex Archaeology staff and recorded immediately. Traces of the original carriage were still attached to the gun barrel along with two iron straps. It is currently housed at the Royal Armouries in Fort Nelson, Portsmouth and is undergoing long-term conservation.

The breech-loading gun and chamber (Figure 4-8) are of wrought iron in a hoop and stave construction. The barrel measures 1.27 m long, with an internal bore diameter of 130 mm. The sleeves measure on average 185 mm in diameter. Owing to corrosion it was not possible to count how many staves constituted the bore. There are 8 sets of hoops, not counting the breech and muzzle hoops, and 8 sleeve groups. The pattern of hoops is described according to their relative size, 1 being the narrowest and counting upwards (Roth, 1989, 194). Counting from the breech forward, the hoops are as follows; breech hoop 21. Hoops: 1; 121; 121; 1; 1; 1; 1; 1. Muzzle hoop 1231 (Figure 4-8). There is a dual ring collar on the fourth hoop.

The barrel of the chamber appears to be of one-piece construction, where the metal is joined by means of forge welding. The chamber barrel is then built up with hoops and sleeves like the gun barrel. A dual ring collar is flanked with two sleeves. The neck is slightly tapered to fit within the barrel breech. The chamber measures 300 mm long, the neck measures 70 mm. With the chamber in place the gun measures 1570 mm long. The vent hole is identifiable on the hoop set of the chamber base and measures 15 mm in diameter.

The barrel and the carriage are currently in a condition which masks many features. The chamber has undergone successful initial stages of conservation, which enabled accurate measurements to be taken. A combination of measurements taken from the Wessex Archaeology sketch and from photographs of the gun when it was first de-concreted allowed the number and codes of the gun's hoops to be accurately counted and the original dimensions to be assessed.

The carriage fragments survived only around the length of the piece, but the shape of the iron brackets suggests that it was a hollowed log with straight sides and that the straps were folded over the edges along its sides, securing the gun barrel. The archaeological reports note rope attached to a lifting ring and wrapped around the muzzle end (Thomsen, 2003, 5). While this may be associated with fastening the gun on board the ship, it is more likely to date from an earlier salvage operation (see Chapter 3.2, page 20).

Efforts have been made to create a typology of wrought-iron guns (Smith, 1988) by arranging the guns according to their form and function. However, not all guns fit into this typology, as there were many different designs and styles that varied by country of origin. Contemporary names of guns are known from documentary sources, but these changed often from country to country and over short periods of time, so that it is difficult to accurately name a piece by its original label (Smith, 1988, 5). According to Lavery's typology, this piece would be a perrier (Lavery, 1987, 97). Within Smith and Brown's terminology this design would be a tube gun with a chamber, even though its dimensions do not fit into their categories of tube guns. The authors admit that this type of gun is the most difficult to classify due to the wide variety in external design.

4.6 Carriages for Cast-Iron Ordnance

A fragment of an elm carriage was recovered from the site with concretions attached (Figure 4-9). The fragment was one of two cheeks, which would have supported a cast-gun on a carriage, most likely one of the cast-iron guns. The timber measured approximately 120 mm thick and exhibited the remains of at least two steps on the upper face. The steps allowed the gun to be elevated to the desired angle. To achieve this, leverage was applied to the breech through handspikes over the steps in the cheeks. Once in position, the gun barrel was secured with a quoin, a timber wedge placed under the base ring (Perrin and Manwaring, 1922, 205).

It is likely that the cheek from the Princes Channel Wreck would have contained more steps when compared to archaeological parallels. A gun raised from the Elizabethan Alderney wreck contained fragments of both carriage cheeks, one in better condition than the other and exhibiting four steps. They measured 100 mm thick and had steps of differing sizes (McElvogue, 1998, 3). Two more examples of well-preserved gun carriages come from the Baltic grain carrier Scheurrak SO1 wreck. They are made completely of oak, except for the forward axles. The cheeks of the Scheurrak SO1 carriages contain three steps on their upper faces (Puype, 2000, 112). Both the Alderney and Scheurrak SO1 examples have holes where bolts to brace the cheeks apart would have been connected.

It is thought that the Alderney example would have rested upon four trucks (wooden wheels), but the two

Figure 4-9: Gun carriage cheek from the Princes Channel Wreck (J. Auer, Wessex Archaeology)

examples from Scheurrak SO1 have two trucks at the front of the carriage bed and one central truck at the rear. The front trucks had a larger diameter to compensate for the camber of the deck and to ensure the carriage would sit horizontally on the upper decks. Puype suggests that the disadvantages of a three-wheeled carriage include less friction to stop recoil and less stability for the gun. This may reveal why the four-wheeled types were more common in the archaeological record (Puype, 2000, 112).

Like the fragment from the Princes Channel Wreck the carriages for cast-bronze guns from the *Mary Rose* (1545) are also constructed of elm; however, they are much larger, with their cheeks constructed of two components, as they were designed for larger guns than the Princes Channel examples (Hildred, 1997, 54).

4.7. Mountings for Wrought-Iron Ordnance

When PC4 was removed from its concretions it had fragments of its carriage still attached to the length of the gun barrel. There are a number of possible carriage designs for these guns based on known examples from wreck sites that include the *Lomellina* wreck at Villefranche-sur-Mer (Guérout and Rieth, 1998), the Anholt wrecks from Denmark (Brown, 1989, 106), the Kravel (Adams, 2003, 80f.) and Riddarholmen wrecks in Sweden (Weidhagen-Hallerdt, 1992 89-92), the Cattewater wreck in Plymouth (Redknap, 1984, 49-57), and the Wittenbergen wreck from the river Elbe (Ní Chíobháin, 2011; Stanek, 2011).

Common to these is a solid wooden bed or sledge, which is carved to receive the gun barrel and breech. A step in the aft part of the bed provided support for forelock and wedges, which secured the removable chamber. The gun barrel was either fastened to the bed with rope bindings as in examples from the *Mary Rose* (Hildred, 2011, 130ff.) or the *Lomellina* (Guérout and Rieth, 1998, 46) or fastened in place with metal retaining straps. Such iron straps were observed on PC4. A good example for a well preserved wrought iron gun mounted on a wooden carriage is HH4, a port-piece from the Wittenbergen wreck which is roughly contemporary with the Princes Channel Wreck (1571) (Ní Chíobháin, 2011; Stanek, 2011) (Figure 4-10).

The wooden beds could either be mounted on trucks or wheels or as rotating swivel guns. Archaeological examples for wheel mounted carriages include the *Lomellina* (Guérout and Rieth, 1998, 46) and the *Mary Rose* (Hildred, 2011, 130ff.). Examples from the Cattewater wreck in Plymouth (Redknap, 1984, 49-57), the Riddarholmen wreck in Stockholm (Weidhagen-Hallerdt, 1992 89-92) and the St Ekön site on the south coast of Sweden (Einarsson, 2008, 6f.) are likely to have been set upon swivel forks which are secured to the carriage with a transverse iron bolt. Swivel guns were usually placed on the upper deck and were used primarily as anti-personnel weapons, to target those attempting to board a vessel or to clear an opponent's deck for boarding. According to Smith, this mounting arrangement is usually for guns of a smaller bore, from 2″ to 4″ (Smith, 1995, 105).

The height of the gunport above the orlop deck on section 3b of 70 cm suggests that a wooden bed would require large trucks or wheels to clear the port. One example from the *Mary Rose* site is placed on large wheels and is supported with a tiller behind the chamber, but when compared to PC4 the *Mary Rose* guns are much larger; so it would seem that PC4 would have either been located on the weather deck on a carriage or mounted on a swivel. It is difficult to draw any solid conclusions about this gun and carriage and indeed the use of wrought-iron ordnance aboard merchant vessels at this time, as there are very few documented parallels to compare them to.

4.8 Shot

Stone shot was purportedly recovered from the site in 1846, but its location is now unknown. No items of shot were recovered during the 2004 excavation, but despite this the analysis of the cast-iron guns makes it possible to ascertain what calibre of shot they would have fired.

Stone shot was most probably used in the wrought-iron perrier ordnance of the Princes Channel Wreck, exemplified by PC4. By the late 16th century most shot was made of iron, as it was much cheaper to make than the hand cut stone shot (Lavery, 1988, 97). Iron shot was cast in moulds of clay and apart from the commonly known round shot, was made in a number of different forms for a variety of targets.

Rigging was targeted with bar shot, a bar of iron with a solid part at each end. Chain shot was similarly made but with a chain connecting the heavy ends (Lavery, 1988, 136). Although writing much later, Falconer states that langrel shot was often used in privateers and merchantmen to target enemy rigging by firing 'bolts, nails, bars and other pieces of iron tied together, and forming a kind of cylinder, which forms to the bore of

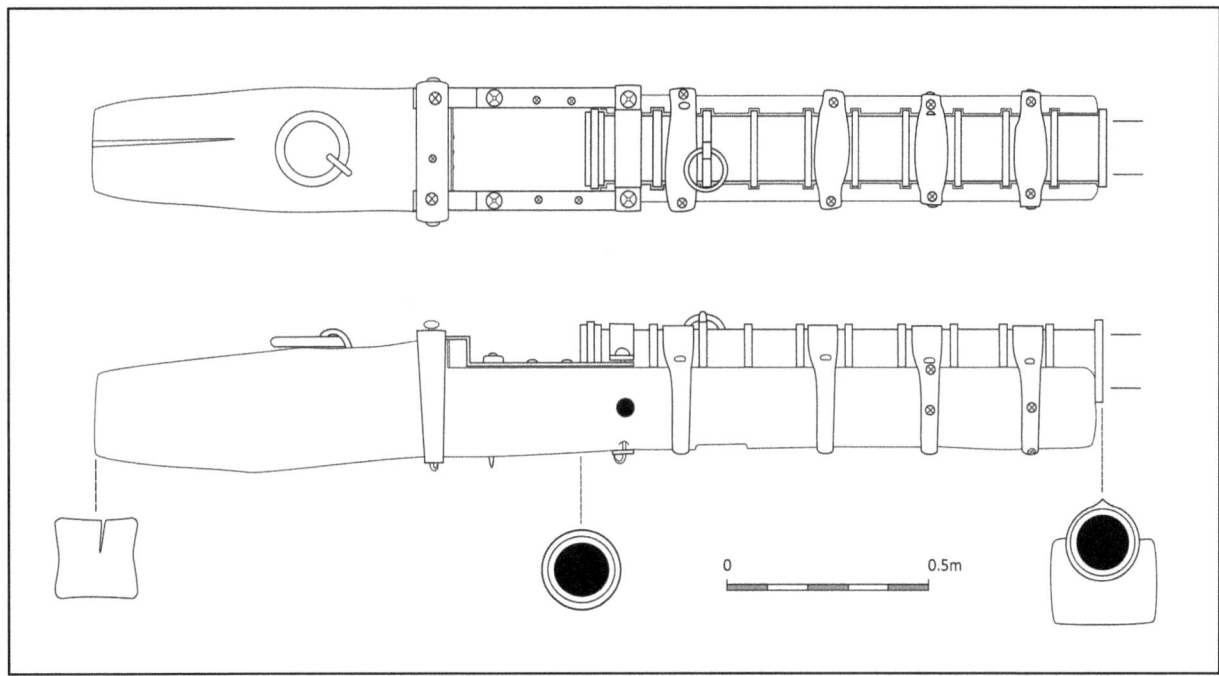

Figure 4-10   Wrought iron-port piece HH4 from the Wittenbergen Wreck (1671) still mounted on wooden bed (D. Ní Chíobháin)

the cannon' (Falconer, 1815, 468). Shot of a variety of kinds was found in the Alderney, Scheurrak SO1 and Wittenbergen assemblages referred to above. Many types may have been intended to paralyse a ship and clear personnel from the decks, rather than sinking it, especially in privateering, where sinking a merchant vessel loses the reward. Circumstances most certainly determined what kinds of projectiles were fired, especially with many merchant vessels at the time being fitted with a variety of gun types.

4.9 Discussion of the Armament Assemblage

With six guns, possibly cast-iron, salvaged from the site in the 19th century (see Chapter 3.2, page 20) and four more guns excavated in recent years, it can be determined that the Princes Channel Wreck would have carried at least ten pieces of ordnance. Trying to re-create a complete assemblage of ordnance, however, is not simple due to the nature of arming vessels at this time. Merchant vessels carried a variety of guns for a number of eventualities, for example swivel guns to target boarders, perriers to shoot at ship's upper structures and heavier culverins targeted at hulls. As many examples of armed vessels from this period carried a mixture of short-range swivel guns and medium-range guns on their broadsides, it could be possible that the Princes Channel ship may have had wrought-iron swivel guns on its upper deck (Ní Chíobháin, 2011; Lavery, 1988, 111).

A close comparison to what the Princes Channel ship may have looked like has been suggested in Matthew Baker's 'Fragments of Ancient English Shipwrightry' (see (Figure 8.1, page 82). The ship in the image, the *Emanuell,* was a 200-ton merchantman of the period. It appears to have six broadside guns, visible from their gunports, and one gun muzzle protruding from its forecastle. The total possible armament of the *Emanuell* would amount to 12 to 14 guns. This number does not conflict with the known number on the Gresham ship. There are no rail-mounted swivel guns visible, which may perhaps reflect the late 16th century view that wrought-iron ordnance was becoming out-dated (Guilmartin, 1988, 40). While the ordnance presented may seem somewhat primitive or plain when compared to guns like the bronze examples from the earlier *Mary Rose*, it must be remembered that these guns were not meant as an embellishments or statements of grandeur. Rather their statement was one of warning and their purpose practical. The guns carried on the Princes Channel ship represent a large range of cheap and effective weaponry that was increasingly necessary on voyages across the North Sea and the Atlantic Ocean for those on the lower end of the trade scale working within tight margins of profit. Therefore ordnance of many kinds wound up on vessels, resulting in 'a hodgepodge of types and sizes of ordnance' (Guilmartin, 1988, 40). When we factor in how much cheaper an alternative for bronze iron had become, the presence of cast-iron ordnance aboard merchantmen would seem appropriate (Padfield, 1973, 47–52). For independent merchants and smaller vessels, moreover, economics were more important than available technology and this may explain the presence of seemingly out-dated and weaker wrought-iron ordnance alongside more powerful cast-iron guns.

Chapter 5: From Record to Model
by Christian Thomsen

To derive the original form and characteristics of a ship from partial archaeological remains, or rather from the data collected during archaeological recording, is a particular challenge. Adequate methodology does exist, however. An important principle in applying it is to analyse the archaeological data for what it is worth and for what it can say rather than making it fit to the image we may already have of a ship of the period. If one jumps to conclusions – however attractive – it will not help our understanding a bit. In this chapter two approaches will be presented, as both were actually used and integrated in creating a research model. One is the manual creation of the wreck sections in wood and cardboard, while the other is a method of directly reproducing the components in a digital three-dimensional environment. Both approaches were combined in an experimental process to model the construction and possible form of the Gresham Ship, and obtain the best possible approximation of its dimensions.

The process started when students of the master's course in the Maritime Archaeology Programme at the University of Southern Denmark in Esbjerg chose the Princes Channel Wreck as a special topic to be studied in the spring semester of 2009. The objective of the course was first to create reconstructions of the individual wreck sections at a scale of 1:20 and secondly to build reconstructions of selected parts of the wreck at a scale of 1:10. Obviously the hands-on exercise was meant to gain an insight into the construction of this particular ship and also to help the students to gain a knowledge of ship construction in general. The course was in many aspects a didactical success and helped in the understanding of what to do and what not to do when approaching archaeological material and data of variable quality. But in terms of research it only showed the way; it did not produce adequate results. The models of the sections were simply not precise enough. It was an eye-opener, however, and served as an inspiration for developing an adequate approach.

As a next step a physical model of the Princes Channel Wreck was built at a scale 1:10, with the aim of producing a hypothetical lines plan, but also of revealing the design ideas that the shipwright had in mind while the ship was still in its initial stages. Although not a central aspect of this chapter, one of the ultimate aims was to make inferences about the underlying thoughts and concepts that guided the shipwright. In that sense archaeology serves as an important complement to and a physical check on our understanding of shipbuilding in late medieval, renaissance and early modern times. So far interpretations have preponderantly been based on historical sources and only very fragmentally on archaeological evidence. That is certainly true for English shipbuilding during the Elizabethan period, for which a rich body of historical material exists. This chapter is just one step and will focus on how to get from the recorded remains of a 16th-century merchant sailing vessel to a lines plan made from a 1:10 scaled working model, ready for further research.

5.1 The Record

As discussed in Chapters 1 and 2, the recording of the Princes Channel Wreck took place in a series of phases, each with their specific conditions and limitations. Underwater recording produced the first overview, but was limited to just that by the environmental conditions on site (see section 5.2). The results fed into the next recording phases, but hardly into the modelling process which needs more reliable measurements. Importantly, however, timbers were labelled with unique numbers and a 1:20 site plan was produced. Individual wreck pieces were subsequently recorded in the (relative) dry, mainly through the use of a total station and descriptions for each timber. However, each wreck section was recorded as part of an assembled structure and therefore it was possible to record only what could be seen from the outside. Measured sketches and scaled drawings were made of chosen components and loose timbers. Under operational pressure the overall record of this phase is not fully comprehensive, although it is complemented by a substantial archive of digital photographs, including a wide range of details from all wreck pieces as well as overview photos from both inside and outside. The archive also contains working pictures documenting the whole project which sometimes provide additional information. Lacunae in the record were specifically addressed in the two field schools in Horsea Lake in 2007 and 2008 (see section 5.2).

5.2 The Methods

The modelling process consisted of a combination of different approaches. The 3D record of the wreck could be used for modelling in wood and cardboard as well as for selective laser sintering of parts. The two approaches will be explained in detail below (sections 5.4 and 5.5). Although one could say that the quality of archaeological recording is what leads to a successful and reliable result (Bischoff *et al.*, 2011), it proved equally true that the modelling process helped to identify and explain discrepancies and distortions in the data.

Traditionally three basic methods for analysis and what has been termed 'reconstruction' have been discerned: graphical, three-dimensional and full-sized models or reconstructions (Steffy, 1994, 214). All three are interlinked. Replica building or complete reconstruction entails all three methods to their full extent. No single method is sufficient to address all the questions and inform all the design inferences and decisions that will present themselves. Designing and building a serious replica is unimaginable without extensive desk-based graphical work and several steps of scaled modelling (Crumlin-Pedersen and McGrail, 2006). Conversely, with the 3D record of the Princes Channel Wreck as a basis, modelling proved to be a necessary step in order to produce a graphical reconstruction.

Inspiration on how to tackle the problems was gained from a variety of projects with different approaches. But it was in no way possible to transfer a single method that could be used in this instance. The work that is carried out in the research department of the Viking Ship Museum in Roskilde (Crumlin-Pedersen and Olsen, 2002) has a series of approaches that were considered, but its specific focus on Nordic clinker vessels left several dilemmas unresolved. The clinker ships are usually reconstructed in ways similar to those used when they were originally built, namely shell-first. This means that cardboard reconstructions of the planking are attached according to their original clinker fastenings, which directly re-establishes the shape of the hull. Since the Gresham Ship was carvel-built, and complexly so, this was not a suitable approach. In this respect guidance was provided by Christian Lemée's use of 'reverse naval architecture' with the ships from the Burmeister & Wain site in Christianshavn (Lemée, 2006). These ships are mostly carvel built and they were recorded using a total station. The record or dataset, however, was different from that of the Princes Channel Wreck, as these ships were recorded in a flat (two-dimensional) top view with additional hand drawings of the moulded dimensions of timbers. Also all these wrecks had been recorded in situ, which meant a fairly limited distortion of the remains and no variability in distortion as recorded. Several of the ships were extensively preserved as coherent structures, which stands in contrast to the Princes Channel Ship, where loose parts were documented whose inter-relationship needed to be established. The choice of using the model as an iterative research tool was certainly adopted and the same materials were used.

The work on the Newport ship shows the possibilities of digital recording and reproduction (Nayling and Jones, 2012). It served as an inspiration for the use of selective laser sintering. This was chosen to gain the maximum level of accuracy in the bow section where the risks and consequences of misshaping were greatest. On the other hand, it was not opportune to deploy this approach for the rest of the ship, as the recording method had been different and data preparation would have been extremely labour-intensive and, last but not least, impractical in view of time and budget limitations. A mixed approach was deemed simply more efficient in view of nature of the dataset and the specific questions to be addressed.

To align the total station recordings of the wreck sections digitally had been tried several times, but all attempts had failed. Translating all the relevant parameters into digital data proved virtually impossible on the basis of the limited dataset. If it had succeeded, the model could theoretically have been completed as a digital 3D object, but the understanding and interpretation of the physical model could hardly have been obtained by a digital model alone.

Because of the broken state of the Princes Channel Wreck and the lack of coherence between the ship's side and the keel, the best option was to make a model of the hull as fragments. This method is particularly fitting for ships that have been broken into pieces after wreckage (Steffy, 1994, 221). Since only the large coherent pieces of the wreck had been recorded systematically, it was not possible or desirable to model each and every loose fragment that had been recovered from the sea floor, so only the major pieces were modelled in this way. Subsequently, the fragments were fitted and joined with long flexible battens fastened to stem- and sternposts. In doing so, the form of the port side of the ship could be assessed and approximated by using all positioning indicators and finding regular and smooth curves. The method was therefore to create a 1:10 half model of the ship that could be used to develop lines drawings of the possible shape.

5.3 Preparing the Data

The first step was to consistently check, correct, complete and transform the 3D data. All this processing was done using the software package Rhinoceros 3D 4.0 (also known as Rhino), a NURBS-based 3D modelling software. What initially needed to be done was to finish the outline of all timbers that had only been partly recorded by the total station. If an outline is not closed, there is only a line in the 3D environment, but no 3D object can be defined. In practice this meant revising every single component of the wreck sections and finishing it as a complete timber (object) that would fit in the structure to be built.

The data needed to be selectively prepared according to two different standards: one for construction in wood and one for the laser sintering, as this requires the creation of solids, a process that will be explained in section 5.6. Preparing the data for modelling in wood and cardboard could be less elaborate. A slightly rough outline, that would be physically finished, was good enough for these timbers and it was not essential that there should be no breaks or bends on the line. It was important, however, to make the outline and the shape of the timber as clear as possible, so that uncertainty and confusion while manufacturing the individual pieces could be minimized.

In the preparation of the digital data it was important to understand how every component indicated and restricted the shape of any adjacent timber that it partly covered. By gradually resolving the lines of one timber it came to define the shape of the timber beneath or next to it. This analytic procedure was necessarily iterative.

Obviously it has a problem of accuracy as to the individual element, but the combined shape of the complete wreck piece is still accurate to an acceptable level.

Most of the data preparation work consisted of cleaning breaks and kinks on the lines and to sort out confusing areas. It was important to make the dataset easily readable and each timber piece clearly distinguishable, for which colour-coding helped a lot. Many of the recorded points had to be deleted and lines re-established in the effort to make the recording clear enough to work with as a basis for the model. As such, data preparation was a simplification of the record that was absolutely necessary for the next steps.

It was essential to flatten out warped planks digitally before creating them as models. In the Norwegian Barcode project a routine for printing a 3D object to a 2D plane was developed, which was adopted for this purpose. A poly-surface was made from a number of cross-sections of the plank. This surface was then unrolled to the 2D plane where the curves, nails and other details flowed along the surface. In this way the model got the right 2D shape and it could then be bent to shape with the other planks. Only the most distorted planks and curved faces of the framing needed to be straightened in this way. The unrolling of a 3D object to a flat surface is incidentally a standard function of the software.

After cleaning and digitally enhancing the data, a system of control lines was applied to the timbers. The control line is a coherent poly-line that reaches from the bottom of a frame on one side over the top face and down the other side. The lines are placed so that they mark the places where strakes cross the frame. Every timber was saved to a separate file that would contain information only on that particular component. A timber file ready for printing would contain the complete outline of the shape, all recorded trenail holes and nail holes, significant breaks in the wood and control lines. Other details such as joints, concretions and repairs would also be shown.

5.4 Wood and Cardboard

The main part of the Princes Channel Wreck was modelled manually from wood and cardboard. This is a well-established method and it is a fairly simple procedure with minimal requirements in terms of workshop facilities and other expenses. The work requires a good working space with proper lighting and a large table. Some essential tools are needed: cutting and carving tools for wood and cardboard, a mini-drilling machine, pencils, glue, a selection of screws and screwdrivers, small hammers, pliers and other basic tools. In this instance a small band-saw with a 180-watt electrical motor and a narrow blade proved indispensable. The small saw with narrow blade gave adequate accuracy in controlling curves when sawing out the frames and other timbers. The wood for the

Figure 5-1: The finished framing timbers on section 3a on top of the outer planking prior to fastening (C. Thomsen)

frames was fir cut from construction timber and floor planks; so the process was cheap in terms of materials.

Although the procedure was based on digital records, work proceeded fairly similarly to the way it is done on the basis of traditional hand-drawn records. Every frame was printed at a scale of 1:10 in three different views, two sides and a top view. Every view was printed out twice, so that there was a spare copy if one view needed to be cut away. The most important shape for getting the reconstructed hull shape right was the moulded shape shown on the side views.

A piece of wood with an appropriate dimension was prepared for making a frame. One of the side views was glued to the wood and the inside curve of the frame was cut out. The top view was then glued to the newly cut surface so that the control lines on top correspond to the control lines on the side.

If the frame was straight and regular, it was sufficient to cut one side of the frame to get the correct sided dimension, but usually both sides needed to be adjusted to get the right shape. When both the sided dimension and the inside curve of the frame were correct, the frame would be completed by cutting the outside face of the frame and thereby finishing the moulded dimension. The control lines are important because they ensure that the views are connected in their correct individual positions. The frames were rarely rectangular in cross-section and therefore the cut often had to go diagonally through the wood to make sure that the outline of the frame was followed.

If it had been necessary to cut away some of the glued print-outs from the frame, the spare print-out could be applied. In cases where sufficient precision could not be obtained with the band-saw, small wood-carving chisels and carving knives proved very helpful. In this way a fairly accurate rendering of the shape of each recorded timber was produced, while the printed views showed all registered details such as nails and trenails, repairs, and markings in their correct positions. The most efficient way to proceed was to organize the work as a

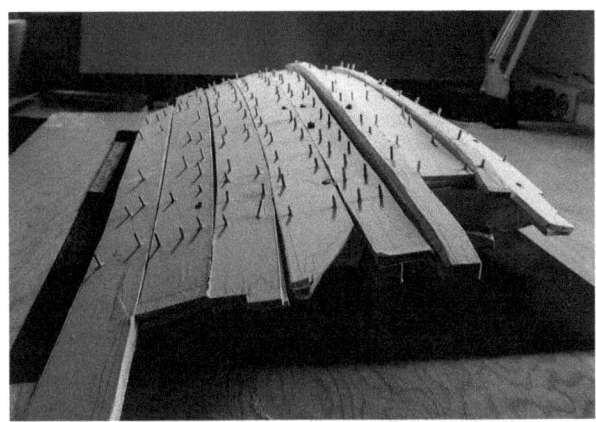

Figure 5-2: The cardboard planks on section 3b fastened with toothpick trenails (C. Thomsen)

Figure 5-3: Cardboard planking under production (C. Thomsen)

serial production, where one wreck fragment at the time was produced in the sequence of their numbers given during the recording (Figure 5-1).

Each reproduced frame was marked with its recorded timber number with a black pen, preferably at a place where it could also be seen after the pieces were assembled. Being relatively systematic in the production of the frames was important so as to keep track of the different components. Furring timbers were attached to the corresponding futtock directly after they were produced. In this way it was fairly simple to line up all the components ready for planking.

Futtocks and furring timbers were connected by imitating the original trenail fastenings. As the printouts showed exactly where the original fastenings had been on the timber, it was natural to use the same places for fastening the reconstructed components. With a mini-drilling machine and a 2-mm drill bit, holes were drilled where they were indicated in the record. Not every single trenail fastening was drilled, but sufficient only for connecting the pieces properly. The 2-mm drill bit corresponded exactly to the diameter of ordinary round toothpicks, which were used as trenail substitutes (Figure 5-2). It is obvious that fastening with a 33-mm oak trenail in a massive 70 mm oak plank cannot be compared with fastening cardboard planks with a

Figure 5-4: The finished scale model of section 1 (C. Thomsen)

toothpick, but it was rather surprising to feel the combined strength of even such minor toothpick fastenings. It certainly indicates the original strength of the fastenings.

Using toothpick trenails had the advantage of being a reversible method of holding the constructional elements together. Despite the relatively strong fastening it was possible to draw the components from each other without damaging the pieces. Where much strain was put on the structure from the curving of the planking and frames it was necessary to use small screws to make sure that components would not come apart.

Like the frames the planks were printed from Rhinoceros 3D at a scale of 1:10. It was often not possible to get a full view of the inside of the planking, since the internal timbers blocked the view during recording. Where reasonable data was available, in the areas with sparse preserved framing, the inside face of the planking was printed. Each side of the plank prints was glued to 3-mm thick cardboard and cut out (Figure 5-3). The two pieces of cardboard were then glued together with wood-glue and held together with clamps until dry. At a total of 6 mm, the thickness of the cardboard planks thus corresponded at 1:10 to the average thickness of the original planking. All the planks had also been supplied with control lines that showed the placement of the frames. In this way it was easy to fit the planks and frames together to their original positions (Figures 5-4 and 5-5)

5.5 Selective Laser Sintering (SLS)

Digital recording and 3D processing open the possibility of using 3D printing as an aid to produce scaled elements for a model. The method is dependent on certain standards of recording, but has been successfully applied in a number of ship-archaeological projects. To create a SLS model of polyamide nylon dust was chosen as the best solution for the bow section. In this way the most accurate reconstruction for this part was ensured. The bow section is particularly important for the reliability of the model, because the run of strakes starts here and therefore defines the positioning of the wreck sections on the ship's side.

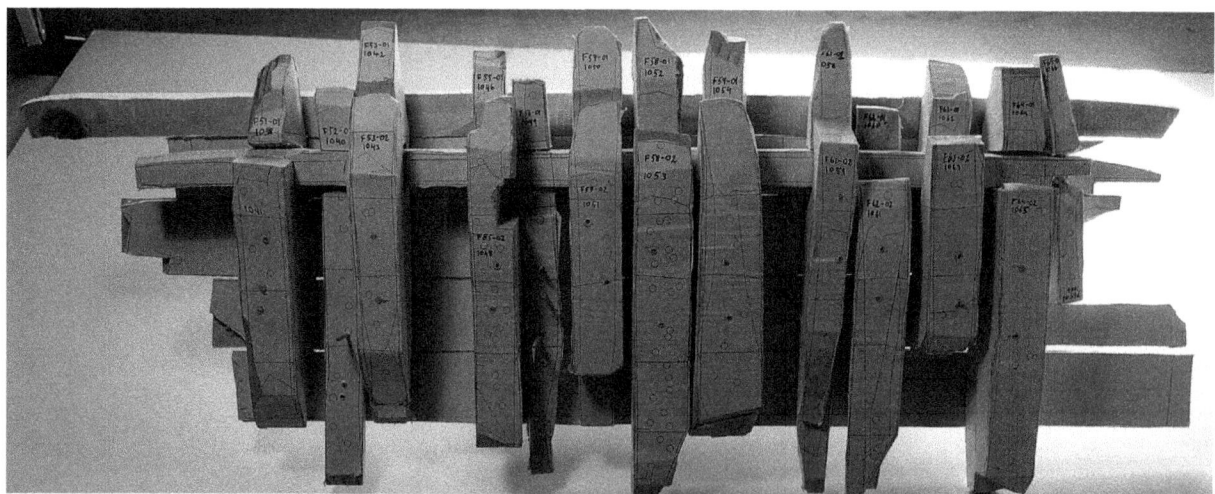

Figure 5-5: The finished scale model of section 2 (C. Thomsen)

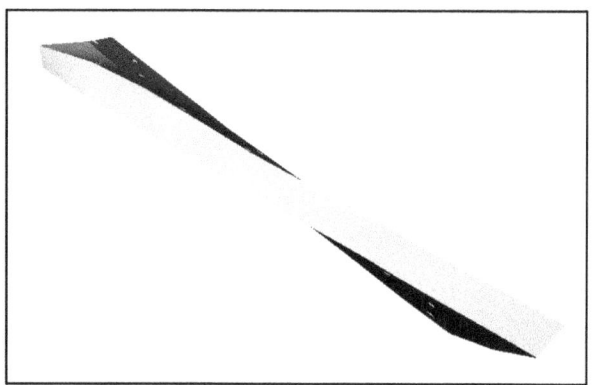

Figure 5-6: Digital solid of one of the outer planks in the bow section; this view clearly shows the amount of distortion in the plank (C. Thomsen)

After preparing the recorded data as explained above, each individual timber had to be recreated as what is called a digital solid. In practice this meant exporting each timber to create a separate file that could be worked upon as a component independent of the rest of the structure. Creating digital solids from the total station recording was a process of simplification of the data to an extent that allowed a smooth digital web to be drawn over the surface of the timber shape. If the shape of the timber recording was too complicated and included too many irregular and complicated shapes, it became difficult to make a completely closed surface that covered the whole piece and further simplification was necessary. The main issue in creating successful surfaces for the solid models was to make the shape simple. This does not mean compromising the shape as such, but an effort should be made to use as few points and curves as possible for making the shape (Figure 5-6).

All the recorded trenails were also created in the solid file. These were made as cylinders with diameter of 26 mm. The cylinders were subtracted from the digital solid by the programme, leaving holes in the timber models exactly where the trenails were originally placed. The record, however, did not include details of the angle of the trenails; so this had to be based on the recorded marking, which would in many cases not have corresponded to the original angle. The markings of each trenail were transferred to the files of all the timber pieces that realistically it could have penetrated and this helped in linking the pieces back together in the right positions.

The processing of recorded data into finished digital solids was a time-consuming process. This was mainly due to the quality of the record since many concealed areas had to be rebuilt completely before creating the solids was possible. The most problematic areas were those parts of the bow section that were extensively covered by other timbers and planking. This was in particular the inner face of the stempost which was completely hidden by the massive apron. In addition the scarf between stempost and keel had to be partially reconstructed, as only the outside part was visible. While rebuilding these areas, hand drawings and detailed sketches along with photographs were crucial. It has to be noted that the process of preparing the data was as much an analysis of how all the elements in the construction related to each other as it was an analysis of form. It was thus an essential step in studying the ship's construction. The process could be compared to a virtual disassembly of the hull sections. However, altogether it can be confidently assumed that the model comes as close as possible to the recorded shape. The planks have the correct curvature and the shape of individual inner timbers reflects that of the originals, even though there might be small deviations.

When a separate file had been created for every timber of the bow section and the digital models had been created as solids, the model needed to be scaled to 1:10. The 1:10 timber model file was saved as a stereolithography or STL file. The STL file was opened in the 3D viewer MiniMagics in order to check the quality of the file. This program would approve the file as ready for manufacturing or indicate which areas needed to be rebuilt. Every step of the process was saved as different files which ensured the possibility of

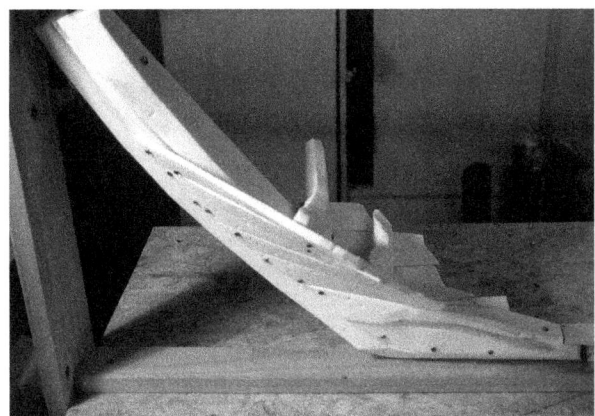

Figure 5-7: The assembled sintered model of the bow section (C. Thomsen)

moving one step back in the process to rectify corrupted areas without having to begin again from scratch. When a 1:10 STL file had been made for every timber, they were submitted for manufacturing.

After receiving the plastic models of the timbers, they were assembled with small 2.7 x 16 mm brass screws. The diameter was just right to bite into the plastic making a strong fastening and they could easily be screwed in with a manual screwdriver. The size of the screws should be considered as early as the digital processing phase and a size that lies as close as possible to the original fastening should be chosen. Pan-headed screws are preferable since these can be screwed further into the plastic and make a tighter connection (Figure 5-7).

5.6 Modelling Problem Areas

Analysing and modelling areas of the hull where the data was problematic was a closely interlinked process between the digital reconstruction, while preparing the data, and the actual physical scaled reproduction of the hull sections. It is a floating and iterative process that makes it impossible to distinguish exactly at what point it is a matter of straightforward data processing or of inference and interpretation.

Section 3a was the most distorted section of the remains. The section was so distorted that the recordings of the inside and of the outside could not be fitted together. The distortion was partly the result of the various lifting operations, but also due to a lack of support during the recording. The uppermost planks were bent inward and needed straightening. It was not possible to see whether the frames had been damaged and whether the angle between floor timbers and futtocks had changed significantly. Modelling the frames in their recorded form made it possible to see what shape the planking would take when attached to the frames. The model then showed a slight distortion as an inward bend of the planking appeared after fastening. Since the original shape was unknown, the distortion was accepted at this point, but would be re-evaluated in connection with the other sections. To preserve the necessary flexibility for later adjustments, the ceiling planks were not yet attached to the inside of the framing. The ceiling planks, after all, would not as such contribute to the shape of the piece and would only require more force in corrective bending.

The ceiling planks on section 3a were covering the area above the joints between floor timbers and first futtocks and these joints were therefore not directly recorded. Examination confirmed that they were connected with interlocking joints, but in the modelling, these joints were simplified, as their precise dimensions could not be obtained. One hull plank was broken and distorted as a result. Consequently the print-out was cut out as two pieces, separated at the break. When glued onto the cardboard the two pieces were connected so that the distinctive edges of the break were aligned and most of the recorded distortion eliminated.

Section 3b represents the uppermost preserved part of the ship and includes two wales and a gunport. The furring was also intact. As opposed to section 3a, it was possible to merge the recordings of the inside and of the outside of the section. Nevertheless, it was clear that the shape of the section had changed when it was turned over to record the other side. The merged file was important for the understanding of the structure, but the distortion hampered the interpretation of the form of individual timbers. Partially recorded timbers were therefore completed on the basis of the inside recording rather than the merged file. As section 3b has a double layer of timbers, the reconstruction of the framing on this part of the wreck was particularly problematic. Several lines defining the shape of each timber had to be improvised and some timbers that had been almost completely covered by other timbers had to be constructed almost completely from artificial lines.

A problem with each of the wreck sections was that the strakes were separated from their original fastening points in the stem and stern. Control of longitudinal curvature was therefore problematic and subject to interpretation of what best fitted the combined data.

5.7 Alignment of the Hull Sections

After finishing the models of the five wreck sections, these had to be aligned in a frame constructed for this purpose. The first section to be fastened was the bow section 4. The idea was to place the other wreck parts in relation to the bow section since the run of the planks would be helpful when moving the sections around to find the best fit. Several attempts were made before the setup was satisfying. In this process it became clear that a range of solutions was possible. The alignment of the sections was thus again a shifting and iterative process in which a range of considerations and interpretations came into play.

Laying a keel was the first step. In order not to deviate from the data in the record and not to prejudice keel length before other indicators were in place, the keel

Figure 5-8: The keel has been laid, consisting of the laser sintered preserved part and a wooden extension (C. Thomsen)

was constructed as a simple extension of the surviving keel piece attached to the bow section. It is quite possible – probable even – that the original keel of the Princes Channel Wreck was flat and broad towards the mid-section of the ship and higher and narrower towards stem and stern. But at this stage it was modelled with the same cross-section from fore to aft. The keel was also assumed to have been straight, although a possible rocker or hogging cannot be excluded on the basis of the archaeological evidence (Figure 5-8).

After the keel had been placed in the frame, the bow section was connected to its forward end. The stempost was fastened with screws and a metal batten to a vertical board at the end of the frame, while the SLS part of the keel was screwed to the frame. With the bow section fixed in place the first and greatest challenge was to find the right distance between it and section 3a. All the others could be directly connected together. This was the only completely missing connection between the fragments. The distance between these two sections was therefore a key factor for assessing the overall hull shape. If this distance could be established with some degree of certainty, the rest of the wreck sections would also be linked to the bow.

When the wreck sections were first investigated on the sea floor there was an approximate distance of 2 m between the end of the keel fragment on section 4 and the nearest frame on section 3a. This distance was not in any way a certain measurement of the original distance between the two points on the hull, but it is nevertheless indicative. The site did not at that stage give the impression of having been greatly disturbed. Both sections were heavy and covered by sediments. It is unlikely that they had moved a great distance from where they had been deposited. The gap between the two sections was most probably caused by the grab used by the harbour authorities when the wreck was discovered. Because of this it was not unreasonable to apply this approximate distance in the model first. It fitted well with a gradual tapering of the planks from section 3a towards the bow. If the section was moved closer to the bow, the tapering of the planks would have been remarkably steep and the twisting of the garboard strake and the second strake would have been very sharp. This would not have been impossible, but suggested nevertheless that the chosen distance was close to the original. A couple of cardboard planks were used to indicate the run of the strakes in the gap between sections 4 and 3a. Prolonging the cardboard planks helped to ensure that a natural run of the strakes was possible between the two sections.

In the preliminary setup the hull sections were held together in a frame with clamps. The frame was equipped with metal bands to which the individual sections could be clamped (Figure 5-9). The second factor that had to be determined before proceeding was the distance from the keel to the lowest preserved plank of section 3a. Different solutions and options were tried. The run of the strakes matched when the third plank from the keel of section 4 corresponded to the first preserved strake on section 3a. This left room for the garboard strake and the second strake as the only missing planks between the preserved parts of the wreck and the keel. There was no direct evidence that indicated the right distance, but it was important to ensure that the lower edge of the lowest preserved plank of piece 3a was running parallel to the keel. A further factor was derived from analogy with the *Sea Venture*, a slightly more heavily built ship of a few decades later, but nevertheless one of the few parallels for the English context of the Gresham Ship (Adams, 1985; Adams, 2003, 109–144). In that case the distance from the centre of the keel to the start of the so-called wronghead sweep was the same as the overlap between the first futtock and the floor timbers. If the same rule had been applied to the Princes Channel Wreck, the distance from the centre of the keel to the lower edge of the preserved plank would be a metre. The distance from the garboard rabbet to the plank edge would then be 90 cm, corresponding exactly to the width of two planks with the same width as the ones preserved. This solution seemed reasonable and was chosen as the basis for aligning the rest of the wreck pieces (Figure 5-10).

The third section to be placed in the frame was section 1. Sections 3a and 1 shared four strakes of which only one plank had been broken and the rest had separated at overlapping planking scarfs. This meant that a good fit between the pieces could be obtained relatively easily. It is clear that the futtocks and floor timbers of section 1 are more upright than the floor timbers of section 3a. This indicates clearly that the narrowing of the ship's breadth towards the stern had begun and the section was located aft of the midships area. The angle of the floor timbers and the rising of overlapping scarfs between floors and futtocks are an indication of the rising line towards the sternpost.

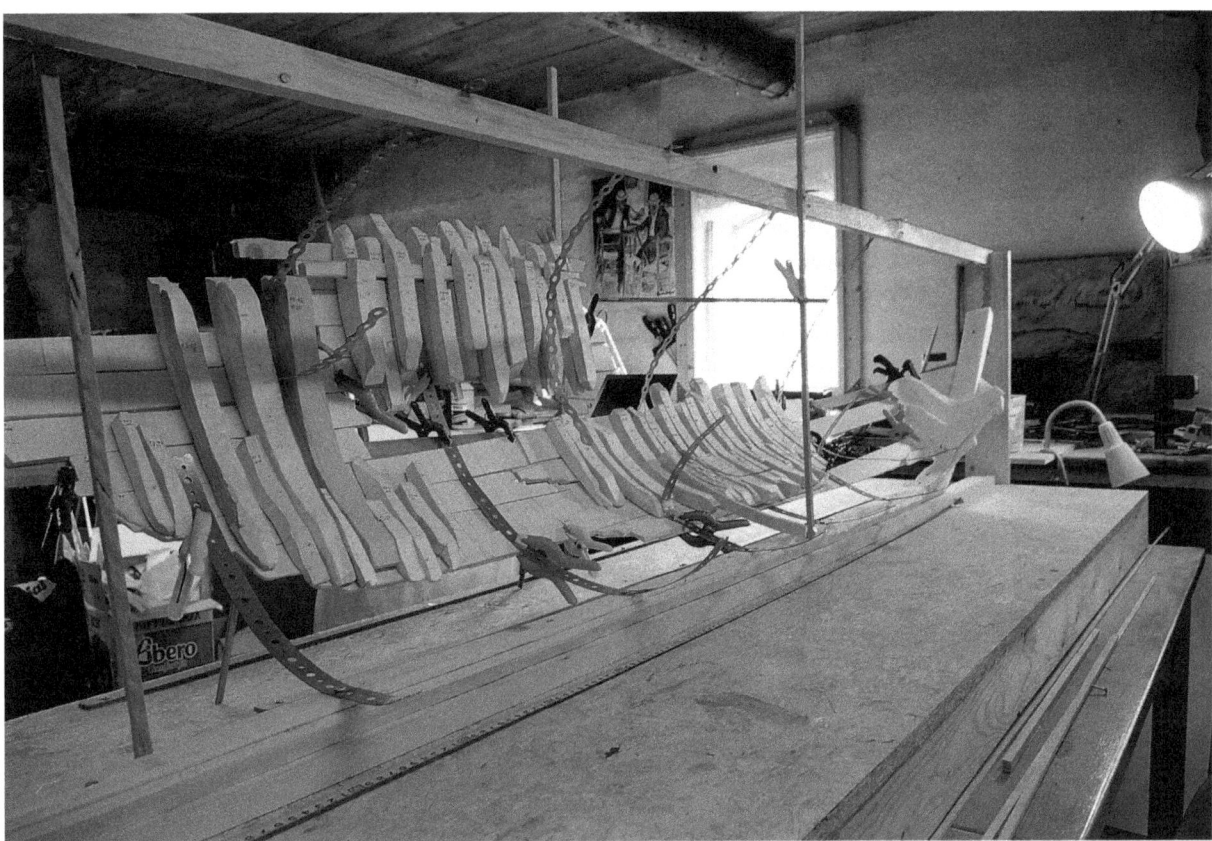

Figure 5-9: *Preliminary alignment of the pieces clamped to metal battens, which were attached to the frame. This solution of the model frame was not stable enough and the way in which the sections were fastened was changed several times (C. Thomsen)*

Figure 5-10: The distance between keel and the lower edge of the third strake on section 3a (C. Thomsen)

Figure 5-11: Broken first futtocks and furring timbers on section 1 aligned with the sandwiched wale on section 2 (C. Thomsen)

Section 2 was attached above and forward of section 1. Both sections could easily be aligned as they share two strakes. Moreover, the wale that was still sandwiched between the frames and furring timbers on section 2 aligned with the top of the broken first futtocks and furring timbers on section 1 (Figure 5-11).

Although a gap exists between sections 2 and 3a, both are connected directly to section 1. In the first alignment the space between sections 2 and 3a was getting narrower towards the bow. This made no sense

and had to be corrected. By pressing in the stern end of section 1 and at the same time lifting it a few centimetres the run of the strakes straightened up and the gap became equally wide at both ends leaving room for the two missing strakes. This also resulted in a more convincing arc for the missing floor timbers.

The last section to be added to the model was 3b. Originally it had been joined above section 3a, but the piece came apart, which resulted in broken futtocks just below the furring timbers. The recording results showed that the two sections were originally connected by eight

Figure 5-12: A view of the sternpost and transom with the flexible battens extending out (C. Thomsen)

Figure 5-13: The bow section with the prolonged stempost (C. Thomsen)

futtocks. It was therefore possible to place section 3b above section 3a with certainty. At this point, however, the distortion of section 3a was very evident. The awkward inward bend contrasted with the relatively fair curve of the planking on section 3b.

Sections 3b and 2 shared four strakes and the lower wale as well as the wale sandwiched between the futtocks and the furring timbers. Three of the planks and the lower wale had been broken and fragments of the planking were missing. One strake was separated at the plank scarf which indicated that the pieces had been directly connected.

With all the wreck components placed in the frame, careful adjustment was necessary to ensure that the run of the strakes was convincing before the hull sections were fixed. In the first setup the sill of the gunport on section 3b had an upward angle, which seemed unrealistic and the shape of the hull was very rounded with significant tumblehome. The angle of the gunport indicated that the shape was wrong and changing this meant bringing the side further out. Naturally the hull shape changed a lot in the process and the result was a shape with a very gentle curve from the bottom of the ship to the lower wale.

After adjusting the model parts, long flexible wooden battens were screwed onto the outside of the model, running parallel to the strakes. The battens continued beyond the extent of the wreck sections. In the after part of the model they were kept longer since the location of the sternpost had not yet been found. On the inside of these battens a double layer of cardboard was attached providing them with the same thickness as the rest of the planking. In this way the surface of the model was extended to areas where nothing of the ship had been preserved. On the inside of the extended planking, vertical flexible battens were clamped to ensure that the inside of the planking was following the same curve. In a way, the battens functioned as a sort of internal framing, but as opposed to stiff moulds the battens would allow for continuous adjustments. In this way the planking was actually defining itself in natural curves. The double cardboard layer on the inside of the battens would ensure that the right distance was kept from frames and that the outer surface would likewise be smooth.

With all the wreck sections finally aligned it was possible to determine an approximate length of the keel. It remains an estimate, but it seems hardly likely that the original keel would have been more than a metre longer or shorter than the estimate on which the reconstruction is based. The main argument is the run of the strakes in the aftermost preserved parts of the hull. By adjusting the curvature of the battens fastened on the outside of the planking the most likely shape was found and this resulted in placing the heel of the sternpost 19 m from the stempost scarf. A supporting argument was found after a sternpost was put up and fixed to the keel with a 20° rake. The distance between the transom and the aftermost preserved location of a beam was exactly four times the distance between beams elsewhere. So on the assumption that they were evenly spaced three crossbeams would fit in between (Figure 5-12).

In the bow section the battens were connected to the SLS model, so that the hood-ends of the prolonged cardboard planks fitted in the rabbet of the stempost.

Above the preserved part the stempost a curved piece of wood was fabricated to continue the arc of the stem. The prolonged planks and battens could then be fixed to this (Figure 5-13).

5.8 The Model

The whole process of modelling, as one will understand, is one in which judging the lines of the hull is as important as integrating those measurements that can be taken as facts. Inference and estimates are not scientific proof, but nevertheless, where inferences strengthen each other, the model becomes the best or most reasonable fit to the data.

The most obvious result is a concept of the basic dimensions of the Princes Channel Ship. Naturally it must be seen in the perspective of a number of uncertainties, but initially, for instance, the length of the keel was expected to be 14–15 m. As modelling proceeded and the modelled wreck sections were placed in the frame it became clear that the length expected when the process started had been a clear underestimate. In fact, the frame used to build the model proved too small and needed to be rebuilt. Based on different considerations the length was finally set to 19 m between the scarf of keel and stempost and the fitting of the sternpost. The lines of the strakes did not leave much doubt that the ship ended in a transom. Just how wide the transom had originally been is another matter. The rake of the sternpost was taken to be 20^0, based on archaeological comparisons and general rules from the contemporary manuscripts concerning shipbuilding. The run of the planks then defined the width of the transom in relation to the keel length that had already been set. The position and rake of the sternpost also determined the length of the ship at deck level to be 24.7 m. The greatest breadth of the ship, measured to the inside of the planking, was found to be 7.71 m of the furred hull and 7.11 m of the original hull. The distance between the upper surface of the keel and the lower edge of the deck beams was around 3.24 m.

Chapter 6 Analysing the Model of the Princes Channel Wreck
by Christian Thomsen and Massimiliano Ditta

Chapter 5 described the way in which the data on the construction of the Gresham Ship, gathered during the various phases of the Princes Channel project, was used to develop a model of the ship's dimensions, construction and shape. The number of unknown variables makes the result open to discussion. Every single angle could have been changed more or less and the outcome would have been different. On the other hand, finding the general shape and dimensions was the central issue and it seems unlikely that these aspects can be changed by minor adjustments. Speculations on the design and shape that go beyond the archaeological evidence were kept to a minimum, although some were both unavoidable and relatively self-evident: the fragments must have belonged to a coherent hull whose lines were faired and as logical as the lines of a ship's hull can be. The model was built only up to the height of the gunports, while everything above this area was left out.

In the present chapter this model will be analysed and interpreted in the context of late 16th-century shipbuilding in England. To make this possible the model, which was developed on the basis of the recorded data, was itself recorded. A lines plan could then be produced, as well as a clean digital hull form. These then become the subject of the next step of the analysis.

As argued above, the keel length was set at 19 m. The overall length of the model at deck level corresponds to 24.7 m in the original. Calculating the relative proportions on the basis of the model as constructed and measured to best fit the archaeological data minimized the risk of circular reasoning inspired by written sources. The greatest breadth of the furred hull measured to the outside of planking is 7.85 m, while the original greatest breadth must have been closer to 7.25 m. If measured to the inside of planking, the breadth is 7.71 m and 7.11 m respectively. The depth from deck level to the upper side of the keel is 3.24 m.

The dimensions and proportions are taken as a basis for inferences about carrying capacity and the size of the ship in terms of tonnage. Subsequently the analysed data on the Gresham Ship will be discussed in terms of the historical discourse on ship design and in terms of the specific characteristics by which the archaeological data – or the model derived from it – can be compared with contemporary texts on the subject of shipbuilding and ship design. First, however, some central features, the midship section, the stem and the stern, will be discussed.

6.1 The Master Frame

Considering the cultural context of the ship with its construction with built-up frames, it is likely that one specific frame was erected as the master frame. On the basis of the archaeological data integrated into the model, the length of keel was decided at 19 m. This goes back to what look like the fairest lines for the run of the strakes and to the assumption that the keel was not lengthened during the rebuilding of the hull when it was furred. Therefore the length is determined as a product of the reconstructed model rather than on the basis of any historical sources, but it is worth investigating if there is some measure of correspondence with contemporary English sources.

Although somewhat later, the anonymous *Treatise on Shipbuilding*, written around 1620–1625, is interesting in this context (Salisbury and Anderson, 1958). According to it the master frame or midship frame is not placed exactly amidships. The broadest mould is placed ⅓ of the keel length from the forward end of the keel. One third of 19 m equals 6.3 m from the forward end. This corresponds very well to the model setup that shows the greatest breadth of the hull just around 6 m aft of the keel and stempost scarf. The role of master frame could then be allotted to the frame registered as floor timber 1177 linked to futtock 206. The two timbers are joined together most probably by an interlocking joint, but the place where the two timbers joined was covered by ceiling planks when being recorded and the exact composition of the scarf was therefore not accessible. Since interlocking joints were recorded on other transitions between floor timbers and futtocks, this can nevertheless be reasonably assumed.

An argument to consider the frame that sits one station further aft as a more likely candidate for the master frame is that this would correspond with the assumed placing of the central athwartships deck beam. The master frame was therefore taken as floor timber 1139 joined to futtock 1179. This places it 7 m from the stempost scarf. As mentioned, nothing was left of the upper framing in this area and therefore there is no actual evidence of the master-frame beam, but the position is exactly in the middle between the aftermost beam-fitting of section 3a and the only preserved beam-fitting on section 2 (Figure 6-1).

6.2 The Bow

Luckily section 4, a composite part of the lower bow of the Gresham Ship, survived. It was of crucial value in modelling the lower parts of the hull from bow to stern. However, the distance between the bow section and the heavily distorted section 3a was problematic. It is brought up again here, as it is a key aspect in the shape of the ship and a sort of 'missing link'. There is a possibility that the distance was originally shorter than suggested by the present model. If that were the case, it would have a considerable influence on the shape of the ship and it would indicate a shorter and proportionally

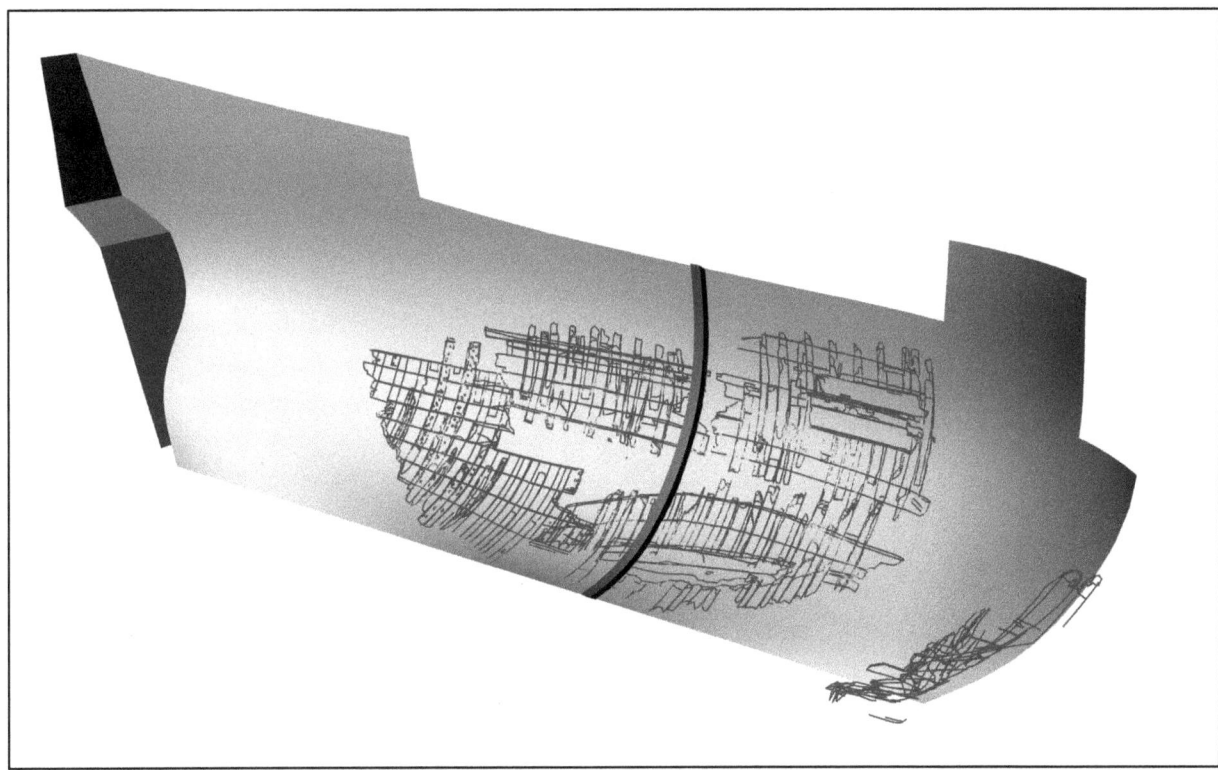

*Figure 6-1:	The location of the master frame in the reconstructed shape of the hull (M. Ditta)*

wider hull. A gradual rising of the heads of the floor timbers in section 3a shows that the last preserved floors are placed on a gradual rising line and therefore not far from the bow. In the unlikely case that the distance was originally greater, this might affect the identification of the master frame, discussed above.

There are no comparable archaeological examples to refer to for comparison. However, during the modelling the conviction became stronger and stronger that the positioning is not far from the original. An important supporting argument is the fact that the tapering of the planks would otherwise have been very steep and that the planks would have to have had a sharp angle towards the hood-ends. A shape like that seems very unlikely when looking at the plank remains from the bow. Also the twist of the garboard and the second strake would have had to be quite extreme in the transition between the bow section and section 3a.

The upper part of the bow, however, is much more uncertain in its modelled shape. The solution that was chosen was a fairly straight run from the preserved planks toward the stem. The run was indicated by the shape of the wale that makes a bend just aft of where it is broken. It is possible or even probable that at deck level the bow was somewhat fuller in shape. This is definitely an area that is open for an alternative solution.

As the aligning of the wreck sections took shape it was necessary to extend the height of the stempost. The lengthening was done by continuing the arc that shaped the stempost and to cut it out in a piece of wood. Extending the stempost by continuing the arc is supported by illustrations in the 'Fragments of Ancient English Shipwrightry', a manuscript dating to the period 1570–1630, started by the shipwright Matthew Baker and continued by his apprentice John Wells (Barker, 1986), and the aforementioned *Treatise on Shipbuilding*, which also explains the construction of the stem as "one or more pieces of large compass timber scarfed and bolted together, swept out by a circle whose radius is the rake forward on" (Salisbury and Anderson, 1958, 7).

6.3 The Stern

In order to allow a better understanding of the archaeological data, the reconstruction model was fitted with a sternpost. Given that there are no remains of the stern, the rake of the sternpost is a qualified guess rather than based on direct evidence. The closest archaeological parallel with evidence of stern rake is probably the remains of a ship from Alderney. Actually, the main constructional element preserved of this ship is the rudder. From analysing its angle, the rake of the stern is calculated to be 16° from vertical (Roberts, 1998, 33). This is slightly steeper than the recommendation in the *Treatise on Shipbuilding*, which advises that the rake of the stern post should never be more than 22° or less than 18° from vertical (Salisbury and Anderson, 1958, 23); similar guidelines are given in the Matthew Baker's manuscript.

A ship of different origin but largely contemporary with the Gresham Ship is the Basque whaler found in Red Bay in Labrador. The ship was extensively preserved including the complete stern structure and transom. Here the rake was 21° from vertical (Grenier *et al.*,

ANALYSING THE MODEL

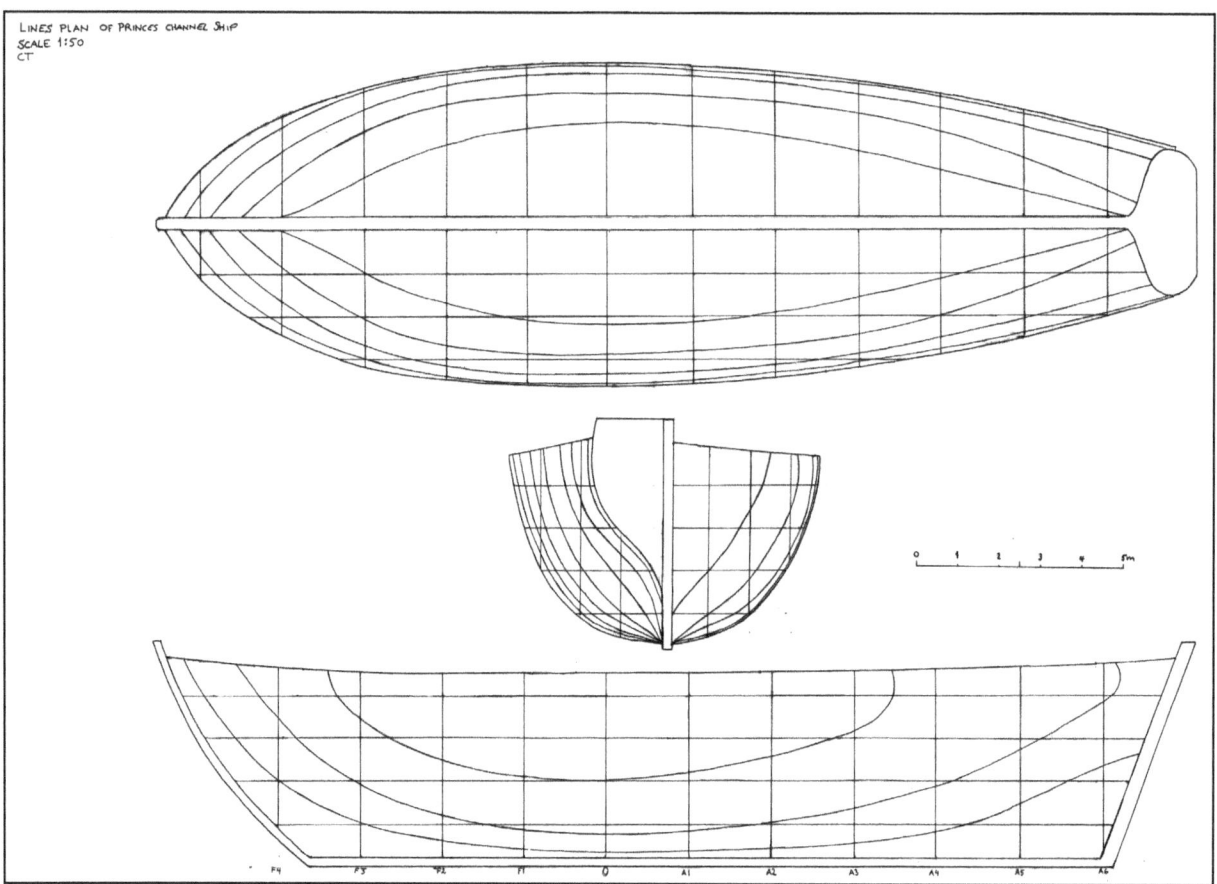

Figure 6-2: The initial lines plan, a result of digital recording and fairing by hand using splines (C. Thomsen)

2007, 48) and thereby within the recommendations in the *Treatise on Shipbuilding* (Salisbury and Anderson, 1958). The possible Iberian-Atlantic vessel found in Studland Bay has a fragment of the aftermost part of the keel preserved and from this the rake of the sternpost is known to be 20° from vertical (Thomsen, 2000, 72). Based on this evidence, it would seem reasonable to propose a rake of 20° for the sternpost of the Gresham Ship as was chosen in the model (Figure 5.12).

6.4 Recording the Model

For the analysis the model had to be recorded. The recording was done by using a total station. The 3D recording would be the basis for developing a lines plan of the hull. A manual approach to measuring the stations along the hull side could have been chosen, but the opportunity of recording the model with the total station would also result in a 3D digital model that otherwise would not have been directly obtainable. Because of the extensive framing it was not possible to gain a clear view of the inside of the planking and therefore it was chosen to record the outside shape of the planking.

The first line to be recorded was the coherent running line of the stempost, keel and stern. After this the transom was measured. A series of the strakes was also recorded with their curving runs. The strake runs function as a control and as an addition to the sections and waterlines. A total of 11 sections were measured, at regular distances of 2 m (0.2 m in the model). The position of the first section, section 0, was chosen so as to coincide with the frame which had been interpreted as the master frame (see section 6.1, page 66). Four sections were measured forward of this, labelled F1, F2, F3 and F4. The six sections aft of it were labelled A1, A2 through to A6. Four waterlines were recorded, parallel to the straight keel on which the model stands. The lowest waterline is at 1 m (0.1 m in the model) above the bottom of the keel, each subsequent one is 1 m higher. With these lines recorded, the whole model could be aligned to a coordinate system that allowed for exact top, side and front views. The model was then scaled so that a set of 1:50 lines drawings of the ship could be produced in a traditional fashion, meaning that all lines were faired with a spline. As only the port side of the ship had been measured, starboard was added by mirroring, making allowance for the width of stem, keel and stern on the centre-line (Figure 6-2).

Besides the lines plan the approach also produced a 3D digital shape of the model. The wreck sections were recorded as individual layers to illustrate their mutual positioning in the hull.

6.5 A Lines Plan, Adjustments and Shape

The lines plan was one of the intended products of the model building. More even than the model building itself, producing a lines plan is a matter of what Lemée (2006) aptly called 'reverse naval architecture'. Lines plans after all are a design tool to describe an intended hull shape in an idealized form. If they are used in reverse, it immediately shows where the plan does not conform. As the lines from the model emerged as the basis for the lines plan, it became clear that some parts of the hull were not quite reliable from a design perspective. The midship bend seemed to be slightly narrower than section F1. The model setup had to be re-evaluated to see if better results could be obtained. The whole structure was twisted by force so that the rear end came out a bit while the bow was pressed slightly further in towards the centre. This made the area just behind section 0 straighter and longer before it started narrowing towards the stern. The twist affected section 0 so that the midship bend was widened by a few centimetres and became slightly broader than F1. Note, however, that this change is not directly based on the archaeological evidence and that the case for the location of section 0, as the master frame, is made above (section 6.1, page 66), but is nevertheless somewhat arbitrary.

Due to the steps in building and recording the model, the lines plan deviates a bit from convention, although this is not exceptional in the context of archaeological (or ethnographical) research. The conventional way to draw lines is to base them on the moulded shape of the hull. This means that the inside face of the planking defines the lines. In cases like the present one there is a problem in getting a clear view of the inside of the planking and hence it was decided to record the outside of the hull instead. Now obviously, the thickness of the planking (6 mm and without variation in the case of the model) could be subtracted from the lines, but in view of other uncertainties this was not considered to be a major issue. Incidentally copying the lines of a ship's hull has often been done historically by measuring the outside of the planking at stations along the ship, since recording the inside of the planking would often be practically impossible.

Altogether the process of analysing the hull of the Gresham Ship was a more or less continuous switching between analogue and digital methods. Digital data capture was followed by partly conventional modelling, after which the model was digitally recorded and the lines plan drawn with traditional splines on a drawing table. However, for final adjustments, the initial lines plan (Figure 6-2) was re-digitized and imported into Rhinoceros. In order to correct inaccuracies some re-fairing and digital reconstruction was performed.

Although Rhinoceros has an in-built feature to fair a curve or surface automatically, the degree and definition of fairness are driven by operator choices and it doesn't necessarily maintain the original shape. In fact no computer program is able to give a good balance between accuracy and faired shape without operator choices. In reverse naval architecture it is therefore important to keep track of the process. A way of doing this is by keeping the original input curves drawing in a different layer to check how far changes affect the final shape as compared to the original. In the present instance re-fairing did not interfere with the lines plan as a whole, but affected only two mid-station lines. They were no more than 0.5 mm out at a scale of 1:10.

The subsequent step was to rebuild the hull surface from the re-faired lines plan. This was possible using the 'surface from a network of curves' function which produces a full digital model of the hull shape as derived from the physical modelling.

At this point it was decided to compare the resulting hull surface with the original recorded hull sections. After patiently merging the recorded sections, the hull surface was corrected to fit the shape of the preserved timbers better. This step was necessary due to the nature of the physical model, which in some areas is affected by the imprecision arising from the nature of the material used. To improve the accuracy of the reconstruction, the model was adjusted according to the shape of the inner planks and frames, which were not influenced by deformations of the outer timber surface. Moreover, the original reconstructed model is missing a small portion above the gunport, which would have given information about the tumblehome. However, a few surviving timber fragments can be used for an approximate reconstruction of the shape of the tumblehome. Using the original total station recordings in the digital model, it was possible to sweep the profile of the preserved part of the tumblehome around the line of maximum breadth, resulting in the reconstruction visible in the final lines plan (Figure 6-3).

Some general remarks

The hull shapes produced by the Elizabethan and Jacobean system of drawing lines tended to be stereotyped (Chapelle, 1967, 17) and the model of the Gresham Ship fits this frame. The keel is straight and relatively short compared to the overall length of the hull. The stem is formed with a long sweep. The sternpost is raked aft and the transom was most likely of a square tuck form. The midsection is formed with a flat floor with no apparent deadrise. The tumblehome reconstructed is only a fragment of the original. It is composed of a smaller sweep, which, if entirely reconstructed, could take two possible shapes: The sweep could be followed by a tangent straight line or a large radius arc in reverse. The initial impression of the hull shape is a relatively sharply defined bottom of the ship, with a slender aft part of the hull.

6.6 The Design of the Master Frame

The design of the master frame is a central issue in discussions about early modern ships in Europe. Deriving its original design from the results integrated in the model is also problematic. The first question is obvious: which design are we trying to recover, the final result or the possibly faulty design that was

ANALYSING THE MODEL

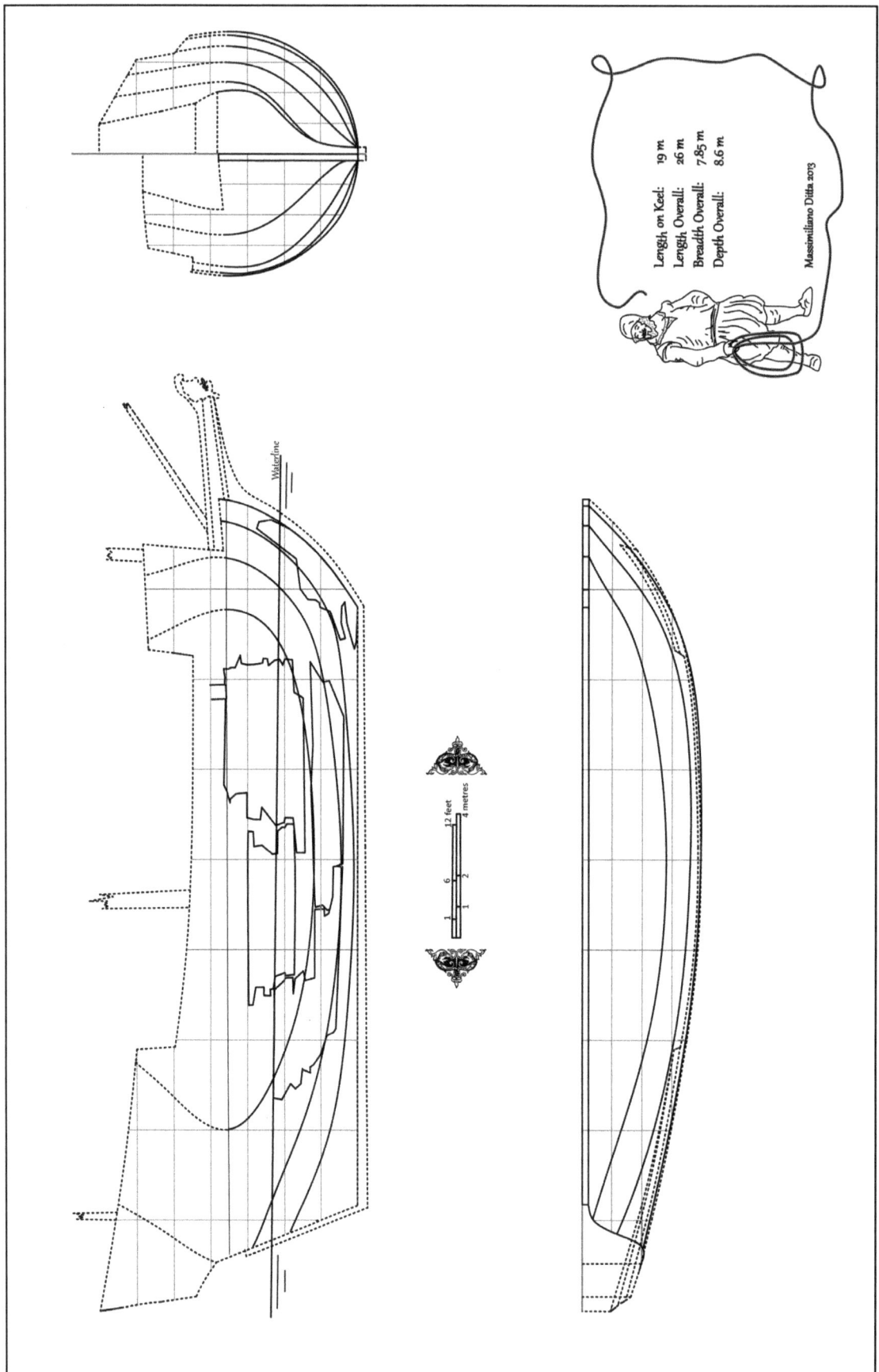

Figure 6-3 Final adjusted lines plan of the furred hull. The dotted outline of the upperworks is derived from the drawing of the Emanuell in 'Fragments of Ancient English Shipwrightry'. (M. Ditta)

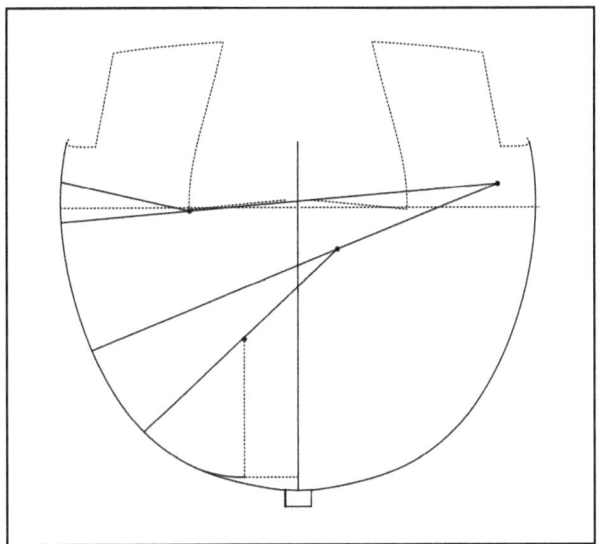

Figure 6-4: A reconstruction of the sweeps that might define the reconstructed master frame (M. Ditta)

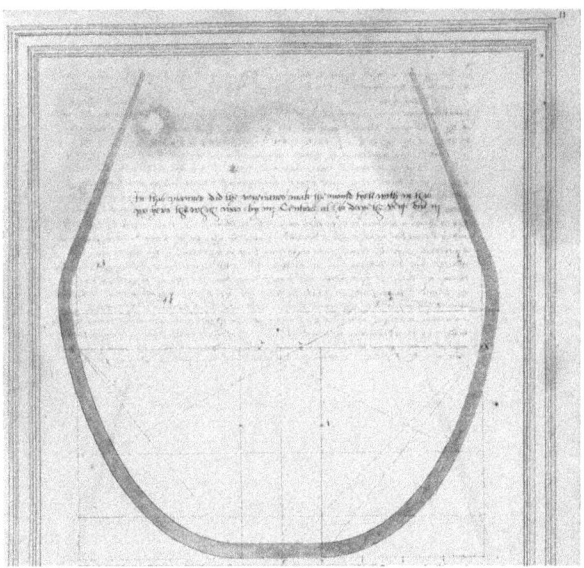

Figure 6-5: The Venetian four-arc method as shown in Matthew Baker's 'Fragments of Ancient English Shipwrightry' (Pepys Library MS 2820, p. 11), by permission of the Pepys Library, Magdalene College, Cambridge

rectified by furring? Is it at all possible to discover the ideas and concepts behind the design? A full analysis of the hull design of the Gresham Ship would be beyond the scope of this study. However, some aspects seem to become evident when the master frame is carefully scrutinized.

Taking the reconstructed master frame shown in Figure 6-4 an attempt was made to rebuild the arcs which might have been used to define its shape and to extract their centres using Rhinoceros 3D. Some care has to be taken when analysing the result, as the reconstruction of the bottom of the hull is based on information about its shape extracted indirectly from the planking and the futtocks and might not represent the true shape of the original floor timbers. The reconstructed floor, shown as a dotted line, represents how the mould would have looked since the bottom line of the midsection has a roundish rise given by the planking. Altogether four arcs could be reconstructed on the basis of the archaeological data. From the bottom these are the bilge arc, which extends from the endpoint of the floor (the point where the two dotted lines meet) upwards, the futtock arc, the breadth arc and the arc of the tumblehome. The arc of the tumblehome is relatively small, but could well have been wider and with a longer straight tangent line. The limited preservation in this area does not allow for a full reconstruction of the original shape (Figure 6-4).

However, when comparing the result with illustrations shown in the 'Fragments of Ancient English Shipwrightry', a similarity with one drawing of a midship bend in particular can be noted. This is shown on page 11 in the manuscript annotated: 'In this manner did the Venetians make the mould till within these xx years, the which was by iiij centres; at this day they use but iij' (Figure 6-5). According to Barker, this Venetian four-arc geometric mould was drawn out by Mathew Baker around 1573–74. Baker does not give any information on the proportions or on the method of drawing and extracting the sweeps. It is also not known if he learned about the method abroad or whether he noted it being used by Venetian shipwrights in England (Barker, 1998).

Such complex geometric methods were to become established in England as well. The midship sections of the merchant vessel *Emanuell* (1571–5?) (Figure 6-5) and of the warship *Foresite* (1570) (Figure 6-6), both built by Baker, were designed following similar four-arc methods (Barker, 1998); and there survives in the National Archives a drawing of the midship bend of the *Hampshire* (1653), also constructed using four arcs (Endsor, 2005, 74–9).

It is interesting to note that the drawing of the midship section of *Emanuell* shows both a design based on the four-arc method and a simplification with only two arcs, which is superimposed and shown as a dotted line (Figure 6-6). There are, however, no annotations to explain the motives of this drawing. The simplified method results in a shorter beam, bringing to mind the original design of the ship from the Princes Channel.

Altogether, it seems clear that the design of the master frame of our vessel was based on a concept of arcs. However, further research is needed to explore the master frame design and, related to that, the design of the remainder of the hull.

6.7 Tonnage

The measurement of tonnage or even its assessment is subject to much debate among scholars dealing with the subject and in fact not only among scholars. It has always been a problematic issue between ship-owners,

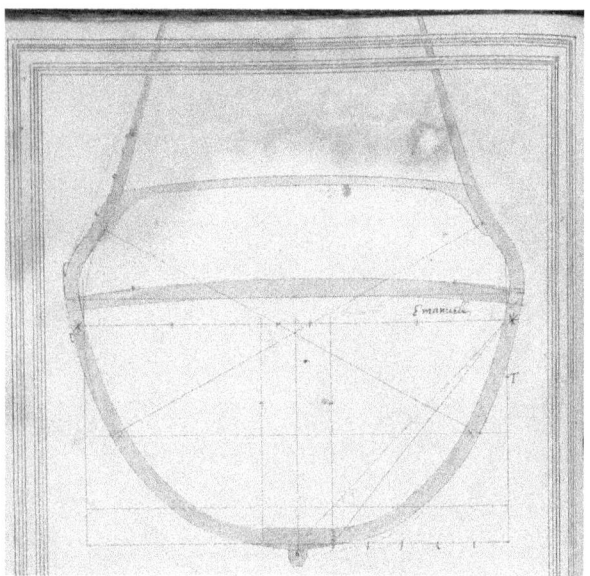

Figure 6-6: The midship section of the merchant vessel Emanuell *constructed using the four-arc method. A simpler two-arc method is superimposed as a dotted line at the left hand side of the image (from 'Fragments of Ancient English Shipwrightry', Pepys Library MS 2820, p. 10, by permission of the Pepys Library, Magdalene College, Cambridge)*

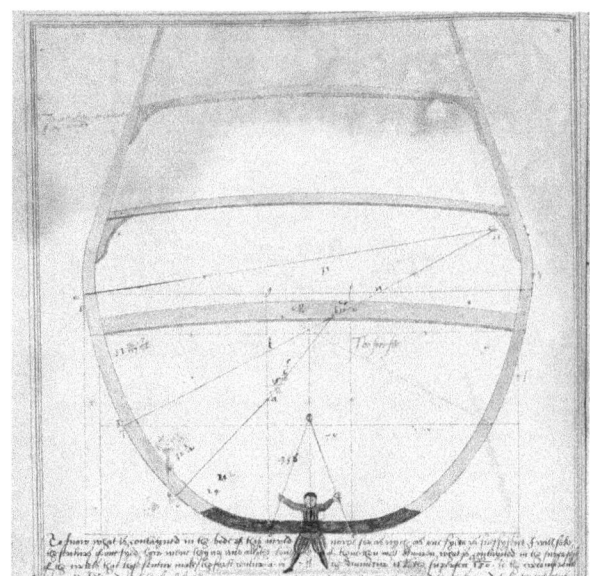

Figure 6-7: The midship section of the Foresite, *designed by Baker in 1570 (from 'Fragments of Ancient English Shipwrightry', Pepys Library MS 2820, p. 14, by permission of the Pepys Library, Magdalene College, Cambridge)*

shippers, underwriters, taxing authorities and their respective surveyors. A central problem is that capacity may refer either to volume or to weight. The debate is too extensive to present in detail in this context. A nice overview can be found in Adams (Adams *et al.*, 1990, 178) and very illustrative is Salisbury (1966), who gives an extensive review of early tonnage measurement in England.

For simplicity, one could say that the tonnage of a ship is the measurement of the amount of cargo it is capable of carrying. The tonnage might not be the actual capacity of the ship, but it is used as a means to compare ships in size and to calculate the rate of port charges and taxes (Steffy, 1994, 144). The development of tonnage as a measurement for ships was related to the development of the merchant fleet rather than for military purposes where the capacity of guns and men would have been a better measure for the ship.

In England from the late fourteenth century and early fifteenth century the standards of tonnage were calculated on the basis of the standard Bordeaux wine cask or tun. The capacity of a ship was estimated based on the number of tuns that could be stowed in its hold (Salisbury, 1966, 43). The tun was a measure of liquid volume and would have weighed in the order of a ton. Salisbury refers to the fact that the cargo capacity might change after major repairing or rebuilding of a ship. This should be kept in mind since extensive rebuilding actually happened to the Gresham Ship.

There were – and are – several ways and reasons for calculating the tonnage of a ship. Besides taxation, port dues and insurance, the shipwright also had a reason to do the calculation, since he was sometimes paid on the basis of the tonnage. These examples imply that there were several reasons for either underestimating or overestimating the tonnage of a ship and therefore that it is not a neutral technical value for a ship (Friel, 1983, 54). Even much later, in 1670, Anthony Deane in his 'Doctrine of Naval Architecture' mentioned that the rule for measuring the tonnage for any ship was a custom rather than the truth. And he argued that in reality ships of different design, but the same general proportions, could have very different tonnage ratings, a fact that is certainly true (Lavery, 1981, 48).

In his *History of the Administration of the Royal Navy*, Oppenheim (1896, 266) refers to a discussion on methods of calculating tonnage in the years 1626–1628, which in his opinion 'would require a whole volume for elucidation'.

According to a text in the State Papers from 1627 (State papers, Dom., lv, 39; 1627), which is reproduced by Oppenheim, tonnage was then and before derived by different formulae. All formulae were similar in that the product of the length of the keel, the breadth and the depth in the hold was divided by an artificial denominator to calculate the 'tons burthen' of a ship. An extra proportion was then added for whatever additional weight in men and munitions might be carried beyond the conventional payload, resulting in the 'tonnage'. However, both the way in which the main dimensions were obtained as well as the denominators varied considerably.

The first way to measure tonnage described in the State Papers is called 'Mr Baker's Old Way' and described as having been established 'in Queen Elizabeth's time'. Using this formula the keel length was measured leaving out false posts (K), the breadth was the greatest breadth measured inside the planking (B) and the depth of hold was measured from the breadth down to the top of the keel (K), with all dimensions in feet. (Oppenheim, 1896, 266). The formula was:

$$\frac{K \times B \times D}{100}$$

To obtain the tonnage one third had to be added to the result. Although a separate note in the State Papers mentions two gentlemen who asserted that the breadth should instead be measured to the outside of planking and the depth to the bottom of the keel (Oppenheim 1896, 266), obtaining the measurements in the way described earlier seemed more logical and was chosen for this calculation.

The required dimensions from the model of the Gresham Ship in its final form with furring in metres and English feet are:

K	B	D
19 m	7.71 m	3.24 m
62.34 ft	25.30 ft	10.63 ft

With these dimensions the equation gives a result of 167.6 tons burthen and a tonnage of 223.5. The breadth used for this example was taken from the furred hull. If we calculate the tons burthen using the originally intended breadth (B = 7.11 m or 23.33 ft) it would be 154.6 tons and a tonnage of 206.1. Obviously the volume of the hold was no smaller before furring than after.

6.8 More proportions and ratios

Here some of the proportions and ratios of the dimensions of the Gresham Ship will be scrutinized in the context of the recommendations of contemporary documents, both for the un-furred hull that proved or was considered unseaworthy and for the final result after redesign and rebuilding. Proportions and regular arcs show that the shipwright was clearly following a set of geometrical rules of design. Obviously the first result was not satisfactory; something had gone wrong in the process. Either the intended control of the outcome was not what it should have been or the design was wrong from the beginning. Interestingly, the furring timbers are shaped on the principles of sweeps based on arcs of circles and the final result reflects desired proportions remarkably well. It is therefore plausible to surmise either an actual redesign or an adjustment to arrive at what had originally been intended.

Keel length, breadth and depth

The model of the Gresham Ship represents a keel length of 19 m, a breadth with furring measured to the inside of the frames of 7.71 m and a depth of hold measured to the top of the keel of 3.24 m. The proportions between these three main dimensions are 100 : 40.6 : 17.1. For the original un-furred hull the proportions would be 100 : 37.4 : 17.1. The *Treatise on Shipbuilding* recommends a ratio of 100 : 36 : 15.5, while Matthew Baker and the mathematician Thomas Harriot suggest a ratio of around 100 : 40 : 20 (Lavery, 1988, 10). With these proportions as a comparison the Gresham Ship must be characterized as of fairly common proportions and close to Baker's recommendations.

Breadth and depth

The furred breadth of 7.71 m is 2.38 times the depth of the hold (3.24 m). According to the *Treatise on Shipbuilding* the best proportion between these two dimensions is to be 7 : 3, which corresponds with the breadth being 2.33 times the depth (Salisbury and Anderson, 1958, 15).

Length and breadth

The ratio of length to breadth is a common way of describing and distinguishing between different ship types. Mostly the approach is a fairly rough description, taking its basis in the length between posts. In the late 16th century ratios of 4 : 1 or higher were attained by lengthening flat-bottomed merchant ships in the Netherlands (Lemée, 2006, 298) and the development from flyboat to flute (Wegener Sleeswijk, 2003). Using an estimated length between the posts at deck level of 24.7 m, the deeper hull of the Gresham Ship would be around 3.4 : 1 in its original un-furred form, with the breadth measured to the outside of planking or 3.47 : 1 with the breadth measured to the inside of planking.

With the master frame at 7 m from the stempost scarf it is tempting to assume that the keel length should be 21 m, since the station recommended in the *Treatise on Shipbuilding* is ⅓ of the keel length from the stempost. It would, however, produce an extremely narrow ship, both with and without furring.

In the English context, and in the context of the English rules for calculating tonnage, it is more common to approach the ratio of length to breadth on the basis of the keel length than the length overall or the length between posts, the more so since calculations on the basis of this measure are frequent in the historical material and have consistently informed later research. In other words the same ratio is used as cited above in the discussion of keel length, breadth and depth (100 : 40.6 : 17.1). The factor 40.6 is important here. If the keel length were to be 21 m, the factor would go down to 36.7 or 33.9 for the un-furred hull. This hardly fits what one might expect on the basis of historical studies.

In his discussion of the *Susan Constant*, Brian Lavery mentions a list of small to medium sized English merchant ships of around 200 tons. The factor is 39.2 for the larger and 41.6 for the smaller ships. The list is dated around 1625, but the proportions seem to have been fairly constant from the 1580s to the 1620s

(Lavery, 1988, 10). The furred hull with a 19-m keel comes very close to this, with a factor 40.6. At 37.4 the factor for the un-furred hull is significantly lower, which makes it understandable that the decision was taken to fur the ship.

Stempost radius

Approaching the ratio of length to breadth on the basis of the keel length obviously presupposes set proportions for bow and stern as well. The rake of the sternpost has been discussed above. The extension of the bow is not only defined by its rake, but also by its sweep. The preserved part of the stempost of the Princes Channel Wreck is approximately half of its original length, but it shows that it was formed as the arc of a circle with a radius of approximately 10 m. This radius is measured on the outside of the stempost, so it would be some 30 cm less at the planking. In comparison the radius of the *Mary Rose* stempost is roughly 27 m (Marsden, 2009, 86). A geometrical rule of thumb in the *Treatise on Shipbuilding* states that the stempost radius must never exceed the width of the ship and that the optimal proportion is ¾ of the ship's breadth. In the case of the Gresham Ship and particularly the *Mary Rose* the radius is far bigger than the width of the hull. In fact there seems to be a major deviation between text and archaeology. In the annotated publication of the *Treatise on Shipbuilding* Salisbury has noted the inconsistency. He believes that an error must have occurred during transcription (Salisbury and Anderson, 1958, 40).

Breadth and flat of the floor

Another principal proportion quoted in 16th- and 17th-century English manuscripts and treatises is the ratio of the main breadth to the flat of the floor timber. The reconstructed master frame shows a flat of the floor timber of 1.1 m, which is 14.27% of the breadth (7.71m). Over time, preferences changed, as has been demonstrated by Adams (2003). Treatises and manuscripts ranging from 1545 to 1670 show a development from a narrow flat of the hull at 14% of the breadth in the earliest manuscript to ratios of 20% around 1600 and of ⅓ or 33.33% of the main breadth in Deane's 'Doctrine' of 1670. The material that Adams included relates mostly to larger merchant ships and warships, but the proportion in the Gresham Ship fits well with a narrower flat of the floor of the earlier period.

Conclusion

Overall the Gresham Ship as revealed by the model is shown to be an average size ship for its time in terms of its dimensions and proportions, particularly in its furred state. The length of the keel compared to breadth and depth is actually remarkably close to the recommendations of both the *Treatise on Shipbuilding* from 1620 and the older 'Fragments on Ancient English Shipwrightry'. It is notable that it is in its furred state that the factor for its breadth in the ratio of its keel length, breadth and depth (40.6) coincides closely with the averages quoted by Lavery.

Chapter 7: Furring in the light of 16th-century ship design
by Cate Wagstaffe

The analysis presented in the preceding chapters demonstrates that the ship of which the remains were found in the Princes Channel had been rebuilt in a manner that is referred to in the literature as 'furring'. In fact the find and its analysis constitute the first tangible evidence of the process, which according to written sources had been a relatively common practice in late 16th-century and early 17th-century England. In view of this there is every reason to look closely at the documents and to describe the process in the light of 16th- and early 17th-century ship design. The material evidence of the ship can thus be integrated with what the written sources allow us to know and understand. In this chapter the sources will be reviewed and discussed. In doing so, the reasons for the process in the context of contemporary design practice will be discussed.

7.1 Mainwaring on Furring

Perhaps the best known and most cited reference to furring is Sir Henry Mainwaring's treatment of the subject in his *Seaman's Dictionary* of 1644, a work that seems to have circulated in manuscript form for many years before under the title *Nomenclator Navalis*. Mainwaring (1587–1653) is assumed to have written the manuscript between February 1620 and February 1623 for the use of Sir George Villiers, first Duke of Buckingham, Right Honourable Marquis of Buckingham and Lord High Admiral of England (Perrin and Manwaring, 1922, 72). As befits a dictionary Mainwaring's work deals with a great many subjects. It explains sea terms and derivative words, but quite frequently expands with advice on how best to operate. Under the entry 'Fur or Furred' the dictionary contains the following description:

> There are two kinds of furring: the one is after a ship is built, to lay on another plank upon the side of her, which is called plank upon plank. The other, which is more eminent and more properly furring, is to rip off the first planks and to put other timbers upon the first, and so to put on the planks upon these timbers. The occasion of it is to make a ship bear a better sail, for when a ship is too narrow and her bearing either not laid out enough or too low, then they must make her broader and lay her bearing higher. They commonly fur some two or three strakes under water and as much above, according as the ship requires, more or less. I think in all the world there are not so many ships furred as are in England, and it is a pity that there is no order taken either for the punishing of those who build such ships or the preventing of it, for it is an infinite loss to the owners and an utter spoiling and disgrace to all ships that are so handled (Perrin and Manwaring, 1922, 153).

Mainwaring distinguished between two procedures for widening a ship and used the term 'furring' for both. The process in evidence in the Princes Channel Wreck is clearly the second of the two procedures described by Mainwaring – 'which is more eminent and more properly furring'. Other sources refer to 'girdling', a word that does not appear in Mainwaring's *Seaman's Dictionary* at all. Although in some instances it is quite clear that the term girdling is reserved for the plank upon plank method, the terms furring and girdling are used interchangeably and are complementary.

It is quite evident from Mainwaring's words that he wholeheartedly disapproved of the fact that the practice was so common in England. He clearly despised the incompetence of shipbuilders who failed to avoid the need for it through proper design rather than by trial and error. On the other hand, in 1627 in the course of his work for Buckingham, Mainwaring had to take stock of the condition of the fleet, several ships being defective or requiring an overhaul. For several of these he advised 'girdling with 4 inch planks' (Manwaring, 1920, 156). The main reason, however, is certainly to strengthen the hull and make the warships more resistant, a reason he also later gives for doing so (Manwaring, 1920, 246). He disapprovingly describes the *Mary Rose* of 1623 (not to be mistaken for Henry VIII's flagship built in 1509) as:

> Tender sided, hard of steering, and said a slug of a sail. She hath been furred and girdled, and lengthened abaft with a false post and false keel (Manwaring, 1920, 159).

That both girdling and furring are compromise solutions is again made very clear by Mainwaring in correspondence relating to the years 1635–1636, in which he advises that it is better husbandry to build new ships then to patch up the old and decayed (Manwaring, 1920, 248).

7.2 Thomas Harriot

An earlier reference to furring is found in the work of Thomas Harriot (*c.* 1560–1621). It is less detailed than Mainwaring's entry cited above. Thomas Harriot is best known as astronomer and mathematician, but his exploits included travels to America and ethnographical descriptions of the habits and languages of Native Americans. In his manuscript 'Mathematical and Scientific Papers' (British Library BL Add. MS 6788, *fo.* 33), he confirms in the following note that furring is a remedy for crank ships:

> The furring of a ship is when she will not beare sayle for want of bredth is to make/build her broader without side with timber and on ye plankes and thin bord below and thicker upward. so far from below as is fit; and housing it in upward to agree with ye upper works by thinner bordes(?) agayne. Many merchant shippes are fyne(?) to be furred.

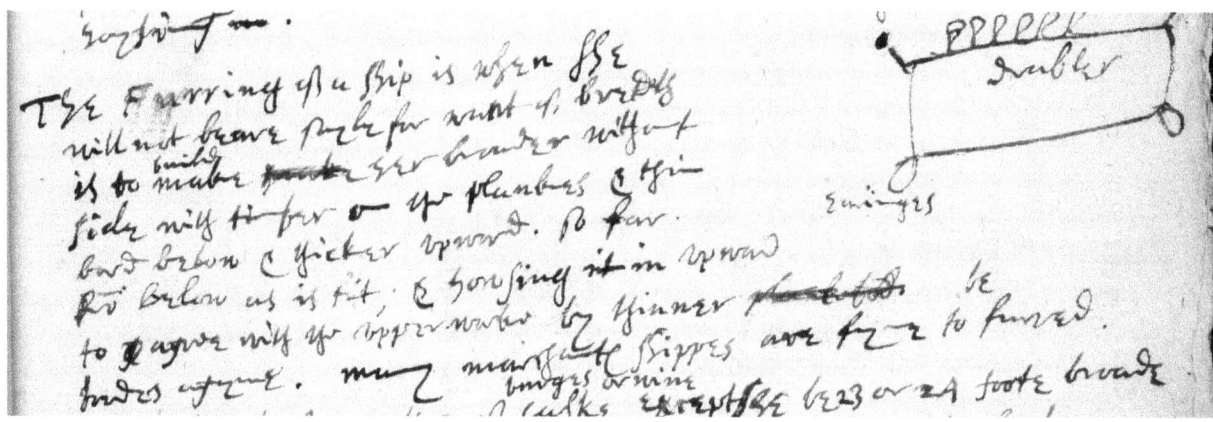

Figure 7-1: Thomas Harriot's definition of furring in his 'Mathematical and Scientific Papers'; © The British Library Board (BL Add. MS 6788, fo. 33)

The text is not easy to decipher or to interpret (Figure 7-1). For example, 'fyne' in the last sentence (which may be read as 'fayne') has been interpreted to mean fine or narrow, thus necessitating broadening (Shirley, 1983, 100); alternatively it has been interpreted to mean 'Many merchant ships are found to be furred' (Wagstaffe, 2010, 29–30)). While the latter may not be correct, the sentence confirms that Harriot, like Mainwaring was aware that, in England at least, furred ships were quite common, more common perhaps than would be desirable.

Harriot's 'Mathematical and Scientific Papers' were written between the years 1608 and 1610 and never formally published. They comprise a combination of rutters, descriptions of nautical courses, anchorages and the like, as well as astronomical research. Various details about shipbuilding, rigging, division of loot between privateers, written down as in a personal notebook, add to the significance of the collection of observations. According to the manuscript, different shipbuilding traditions were adapted for the various geographical climates, allowing each country's design and construction to vary. This could perhaps explain why the English shipbuilding tradition in particular succumbed to rebuilding ships after construction in the way the Princes Channel Wreck did. Harriot was anyway concerned about the practice:

> ... our English ships are intended to have such perfection, that (according to the intent of the builder) they hold burden with the Fleming; bearing with the Spaniard; going well with the French, &c ... Every Nation aymeth at this: to have there ship go well and steer well. Which proceedith especially from the well weying of a ship fore & aft; for the Runne [that part of the ship's bottom which rises from the keel and bilge and narrows toward the stern] and Tuck [the gathering of the ends of the bottom planks under the stern] ... These are the chief proper types of a ship in the sea. To go well; to steer well, and bear a good sail. As for the burthen that belongeth to the owners profit, which some to much affecting hath made us to have so many furred ships (Shirley, 1983, 100).

Harriot's concise descriptions are the oldest reference to furring found to date. As furring is probably the most significant aspect of the Princes Channel Wreck assemblage, it would be just as adequate to call the ship after Thomas Harriot as it is to name it after Thomas Gresham. Anyway Mainwaring's as well as Harriot's emphasis on the deficiencies of English ships seem to be quite appropriate in the present context.

7.3 Matthew Baker and Phineas Pett

A more elaborate source on the process and implications of furring is the autobiography of Phineas Pett (1570–1647), published by the Naval Records Society (Perrin, 1918). It describes his life between 1570 and 1638. Pett was born into a famous family of shipwrights and became a high-ranking shipbuilder contracted by the Royal Navy. Pett's story is one of conflict between him and his former tutor Matthew Baker and the intrigues as well as the technical aspects of contention have kept generations of naval historians in their spell (Oppenheim, 1892, 487; Perrin, 1918; Abell, 1948, 41–3; McGowan, 1971, xv, 231; Winfield, 2009, 3; Wagstaffe, 2010). Matthew Baker (1530–1613) had been Master Shipwright of the Kingdom since 1572 and Pett's tutor. He is best known for his 'Fragments of Ancient English Shipwrightry', a collection of documents, drawings and maps he started around 1570 (Barker, 1986). It is without any doubt the most important collection of historic documents that has informed naval historians about English shipbuilding of the period, from Oppenheim (1892), through Abell (1948) to Lavery (1987). While acting as witness for the Navy Commission, Matthew Baker refers to the fact that Pett had repaired a 223-ton ship that was in worse condition after he had completed it and that such an example alone made him a quite unsuitable choice for the building of the prestigious *Prince Royal* that was being discussed:

> '. . . so that with his first repairing and furring up them he doubts not but it doth appear by the accounts that his workmanship with stuff was more chargeable than a new ship of that burthen might have been new-built for; which are enough to

persuade any man that he cannot be sufficient to perform the building of so great a ship, when he hath performed the reparation of a small ship so ill, as of a good ship he made a bad' (McGowan, 1971, 231).

It is the only instance in which Matthew Baker addresses the subject of furring. But it is a salient point in the present context that Pett, who had been given the commission of building the 55-gun royal ship anyway, was later subjected to an inquiry, during which he was accused of having furred this *Prince Royal*, when he built her at Woolwich in 1609–1610. Whether true or not (Pett was acquitted after all and was commissioned to build the *Sovereign of the Seas* in 1637), the episode shows the very derogatory terms in which furring was presented as almost equivalent to abuse, deceit, fraud and incompetence. As such, furring was just one of the awful practices Phineas Pett was accused of having engaged in. It is on a par with accusations of using unseasoned and substandard timbers. It is on a par with 'working the frame bend incorrectly' and 'not having enough scarf between futtocks and floor timbers'. Basically it is presented on a par with being completely and utterly useless.

Although both Matthew Baker and Phineas Pett were practising shipbuilders, the information they offer on furring is by no means more technical than that of the pirate-politician Mainwaring or the scientist Thomas Harriot. In fact, it is not the details that are discussed, but the relationship of furring to competence. And in the context of the debate it is not the competence as a resourceful craftsman that is at stake, but competence in mathematically designing the ideal hull form without having to resort to adjustments while building or later.

The same argument occurs in the *Treatise on Shipbuilding* that has been referred to extensively in Chapter 6. As it was written around 1620–1625, it dates from Pett's lifetime:

> . . . merchants covet to have great floors in their ships for gaining of stowage, but thereby they spoil the ship's bearing for most of them grow tender-sided, and after they are built come to be furred (Salisbury and Anderson, 1958, 16)

Here, however, it is not the mathematical designer whose competence is questioned, but the client, the merchant, who is blamed. It resonates the argument brought forward by mathematician Thomas Harriot in the last sentence of his quotation in the last section.

7.4 John Smith and Nathaniel Butler

John Smith (1580–1631) was an English mercenary and adventurer who settled in Virginia and called himself Admiral of New England. He is better known as 'Captain John Smith' after his rank as soldier in service of the Austrian Habsburgs. He wrote several books, describing his travels and adventures and promoting settlement in Virginia. Educational in purpose they focus not only on how to take one's fate in one's own hands, but for instance also on how to become a good seaman. In his *Sea Grammar* of 1627 Smith tries to explain everything a practical navigator and gunner needs to know. In doing so, he refers to the practice of furring in relation to a crank ship:

> If a ship be narrow, and her bearing either not laid out enough or too low, then you must make her broader and her bearing the higher by ripping off the planks two or three strakes under water, and as much above, and put on the Timbers upon the first, and then put on the planks upon those Timbers, this will make her bear a better sail, but it is an hindrance to her sailing, this is to be done when a ship is Crank-sided and will bear no sail, and is called furring (Smith, 1627, 53).

Although less elaborate, mostly by not referring to the procedure described as 'plank upon plank', this entry in Smith's *Sea Grammar* is nevertheless quite similar to Mainwaring's text. It was published seventeen years before the formal publication of Mainwaring's *Seaman's Dictionary*, but it is generally assumed that Smith incorporated much of Mainwaring's text (Barbour, 1964, 91). We can therefore assume that Smith's definition of furring derives from Mainwaring's description, despite its slightly different wording. With the latter being more detailed, Smith's text is less interesting. It just adds to our understanding that furring was quite a commonplace practice, the principles of which were quite commonly known.

Nathaniel Butler or Boteler (c. 1577–after 1639) was a contemporary of John Smith, who like him had a seaman-soldier career and was involved with Virginia. After sailing to Bermuda in 1619 – incidentally on board the *Warwick*, the ill-fated ship presently under archaeological investigation (Bojakowski and Custer-Bojakowski, 2010) – he became Governor of Bermuda. His work *A Dialogical Discourse* (1634 – Perrin, 1929) takes a more literary form than John Smith's *Sea Grammar*. Its purpose seems to have been to brief the head of the Board of Admiralty on naval matters through a series of six dialogues between an admiral and a captain. The purpose of the book is educational and it sheds light on operations and life at sea in the context of the Navy. Furring is mentioned in the Fourth Dialogue, where the Admiral asks the captain: 'What is the furring of a ship?' The Captain answers:

> There are two kinds of furring. The one is after a ship is built, and then it is done by laying on of double planks on her sides, and this is called plank upon plank. The other way (which is properly furring) is performed by ripping off the planks, and putting second timbers upon the first timbers, and upon them again other planks. And all this is done to make a ship to bear the better sail (Perrin, 1929, 92).

The close similarity with the entry in Mainwaring's dictionary, given at the start of this chapter, is striking.

In fact Perrin thought that all the detail in Butler's text is extracted from Mainwaring and he concluded that the fourth dialogue is 'of little independent value' (Perrin, 1929, xxvii). The fact that it was written ten years before Mainwaring's book was published is an argument supporting Perrin's inference on wide distribution of Mainwaring's *Seaman's Dictionary* before publication (Perrin and Manwaring, 1922, 70). Overall Perrin is not very impressed by Butler or his ornate style. Unlike Mainwaring, who was ten years younger and trained as a lawyer, Perrin – justified or not – derided Butler as not being a seaman, but one of the 'gentlemen captains,' who hardly knew stem from stern (Perrin, 1929, xxvi). Whoever of the two, Mainwaring or Butler, was more gentlemanly is not for us to decide, but the verdict is not in complete agreement with what little is known of Butler's biography (Carr Laughton, 1911). One can hardly operate as privateer or in salvage if one lacks hands-on understanding. This is true as much for Butler as it is for Mainwaring. For our present study it hardly matters who paraphrased whom. Butler continued the dialogue with the following:

> To which end also, especially if the ship be anything wall-raised, that is, raised out straight up, they use to spike on some thin timbers or narrow thick planks all alongst her main bends and wales; which adds somewhat towards her better bearing though not much (Perrin, 1929, 92).

As this text follows directly on the previous quotation, it is not completely clear whether it is just elaboration or whether Butler means to distinguish this spiking on of some timbers from the plank-upon-plank process he describes earlier. 'Wall-raised' could be interpreted as the ship's sides rising from the water as a straight wall, rather than with tumblehome. It appears to be synonymous with 'wall-reared', of which the dialogue treats a bit further and which specifically seems to refer to the absence of tumblehome. Here, the Admiral asks 'What mean you when you say a ship is wall-reared?' and the Captain answers:

> Of this I spake somewhat formerly, and even now I made mention of a ship being housed-in, in her upperworks; quite contrary to which when a ship is built over-right or directly up, after she comes to her bearing, she is said to be wall-reared; the which though it be unsightly, and as the sea phrase is, not shipshapen, yet it causeth a ship to be very roomy that is large within board, and withal makes her a wholesome ship in the sea, especially if her bearing be well laid out (Perrin, 1929, 96).

It is clear from this text, that such absence of 'tumblehome' or narrowing in the upperworks is not considered 'shipshape' at the period, but that it is not necessarily a fault either.

It has been suggested that 'to spike on some thin timbers or narrow thick planks all alongst her main bends and wales' in this case should be distinguished from the two systems that Mainwaring and Butler otherwise describe, in specifically addressing the tumblehome (Wagstaffe, 2010, 56–7). However, this form of girdling can hardly be distinguished from plank upon plank furring as described by Mainwaring and the less so if it is applied all around the ship. Girdling, after all, is to be understood as a permanent adjustment method that consisted of extra timbers (that is to say planking) fastened outside the hull at the widest breadth of the frames, increasing the beam measurement and giving more buoyancy (Nelson, 2001, 220).

In short, Butler's text gives rise to some discussion, as it provides some additional notes, even though it has been received opinion that Butler just reproduces Mainwaring.

7.5 Later References

Evidence for the continued practice of furring, as well as for the continued debate on its disputable attractiveness is for instance found in the papers left by Charles Sergison (1655–1732). A selection of these, referring to the years 1688–1702, have been published by the Navy Records Society (Merriman, 1949). They include correspondence between the Navy Board and the Admiralty on the various aspects of naval administration, such as shipbuilding and practice in the dockyards. Faulty design and ways to correct this are discussed at some length in the context of a dispute that arose in 1693 in relation to new demands on the performance of the *Royal William*, built in 1670. Although the publication presents the relevant correspondence in such a way as to illustrate the antagonisms that hampered the naval administration of the day, they also provide technical discussion of methods for bettering a crank ship. A letter from the Admiralty to the Navy Board (No. 27, dated 26 January 1694) gives the reasons for girdling the ship as follows:

> (I) Her foundation not being sufficient for her upper works 'twill be such an addition as will make her carry sail enough to work her, whereas she is now not able to do it.
>
> (II) 'twill cause her to be more floaty and for that reason carry her guns better.
>
> (III) That it will make her a more circular body and consequently work much better.
>
> (IV) That she will sail better, because her straight side being made circular she will carry a great deal less dead water.
>
> (V) That it will make her almost shot-proof between wind and water and consequently not in so much danger of being sunk (Merriman, 1949, 87–8).

The papers discuss the time constraints and conditions to be met if the ship is to be girdled and the practical as well as the more theoretical aspects are brought to bear.

How much wood is applied when a ship is to be girdled may vary significantly depending on the specific issues with the ship's buoyancy. Calculations can then be made as to how much wood is required, taking account of the difference in density between sea-water and fir timber of equal volume. In the emerging art of hydrostatic calculations, moreover, the difference between the squares of the half breadth of the ship in its present condition and the same with the addition of girdling are compared (Merriman, 1949, 89–90).

It is interesting to note that furring as opposed to girdling (or plank upon plank furring) is also discussed. In fact, as a result of long service and previous repair the ship was already 'chocked out 6 inch of a side with dead wood' if we are to believe Edmund Dummer, Surveyor of the Navy during the years 1692–1699. He is cautious of putting ever more weight on the sides, and prefers better trimming or a more fundamental rebuild. The latter solution is rejected because of the delay it would cause, as the fleet needs to be deployed urgently (Merriman, 1949, 92). But much like Mainwaring, Edmund Dummer describes the repairs of crank vessels as being 'present evils' that should be remedied, explaining that the service done to the ship, whether she had been girdled or furred for that matter, should not have been done.

A strong additional argument he brings to bear is that

> ... it is experimentally found that the thickest part of a ship first rots, and consequently that prodigious thickness this ships side will be when a girdling is added to her former doubling will inevitably occasion a very speedy decay of all the timbers, planks and trenails contained within it (Merriman, 1949, 102).

The Sergison papers are the last English reference to furring and girdling to be discussed here, as very few ships were girdled after the *Royal William*. The contrast between girdling and furring in the papers is to be interpreted as similar to the contrast between 'furring plank upon plank' and what 'is more eminent and more properly furring' that has been discussed above in relation to the earlier sources. The sources also make it clear that the process for which we see evidence in the Princes Channel Wreck ('which is more eminent and more properly furring') was a specific, most drastic and specifically debated procedure that were among a range of measures to improve a ship's stability by extending its waterplane area.

7.6 Other References

Debates on the occurrence of furring in the English context of the late 16th and 17th centuries are the most relevant to the present study and hence it is these that are focussed on in preference of any other information. It is clear that problems of trimming and improving sailing capabilities occurred elsewhere as well. Also, despite the absence of archaeological examples and despite Mainwaring's assertion that 'in all the world there are not so many ships furred as are in England', we may fairly assume that what the English sources describe as girdling or plank upon plank furring occurred elsewhere as well. French texts refer to doubling (*doubler*), but they also use the word *soufflage*, which might 'more properly' reflect furring. In Spanish one comes across the word *fórro* in connection with any covering or sheathing, also of a ship, and the practice of lavishly doubling and broadening a ship if it is too slender in its wetted area or to make it sail well is known from the Netherlands as well, although Nicolaes Witsen only mentions it in the second edition of his book (Witsen, 1690, 343, 344). It is an addition that reflects his efforts to think things through and incidentally it is added in the limited print-run that he created after having spent most of a year in England (Maarleveld, 2013). Van Yk (1697, 352–8) goes at some length to discuss sailing capabilities and improving them. But his focus is on trimming, on the right positioning of sail-surface and on the form of the wet area fore-and-aft, rather than on a well-designed cross-section and adding to it for improvement.

It therefore seems fair to say that the specific procedure followed in the Princes Channel Wreck seems to be typically English, just as is the ship, but of course this is easily said in the absence of any other material evidence of the practice.

7.7 Early Modern Ship Design in England

As has been indicated above, the most relevant informants on furring are also those that provide the most cherished historical information on the design and construction of ships in late 16th-century and early 17th-century England. Matthew Baker's 'Fragments of Ancient English Shipwrightry' are central to the debate on the application of theoretical constructs for the design of frames or cross-sections in a frame-based approach to shipbuilding. The system he employed and illustrated in principles and variations is an architectural approach, based on the techniques of whole-moulding (Barker, 1991; Ferreiro, 2007, 40). Phineas Pett was his apprentice. Whether he was a good apprentice or not is not for us to decide. Both, however, stood in the same tradition and it transpires from Baker's manuscript that he was describing accepted approaches rather than radically new ideas (Hocker and Ward, 2004, 82). The approaches were deeply enshrined in the theoretical concepts of the day. If we look at the references to furring, they seem consistently to imply that furring may have been a resourceful solution, but one that was rather to be avoided. Better trim by adjusting weight distribution, including masts and spars, but also guns or adding ballast was the more obvious approach to improving stability and correcting the centre of gravity of a ship that does not perform so well. Nevertheless, the sources also seem to indicate that in practice many ship-owners and ship-builders resorted to increasing the beam of their ship in one way or another. The practical ways of doing this varied from girdling (or plank upon plank furring) to the system more properly named furring by Mainwaring. And it seems reasonable to assume that this occurred more frequently in England than anywhere else (although admittedly this has also been the focus of this study).

It is not a big step then to suppose that there is a relationship between the concept and practice employed in early modern ship design in England and this high rate of occurrence of furring. Indeed, the sources suggest this. As we have seen, both Thomas Harriot and the anonymous *Treatise on Shipbuilding* seem to try and blame the greediness of merchants rather than any flaw in the mathematical system as such or in its practical implementation. But for one thing the same problems seem to occur in the context of the Navy, where greedy merchants had less of a say, and for another it would be very counterintuitive to suggest that merchants from for instance the Low Countries would be any less greedy than their English counterparts.

The theoretical constructs that informed Baker, Pett and contemporary shipwrights in England led to beautiful theoretical work, but also to a fruitless effort in chasing of the ideal hull form, in which the solutions for making a ship faster and more manoeuvrable were expected to lie in making the ship narrower. That breadth is only one factor was not yet fully understood (Abell, 1948, 53). And many ships needed to be made broader as a consequence.

Archaeologically, the theoretical constructs can be recognized most directly through pre-erected and therefore pre-designed frames, whereas other elements have gradually been recognized as indicative of approaches in which such a theoretical phase of design is absent or less prevalent. On the basis of comparison of wreck-find material, it has been suggested that the immediate advantages of the theoretical constructs were few (Maarleveld, 1992, 167). They allowed for more division of labour between the designer and different parts of the workforce than an approach in which one resorted to 'design-and-construct', to borrow a term from present-day contracting of development projects. But it is only by virtue of later marine architecture that the theoretical approach to design can be assessed as positive. The risk of ending up with a badly performing ship was very real.

From a naval architectural perspective there has been an ongoing debate, partly oblivious of the archaeological reality. On the one hand the argument is promoted that the theoretical contructs of the day are perfectly sound, and stand in a continuous tradition of western thinking (Barker, 1986; 1991; 2003). On the other hand it has been suggested that the elaborate geometric procedures to design frame bends in advance might result in hull forms that were only remotely related to good sailing performance (Gillmer, 1985, 261). Adjustments then needed to be made.

Mainwaring, Harriot and many others considered it a sign of incompetence for a shipwright to mess up in the process of designing and constructing a ship. Furring solved some problems, but was nothing to be proud of, as it was a makeshift correction of poor ship design (Shirley, 1983, 100). In review of the historical sources there can be little doubt, however, that there is a tight relationship between the weaknesses of the theoretical approach to ship-design in England and the many English ships that Mainwaring and Harriot refer to as needing this ultimate remedy.

Chapter 8: The Ship from the Princes Channel: A Typical 16th-Century Merchant Vessel?
by Jens Auer and Thijs Maarleveld

In the preceding chapters, the construction and armament of the Princes Channel Wreck have been analysed and an attempt has been made to derive or reconstruct the original dimensions and form of the ship on the basis of the archaeological material. This chapter aims at going a step further. The dataset generated by the present study will be compared with other relevant and contemporary archaeological finds and the results will be discussed in relation to what we currently know about 16th-century ship design and construction.

8.1 From Princes Channel Wreck to Gresham Ship: A Summary

In the course of the study of hull and contents of the Princes Channel Wreck, the ship was assigned a working term, based on the gun-founder of one of the guns found on board: the Gresham Ship. And although there is no proven historical association between the English merchant and financier Sir Thomas Gresham and the wreck in the Princes Channel and in fact, as mentioned in Chapter 7.2 (page 76), the vessel could equally be called after Thomas Harriot who wrote the earliest work referring to the practice of furring, the term Gresham Ship became firmly associated with the ship from the Princes Channel and will be used here for continuity.

But what did the Gresham Ship look like?

The Gresham Ship had an approximate overall length at deck level of 24.7 m. The keel length, which in England was the basis upon which tonnage was calculated, as often stated in contemporary English sources, was about 19 m. The maximum breadth or beam of the furred vessel, measured to the outside of planking, was 7.85 m and the depth in hold, measured from the top of the keel to the underside of the deck beams, was 3.24 m. These dimensions result in 167.6 tons burthen or a tonnage of 223.5 (see Chapter 6.7, page 73). This would have made the Gresham Ship a medium sized trading vessel, which could certainly sail in European waters, but for which journeys further overseas were not out of reach either. Shipping returns showing the number of merchant ships constructed in English cities list ships ranging from a tonnage of 100 tons to 500 tons. Between 1571 and 1576, besides many smaller vessels, one ship built in London was recorded as being of 180 tons and a further two of 260 tons. The returns for merchant ships for the year 1577 include seven ships in the size range of the Gresham Ship: four of 200 tons, two of 220 tons and one vessel of 240 tons. The largest ships in the list are a vessel of 300 tons built in London and one of 500 tons constructed in Bristol (Oppenheim, 1896, 173f.).

The quantity of metal cargo which was probably salvaged from the site in 1846 (see Chapter 3.2, p. 19), as well as the large number of iron bars removed in the various stages of the project, give a good indication of the cargo capacity of the ship.

We know little about the internal layout or appearance of the vessel. It is clear that at least one deck was present and that this deck also carried armament. Judging by the overall dimensions, this might well have been the only deck in the vessel. Not surprisingly for the time, the Gresham Ship was armed. Oppenheim states that it was a usual clause in a charter-party that a merchantman should be armed with ordnance and small arms (Oppenheim, 1896, 171). With four guns found on the wreck and a further six reported to have been salvaged in 1846, a total of 10–12 guns of varying types and sizes does not seem unrealistic (see Chapter 4.9, p. 53).

As no material related to the rigging is preserved, any reconstruction of the rig of the Gresham Ship would be based on conjecture. However, to judge from contemporary illustrations, a three-masted rig would be fairly typical for a vessel of this size. Such a rig is also depicted in the illustration of the *Emanuell* in the 'Fragments of Ancient English Shipwrightry', mentioned earlier in this volume (Figure 8-1). About the *Emanuell* Baker says: 'I have made a ship called the *Emanuell*, which is 26 ft [7.9 m] broad; this ship will bear in merchants' goods 200 tons, and not being overcharged with the same.' (Pepys Library MS 2820, p. 21). Looking at the reconstructed size of the Gresham Ship, the *Emanuell* would certainly be a close comparison, not only in size and armament, but also in the design of the master frame (see Chapter 6.6, page 71).

We also know that the Gresham Ship was built after September 1574 from timber sourced in eastern England, most probably East Anglia and Essex. At some point in her career the vessel was rebuilt to correct a flaw in the original design, perhaps at the yard which had been responsible for her original construction.

Based on this analysis, was the Gresham Ship a typical merchant vessel of her time? The few preserved historical sources would certainly suggest this. And while the furring has been highlighted as unique from an archaeological point of view, to judge from Mainwaring's comment reported in Chapter 7.1 (page 75) – 'I think in all the world there are not so many ships furred as are in England' – the phenomenon was definitely not uncommon at the time.

Figure 8-1: *A 'ship called the* Emanuell, *which is 26 ft broad; this ship will bear in merchants' goods 200 tons, and not being overcharged with the same' (from 'Fragments of Ancient English Shipwrightry', Pepys Library MS 2820, p. 126, by permission of the Pepys Library, Magdalene College, Cambridge)*

8.2 The Gresham Ship in the Context of Early Modern Ship-building

If the dimensions and appearance of the Gresham Ship are typical for the time we should take a look at the construction, the main subject of most ship-archaeological studies. An introductory overview of early modern merchant ship construction based on archaeological evidence (Maarleveld, 1992, 81ff.) discusses the then available data and defines five distinctively different regions of ship-building: the Ibero-Atlantic region, France, the British Isles, Germany/Scandinavia and the Netherlands. Each of these regions is characterized by a number of features, which seem to be typical for the related ship-building traditions. Based on the limited availability of well-studied archaeological ship finds and the omnipresent bias towards the investigation of warships, there are, however, large gaps in the overview presented. While built-up and interconnected frames could be defined as a typical feature of Ibero-Atlantic ship-building, just as shell-first construction and irregular non-connected framing are typical for Dutch ships of the period, features of French, English and German/Scandinavian ship-building traditions are less well-defined.

A later study by Oertling (2001), took a closer look at the Ibero-Atlantic ship-building tradition and defined eleven characteristics, which could be used to define the 'Atlantic Vessel'. Adams' overview of carvel ship-building in Northern Europe (2003) does not focus on ship-building traditions as such, but provides a wider analysis of the developments in the area in question between 1450 and 1850. It does, however, also serve as an excellent introduction to English ship construction in the early modern period. Since the publication of these studies, the dataset has been constantly growing with some of the earlier ship finds being fully published (Marsden, 2009; Grenier *et al.*, 2007), while further ships have been discovered and described (e.g. Lemée, 2006; Bojakowski and Custer-Bojakowski, 2011).

In order to compare the specific construction features observed in the Princes Channel Wreck, it is necessary to define a range of comparative wrecks as well as constructional features or technological parameters. Although we know that the Gresham Ship was built in England, we would have limited ourselves and the analysis by including only wrecks known to be English. It was therefore decided to choose wrecks from all ship-building regions discussed by Maarleveld for a broader view. The date range is another point of discussion. In the light of the relatively rapid changes in ship-building technology in the early modern period, comparative wrecks should probably be limited to a time window of 100 years around the construction date of the Gresham

Ship. This would, however, exclude the Genoese trader *Lomellina*, which sank off the French coast in 1516 and which exhibits a number of similarities with the Gresham Ship (Guérout *et al.*, 1989; Guérout and Rieth, 1997). It would also exclude the *Mary Rose*, a warship, but at the same time a well-preserved and well-studied English comparison with the Gresham Ship. This takes us to another question: should the comparison be limited by the function of ships? It is clear that warships are built for a different purpose than merchant vessels, a fact that will certainly be reflected in their construction as well. However, if the comparison is purely limited to the technicalities of construction, it is probably acceptable to include warships, especially given the limited availability of data.

Last but not least, size is an important factor. The size of a ship will certainly have an influence on the scantlings of individual timbers and the way they are joined. But the relationship is a complicated one (Maarleveld, 2013, 352–4). Moreover, the reconstruction in Chapters 5 and 6 has shown that it is difficult to derive the approximate hull form and dimensions from an archaeological ship find. And even if the size is stated in historical sources, it is problematic to compare ships, for example, on the basis of tonnage due to the wide variety of ways and formulae to calculate this value and other ways of assessing size. The comparative table (Table 8-1) therefore does not take scantlings into account, but these are referred to where appropriate.

The table is organized chronologically by ship-building region. The first three ships, the *Mary Rose* (Marsden, 2009), the *Sea Venture* (Adams, 2003) and the *Warwick* (Bojakowski and Custer-Bojakowski, 2011) were built in England. The Basque whaler *San Juan* (Grenier *et al.*, 2007) and the so-called Pepper Wreck, probably the remains of the *Nossa Senhora dos Mártires* (Castro, 2003) represent the Ibero-Atlantic ship-building tradition. The *Lomellina*, a wreck found near Villefranche in southern France was probably built in Genoa and is thus representative of Mediterranean, rather than French, ship-building (Guérout *et al.*, 1989). The Vejle Hafnia Wreck (pers. comm., Aoife Daly and Alexander Cattrysse), the B&W 1 Wreck (Lemée, 2006) and Scheurrak SO1 (pers. comm., Thijs Maarleveld) were built in the Netherlands. For the last comparative wreck, the Wittenbergen Wreck found in the river Elbe, it is more difficult to define the place of construction. The sampled timbers derive from Lower Saxony, an area which also supplied timber to the Dutch ship-building industry (Stanek, 2011, 18). However, this wreck had caulking battens on the inside of the outer planking, a feature otherwise known from Scandinavian and northern German wrecks (Adams, 2003, 89f.; Stanek, 2011, 46). It is therefore tentatively used as representative of this ship-building region.

The constructional features used for comparison are dictated by the evidence recorded for the Princes Channel Wreck. Most of these are self-explanatory. As the provenance of construction timbers and place of construction do not always coincide in the period in question, both are listed. The timber provenance has usually been established through dendro-provenancing, while the country of origin might be indicated by cargo or find material or relevant historical sources.

Vessel dimensions are, depending on the level of preservation, inherently difficult to establish. In this case they are based on the investigators' estimates and have been included to give a rough impression of vessel size.

Construction method refers to the method or process of ship-building, generally indicated by features of the archaeological remains. Here, three methods have been differentiated: skeleton-built, which implies a skeleton of pre-assembled and pre-erected frames; frame-led, a method in which individual frame components are not pre-assembled, but still erected before the application of planking; and shell-first, also called Dutch flush (Maarleveld, 1992, 121f.), a method in which the bottom hull planking is put into place before inserting the framing timbers.

The picture that emerges from the table is anything but clear. While it is possible to recognize some similarity between vessels constructed in the different ship-building regions, there are also notable exceptions. There is a clear division between ships built in the Dutch flush or shell-first method and those built on the basis of frames. The Dutch vessels share loose irregular framing and the presence of *spijkerpennen*, plugs which fill the holes left by temporary fastenings of the planks, features identified as typical for this construction method (Maarleveld, 1992, 125). An exception among the three Dutch wrecks is the Vejle-Hafnia Wreck, which is built on a T-shaped keel with vertical scarf joints between outer planks.

The two ships from the Ibero-Atlantic area also share features based on their method of construction. Both have regular framing and interconnected floor timbers and first futtocks, a sign of pre-assembled framing, but again, the ships differ substantially in the details, such as fastenings, caulking method and keel construction. The Genoese *Lomellina* is closely comparable to the Ibero-Atlantic vessels, but here even more framing elements are joined and were probably assembled prior to the frames being erected.

A lack of well-studied sources makes the German/Scandinavian area harder to characterize. The Wittenbergen Wreck shares some features with the Dutch wrecks, while the presence of a joint in a futtock might point to some pre-erected frames. The only feature not seen on any of the other wrecks are caulking battens on the inside of the outer planking, which are notched into the frames. Similar battens have also been observed on the wreck of the Swedish warship *Elefanten* (Adams, 2003, 89) and the Mukran Wreck, found on the German island of Rügen (Förster, 1999, 15). This is a feature we will return to at a later point.

As a group the English ships exhibit surprisingly few similarities. All the vessels included were built either frame-led or with pre-erected frames, but the individual framing solutions vary considerably. Besides the rabbeted beam keel, the only feature shared by all English vessels is the way in which the oak trenails in the outer planking have been expanded by driving oakum into their heads. Based on the scarce evidence preserved, this would make the group of English ships the least homogenous of the three for which there are a sufficient number of wrecks preserved.

However, within the group of English vessels, the Gresham Ship shows a number of similarities with the older and considerably larger warship *Mary Rose*, namely the framing system with filling timbers around the bilge and joined floor timbers and first futtocks and the stem construction.

Although floor timbers and first futtocks in the *Mary Rose* are in many cases joined, the morphology of these joints cannot be fully described, as they are either eroded or hidden by ceiling. The investigators point out that many joints might be a result of the narrow space between floor timbers, which does not allow the insertion of full size futtocks (Marsden, 2009, 49). In that case the observed lap joints would be a constructional adjustment, rather than an indication for pre-assembled frames. However, at least five floor timbers and first futtocks were fastened with trenails (Marsden, 2009, 48f.) In the discussion of the assembly sequence of the *Mary Rose*, a staged or 'stepwise' approach is proposed. A central group of floor timbers and futtocks is thought to have been assembled, but, as opposed to the Gresham Ship, there is no direct proof for a pre-assembly, as there is enough room between floor timbers to allow them to be assembled in situ (Marsden, 2009, 50).

The bow construction of the *Mary Rose* is very similar to that of the Gresham Ship. The keel and the stempost are connected with a vertical scarf joint and reinforced by an apron on the inside. The stempost of the *Mary Rose* is, however, considerably more substantial (Marsden, 2009, 84f.).

When comparing the Gresham Ship with the *Sea Venture*, which is closer in date, size and function, it is surprising to note that the two vessels have little in common. There is no connection between the framing elements of the *Sea Venture* and filling timbers are not present.

Due to the location in the hull of the preserved section of the *Warwick*, it is difficult to compare the Gresham Ship with it, but the investigators of the *Warwick* conclude that its construction is quite different to that of the slightly younger *Sea Venture* and more like that of the older *Mary Rose* (Bojakowski and Custer-Bojakowski, 2011, 27f.).

If the Gresham Ship does not compare too well with other English vessels, do its features have parallels in other ship-building traditions? To answer this question it is worth taking a closer look at the framing system, the outer hull planking and the deck construction.

It could be argued that the floor timbers and the first futtocks, which spanned all the way up to deck level in the Gresham Ship, were pre-assembled prior to being erected on the keel (see Chapter 3.4, page 39). While this certainly indicates a frame-first construction, it is unclear whether the main function of the joints between these components was to strengthen the hull or whether they are evidence of pre-moulding. This matter has been the subject of discussion among researchers (Redknap, 1984; Barker, 1991; Marsden, 2009; Grenier et al., 2007) and an answer has not yet been found. With the exception of the *Mary Rose*, this characteristic is mostly known from ships built in the Ibero-Atlantic or Mediterranean area (Oertling, 2001; Grenier et al., 2007, III-62f.). Joint morphology varies, with pure dovetail joints being the most common form. Interlocked or knuckle joints like those on the Gresham Ship are, however, also known from the early 16th-century Yassi Ada Wreck from the Islamic area (Steffy, 1994, 134), from the Genoese *Lomellina* (Guerout et al., 1989, 35f.) and from the *Mary Rose*, albeit here as a connection between first futtocks and second futtocks (Marsden, 2009, 47). In the majority of Ibero-Atlantic wrecks, the mortises are on the floor timbers and face away from the master frame, which might have mortises on both faces (Grenier et al., 2007, III, 62f.). In the Gresham Ship, there is no change of direction around the master frame, all futtocks are attached aft of the floor timber. The only other wreck to display a break from the Ibero-Atlantic pattern of mortises facing away from the master frame is the *Lomellina*. Here no consistent joint direction could be observed (Guerout et al., 1989, 35f.). While in some wrecks only the master frame and a selected number of frames forward and aft were joined, all ten preserved floors in the Gresham Ship are joined in the same way. Taking into consideration the missing floor timbers in between the individual hull sections, the number of joints would easily increase to 20 or more. Again, only *Mary Rose* (21) and *Lomellina* (20) display a similar number of connected floor timbers and first futtocks (Guérout et al., 1989, 35f.; Grenier et al., 2007, II-63).

The regular occurrence of filling frames is otherwise only known from the *Mary Rose* (Marsden, 2009, 47, 93). The frame knees on the Dutch B&W 1 Shipwreck seem to have a similar function, but are not really comparable, as the framing on this ship is fairly irregular.

This means that, in terms of its framing system, the closest comparisons with the Gresham Ship are the substantially older and larger English *Mary Rose* and the likewise older and larger Genoese merchant vessel *Lomellina*. In Chapter 6.6 (page 71) the possibility of Venetian influence on the design of the master frame of

Comparative Analysis
Princes Channel Wreck/ Gresham Ship

Wreck / Find Features	Mary Rose	Gresham Ship	Sea Venture	Warwick	San Juan	Nossa Senhora dos Mártires	Lomellina	Vejle Hafnia	B&W 1 (Verlanger)	Scheurrak SO1	Wittenbergen
Date	Built 1510	Built 1574/5	Wrecked 1609	Wrecked 1619	Wrecked 1565	Wrecked 1605	Wrecked 1516	Built 1567–77	Built 1582–84	Wrecked 1593?	Built 1571
Raw Material											
Timber Type	Oak	Oak	Oak	Oak	Oak/beech (keel)	Cork oak/pine	Oak, pine (planking), etc.	Oak	Oak	Oak	Oak
Timber/Vessel Origin	England/England	England/England	NA/England	NA/England	NA/Basque Country	Portugal/Portugal	Diverse/Genoa	Dutch/NA	Western Germany, Sweden/Dutch	Lower Saxony/Dutch	Lower Saxony/NA
Dimensions											
Estimated Length (L) or Keel Length (KL)	KL 32 m	L 24.5 m	KL 22 m?	L 30–34 m?	L 22 m	L 40 m?	L 32 m	L 18 m	L 26 m	L 34 m	KL 22 m?
Estimated Beam	B 12 m	B 7.85 m			B 7.75 m		B 12.5 m	B 5 m	B 6 m	B 9 m	NA
Construction											
Construction Method	Frame-led	Skeleton-built	Frame-led	NA	Skeleton-built	Skeleton-built	Skeleton-built	Shell first?, spijkerpennen present	Shell first, spijkerpennen present	Shell first, spijkerpennen, double planking	Shell first?, spijkerpennen on one plank
Keel Type	Rabbeted beam keel	Rabbeted beam keel	Rabbeted beam keel	NA	Keel with incorporated garboards (except at bow and stern)	Rabbeted beam keel	Rabbeted beam keel	T-shaped keel	Rabbeted beam keel	Rabbeted beam keel (double rabbets)	NA
Joint between stempost and keel	Vertical scarf joint	Vertical scarf joint	Vertical scarf joint	NA	Vertical scarf joint	NA	NA	NA	Original keel: horizontal scarf joint	Composite post, keel end replaced, vertical lipped stempost, scarf and mortise for inner post	NA
Apron present?	Yes	Yes	NA	NA	No	Yes	NA	NA	No	Yes	NA
Framing System	Regular, floor timbers (in some cases) joined to first futtocks.	Regular, floor timbers joined to first futtocks, second futtocks between the ends of first futtocks, filling timbers at bilge	Regular, first futtocks between and overlapping floors	NA	Regular, floor timbers fastened to first futtocks, second futtocks overlap first futtocks, third futtocks overlap second futtocks	Regular, floor timbers fastened to first futtocks	Regular floors fastened to first futtocks, first futtocks fastened to second futtocks	Irregular	Irregular, presence of floor timbers, frame knees and futtocks	loose	NA
Connection between floor timbers and futtocks	Master frame, five forward and 15 aft (21), square and diagonal lap joints, knuckle joints	All visible frames connected with interlocked joints	No	NA	Master frame with two futtocks attached and 7 aft and 6 forward connected with dovetail joints (14)	Knuckle joints fastened with countersunk iron nails	Dovetail and knuckle joints	No	No	No	None, although a single futtock has a dovetail joint preserved
Connection between first and second futtocks	Yes in some cases (24)	No	No	NA	No	NA	Dovetail and knuckle joints	NA	NA	No	NA
Presence of filling timbers	Yes	Yes	No	NA	No	No	No	NA	Yes, here called frame knees	No	NA
Connection between outer hull planks	Butt joint	Vertical scarf joints	NA	Butt joint	Butt joint	Butt joint	Butt joints	Vertical scarf joint, garboard attached to keel with combination of rivets and small wooden nails	Diagonal nipped scarfs in most planks, a single vertical scarf joint in garboard strake	No	None, but joints
Waterproofing of outer hull planks	Caulking, caulking battens on outside	Inlaid waterproofing in groove at bottom of plank	Caulking	NA	Caulking	Caulking with lead and oakum, seams sealed with lead strip	Caulking	Caulking	Inlaid waterproofing (moss)	Caulking	Caulking, with caulking battens on inside
Fastening of plank/ frame joints	Trenails, caulked (3)	Trenails, irregular pattern below furring line, regular (2–3) above furring line, all caulked	Trenails in irregular pattern, caulked	Trenails (2–4)	Trenails/iron nails (2, 2)	Iron nails	Iron nails	Trenails	Trenails	Trenails	Trenails, some wedged
Fastening of plank butts/ joints/ hood ends	Iron nails	Trenails/iron nails	NA	NA	Trenails/iron nails	Iron nails	Iron nails	Iron nails	Trenails	Iron nails	Trenails/ Iron nails
Deck construction	(Orlop deck) beams lodged on beam shelf, standing knees on upper surface	Beams lodged on beam shelf and heads of futtocks, butt against outer planking, supported by standing knees	NA	Beams lodged on beam shelf and supported by lodging knees	Double beams resting on beam shelf, standing knees	NA	Doubled deck beams on top of each other with standing knees scarfed to the top, supported by beam shelves	NA	NA	Beams supported by hanging knees, joggled waterway	NA
Sources:	Marsden, 2009		Adams, 2003	Bojakowski and Custer-Bojakowski, 2011	Grenier et al., 2007	Castro, 2003	Guerout et al., 1989	pers. comm., Aoife Daly and Alexander Cattrysse	Lemée, 2006	pers. comm., Thijs Maarleveld	Stanek, 2011

Table 8-1: Table of comparative sites; the Gresham Ship is marked in light grey (J. Auer). Please note that a larger version of this table is available to download from www.barpublishing.com/additional-downloads.html

the Gresham Ship was noted. The joints between floor timbers and first futtocks are certainly connected to the design of the ship, even if their primary function might have been a strengthening one, but at least some of the pre-assembled frames are likely to also have been pre-designed. Could the similarity in framing system between the Genoese *Lomellina*, the *Mary Rose* and the Gresham Ship be an indication of Mediterranean or more specifically Italian influence on ship design?

The outer hull planking of the Gresham Ship also displays a number of constructional oddities. Hull planks within a strake are carefully joined with vertical scarf joints and the planks are waterproofed with strands of tarred animal hair laid into a groove at the bottom edge of the planks. Both features warrant further discussion.

The joining of strake planks with scarf joints is a well-known characteristic of clinker or lapstrake ship-building. Here the overlapped and joined planks of themselves do not only provide a watertight shell, but also represent an important element of structural integrity. The framing system is secondary, and the frames are being only inserted only after the shell has been completed. The Gresham Ship, however, as has just been shown, is a frame-first construction with a skeleton of pre-assembled and pre-erected frames, which determine the shape of the hull and are the main element of structural integrity. In such a construction, the joining of strake planks with scarfs would technically be unnecessary, butt joints aligned with timbers being adequate. A look at our table of comparative wrecks shows that the only contemporary wreck with scarf-joined strakes is the Vejle-Hafnia Wreck, a Dutch merchant vessel built shell-first. And yet, while the concept of joining strake planks with scarfs seems to make more sense in the context of shell-first construction, none of the other shell-first built wrecks in the table displays this feature.

Does this make the vertical scarf joints between planks an archaic legacy of clinker ship-building? In this context it is interesting to note that the Vejle-Hafnia Wreck also had a T-shaped keel, to which the garboard strake was attached clinker-fashion with iron nails clenched over rove plates and small wooden nails (Cattrysse, 2014).

What about waterproofing? Clinker shells are made watertight using material laid between the overlapping strake planks, while carvel hulls are generally caulked with waterproofing material hammered into plank seams after assembly. The solution seen on the Gresham Ship seems to be a crossover between both techniques. The shipbuilders were certainly aware of caulking, as they used it around the wale and in repairs, but seemingly made a considered choice not to use caulking to seal the outer hull planks. Did they not trust the caulking technique?

Here it is worth taking a look at the discussion presented by Adams (2003, 89f.) in his overview of carvel ship-building in Northern Europe. Adams refers to the caulking seam battens on the outside of the hull planks observed on the *Mary Rose* and to the caulking battens, already mentioned, notched into the sides of the frames on the inside of the outer hull planks as observed on the Swedish warship *Elefanten*, as well as the Mukran Wreck and the Wittenbergen Wreck. He sees these solutions as an expression of the lack of skill of early carvel shipbuilders and their 'creative search for new solutions even within a tradition with skills-based rules about how certain tasks should be performed' (Adams, 2003, 90). This might well be the case in the Gresham Ship as well.

One last constructional feature, for which no direct contemporary archaeological comparison could be found, is the support of the deck beams. In the Gresham Ship, the deck beams rest not only on the beam shelf as in most other ships, but also on top of the first futtocks. The deck beams butt directly against the outer planking. While this arrangement certainly presents a higher degree of support, it seems unique and is vaguely reminiscent of the projecting beam heads in large clinker vessels such as Aber Wrac'h 1 (L'Hour and Veyrat, 1994, 174). Again, it is not difficult to see the reason behind an arrangement such as that found in the Gresham ship, but it seems slightly archaic as well.

Altogether, it remains to conclude that the Gresham Ship does not easily fit into our current picture of early modern ship-building. With the exception of the earlier *Mary Rose*, there is little similarity between the Gresham Ship and other contemporary English wrecks. Instead constructional features found on the Gresham Ship are reminiscent of Mediterranean ship-building, and the only contemporary parallel to the scarf-joined outer planks was built in the Netherlands. Many other features are reminiscent of clinker building techniques.

To come back to our initial question: is the Gresham Ship a typical 16th-century merchantman? Maybe the answer here is yes. Maybe the contrast between design and construction, and the puzzling mix of seemingly archaic construction features is even very typical for a period of transition and a change from the old but proven way of constructing ships to a new 'scientific', but not yet trusted way of designing and constructing a ship. Only a little more than 100 years before the construction of the Gresham Ship, large clinker-built seagoing vessels were still a common sight around the shores of Britain, as witnessed by the Newport Ship (Nayling and Jones, 2014). And, although most probably built in Poland, the large clinker-built merchant vessel U34 predates the Gresham Ship by only some 46 years (Overmeer, 2008). Maybe the features seen on the Gresham Ship also represent the social division on the shipyard between the educated master shipwright, who is trying to implement 'modern' ship design and the workforce of carpenters who do not trust these methods and come from a tradition of building clinker vessels.

Considering the major rebuild, necessitated by the flawed original design, one can almost hear the shipyard carpenters chuckle ... .

Chapter 9: In Conclusion: Looking Back and Looking Forward
by Jens Auer and Thijs Maarleveld

In the present monograph a range of topics related to the archaeological data on the Princes Channel Wreck and the construction, armament and equipment of this so-called Gresham Ship are addressed. They are analysed in the context of our present understanding against the background of on-going historical and archaeological discourses; not all discourses obviously, but those that the present authors have deemed relevant in the context of the aspects addressed here. The ship's cargo is the subject of another volume. In rounding off, it seems useful to look back to the results and deficiencies and to look forward to refining research questions and ways of improving our ability to address them. The one aspect that stands out – with the Princes Channel Wreck as the first discovered example – is the furring of the ship and the way this process has been performed. It is addressed throughout the study and notably in Chapter 7. Equally important, however, is how furring and the research that could be undertaken could inform our understanding of the developments of ship-building at the start of Modern History. Here those aspects will be summarized and assessed in section 9.1 under the heading of 'Results'. Another theme, pervasive throughout the study, consists in the limits to our ability to observe and to record reliable archaeological data. It will be addressed in sections 9.2 and 9.3 under the headings 'The Archaeological Process' and 'The Role of Universities'. It will be followed by some 'Final Remarks' (section 9.4).

9.1 Results

Shipping and ship-building are as central to the history of exploration (Fernández-Armesto, 2006) as they are to the early modern integration of international markets that created what in modern approaches to comparative global history has been called the Modern World System (Wallerstein, 1974; Wallerstein, 1980) and the Great Divergence (Pomeranz, 2000). But central as these may be, it is equally true that our present understanding of developments in ship-building technology in this crucial period in European and world history is far from satisfactory and needs informed and detailed archaeological study to move forward (Adams and Flatman, 2013, 157). General trends relating to the adoption of new technologies can be discerned. But innovation and entropy go hand in hand in a problematic relationship, while explanations tend seemingly to favour so-called modern and scientific solutions in a teleological way. In practice, however, the role of innovation and transfer of technology proves not to be straightforward at all (Schweitzer, forthcoming). Developments follow their own logic and a different one for the different regions of Iberia, the Atlantic seaboard, the British Isles, the Low Countries and Scandinavia. The envisaged operational environments play their part. More importantly, however, developments and differences are linked to socio-economic factors, such as the organization and control of shipping and ship-building as a strategic endeavour, both politically and economic.

For England, the political concerns relating to the sector in the second half of the 16th century are relatively well studied (Oppenheim, 1896; Perrin, 1918; Manwaring, 1920; Perrin and Manwaring, 1922; Merriman, 1949; McGowan, 1971; Nelson, 2001). Technological aspects have been part and parcel of these discussions and have in some measure contributed to the formulation of archaeological research questions (Barker, 1986; Adams, 2003; Hocker and Ward, 2004). What transpired is that the adoption of theoretical design rules for ships actually preceded the necessary understanding of the mathematics of complex three-dimensional shapes, let alone of their hydrodynamic behaviour. Consequently 'As the frame-first system of building became refined the shapes of the frames were "designed" by elaborate geometric procedures that resulted in hull forms that were only remotely related to good sailing performance' (Gillmer, 1985, 261).

The Princes Channel dredging incident and the work that followed produced one of the rare opportunities to check such assertions and to assemble detailed new data that can be fed into the discussion. To confront new ideas and received wisdom with inferences based on this new tangible dataset is what the research in this volume tries to do in addition to the consolidation of direct evidence.

What the research shows in relation to English ship-building of the period can be interpreted as follows:

- a clear inconsistency between efforts at theoretical design and practical craftsmanship in the English dockyard;
- the clear lead of the theoretician(s) over the actual woodworkers, despite the latters' practical experience and probably successful routines in building shell-based (clinker, lapstrake) boats and ships on the one hand and their uneasiness with waterproofing a hull in which the planks are not interconnected lengthwise on the other;
- in taking the lead, the designer made sure to mould every single frame;
- the advantages of design in advance, based on transfer of theoretical knowledge, rather than transfer of true technology, were by and large cancelled out by its risks and disadvantages, including:
  - the production of crank or otherwise unsuccessful ships, which in this case led to furring;
  - putting a disproportionate demand on wood resources (Maarleveld, 1992, 169);

- and
- the introduction of inherent weaknesses in the overall strength of the hull through a systematic ordering of framing timbers, including short filling timbers and second futtocks that start from a high position.

Although these are significant assertions that find their basis in the arguments developed throughout this monograph, it is obvious that the study of one dataset, even in comparison with other published data, does no more than take the discussion a little step forward. Arguments will be criticized and many issues remain unresolved. All in all, however, it is not just at the level of technical detail that the approach has relevance, but also at the level of how practice shapes concepts and how hard it is to impose new concepts, whatever their scientific status, on long-established practice in the crafts. In the present instance new concepts of design are imposed on wood conversion, ship-building and creating a watertight hull, but the process and its lack of success has a clear parallel in the introduction of scientific navigation. There also the process could not really be imposed as older methods continued to be thought more reliable (Davids, 1985, 308). At a further level of abstraction this has consequences for our understanding of all processes of cross-cultural craft-encounters, so easily referred to as transfer of technology. It is in confrontation that very different solutions are found and often – the waterproofing between planks in this instance – in a spirit of applying solutions that have worked within the experience of the craftsman (Crawford, 2009, 161–79). The process is thus basically conservative rather than innovative. Nevertheless, one could argue that the wider the repertoire of experience, the greater the ability to adapt to new demands and find creative and innovative combinations (Van der Leeuw, 2011, 216–17). Doing is thinking and the crafts and technologies involved in boat and ship-building are simultaneously so basic and so complex that their study provides the best clues to the mind of *homo faber* that an archaeologist can ever expect to find. But those clues lie in the detail (Schweitzer, forthcoming). And although some detail was available in this instance, a lot of detail has also been lost or gone unrecognized.

9.2 The Archaeological Process

The popular image of archaeology, but especially the archaeology of ship-finds offshore, is probably still the image of the self-contained expedition or project. It is an image that finds its basis in the exemplary research with which the discipline of underwater shipwreck archaeology proved its worth (Martin, 1975; Rule, 1982; Green, 1989; Bass, 2005; Grenier *et al.*, 2007; Maarleveld and Overmeer, 2012). And the image is in fact preserved by the many volunteer-based public archaeology efforts around the British Isles and elsewhere (Beattie-Edwards and Satchell, 2011) as well as by university field schools (Auer *et al.*, 2013).

Nevertheless, that image is far removed from everyday reality (Dellino-Musgrave, 2012; Firth *et al.*, 2012).

In practice self-contained archaeological projects are embedded in a mesh of trying to make the best of everyday contingencies that affect the future existence of archaeological material and information. The dredging of the Princes Channel in 2003 is just such a contingency. Although it is important to stress that in exceptional cases significant research questions can be reason enough to sacrifice a stable site or part of it through excavation, it is – and should be – the exception rather than the rule (Maarleveld *et al.*, 2013, 26). In that sense, contingency- and development-led activities are far more typical than projects that stand alone. The majority of archaeological interventions are – and should be – targeted at mitigation, either by reducing negative impacts or by turning potentially negative effects into positive and creative research. On land, and likewise at sea, the whole process has become regulated in accordance with the European Convention on the Protection of the Archaeological Heritage (Revised) of 1992. And England is rich – perhaps even more so than other parts of Europe – in guidance on how to do this.

Despite all this guidance, however, it is hard to look back on the process that started in 2003 as a project which followed any of the basic principles of project management, archaeologically or otherwise. Projects have a clearly defined objective, a clearly defined starting point and a clearly defined conclusion. Archaeological projects serve one or several aims to the benefit of one or several stakeholder and interest groups. These need to be identified, the proper approach chosen and funding allotted accordingly. A good project design is probably the best avenue to a broad basis and a good result (Carver, 2011, 119 *et seq.*) both in development-led and self-contained projects. But the research described here had nothing of that. Rather it has been 'A Series of Unfortunate Events', to use the title of Lemony Snicket's hilarious series. Obviously not wholly unfortunate, otherwise there would not have been any data or scientific results to report. But the cumulative data and decisions clearly indicate that at no point in the trajectory did any two persons, authorities, institutions or interested parties have identical ideas on what the overall trajectory actually was and where respective responsibilities lay or were to be placed, whereas nobody would or did deny that these are quite crucial characteristics for any approach to project management.

There are several explanations for this. Some will be highlighted here, as they represent underlying rather than contingent factors. In Chapters 1 and 2 the field activities undertaken at the start are presented as a relatively novel example of development-led intrusive shipwreck archaeology in a maritime environment. In a way this is true, in a way it is not. And that is the first point to highlight.

Development-led activities are organized as part of development projects. They are thus rigorously planned in advance and, in response to the contingent nature of some rescue archaeology in the post-war period, the practice of archaeology has become an integrated part of the planning of development projects (Rahtz, 1974; Cleere, 1984; Trotzig and Vahlne, 1989; Cooper et al., 1995). But not all activities in maritime waters are new developments in the sense of planning practice and planning legislation. Maintenance dredging to ensure the accessibility of maritime ports is an ongoing concern. Evidently it is subject to day-to-day planning, but basically it reacts to the contingencies of erosion and accretion in harbour approaches. It can hardly be otherwise. In consequence, however, the practice is in some measure exempt from the rigorous project approach currently associated with truly new developments.

All parties directly concerned with the 2003 contingency were prepared to go a long way to cater for a significant archaeological discovery. If that had not been the case, it would have been just another example of clearing wreckage of different ages of which nobody would have taken any notice, as was routine 20 years before (Redknap, 1990). This book would never have been written and the Princes Channel Wreck would never have had any significance at all. This is the second point. Significance is not an intrinsic value, even though it is often perceived as such. It simply does not exist without a sponsor. Consequently, to assess the significance upon discovery was not easy, if it ever is. Despite contradicting views on integrity and dating, it was significant enough for the Port of London Authority to decide to fund more than just the clearance. Practices and procedures that are tuned to development projects were tentatively adopted to organize this. Plans were written that would take the archaeological 'project' through a range of phases and possible satisfactory outcomes. But the absence of the basic structure that characterizes the organization of a development project meant that these were more or less implemented in a void. This was the more critical, since the structure of a self-contained project that could warrant continuity was not in place either.

The issue of significance, even if not static and hard to define, has quite a bit of consequence. In the time-pressed structure of development-led archaeology, it is the curator's role to make sure that the archaeological efforts a developer agrees to integrate into a development project and the quality of the activities deployed in that context reflect sufficiently the significance of the heritage affected (Willems and van den Dries, 2007). In a self-contained project this is less of an issue. Obviously, significance and the attainment of significant results are at the basis of such a project in the first place, but there is more leeway for significance to develop gradually. The role of the curator or 'competent authority' is equally central, but less of an issue (Maarleveld et al., 2013, 21). Permitting or withholding approval is what it comes down to.

Whatever their function and competence, the position of competent authorities is determined and controlled politically and therefore fundamentally influenced by public opinion. General policies and rules – politically approved – consolidate approaches. Choices are accounted for vis-à-vis political constituencies and the public. But what of public opinion in this instance? The initial contingency (and the services that were hired to deal with it) happened at a location where nobody could see or form their opinions. No feedback occurred. This is very different from the contingency that brought the so-called Newport Ship to light during the construction of the Riverfront Arts Centre, a find that acquired immediate significance through the attention of the city's population (Trett, 2010, 8). Inherently and scientifically the two finds were certainly equally significant, but significance was added in very different ways by the archaeological processes that followed. It shows a fundamental problem with the management of archaeological resources offshore, where typically there is very flimsy information to go by to begin with, where no local population or local government exists and where other stakeholders do not present themselves (Satchell and Palma, 2007, 3–30, 49–58; Maarleveld, 2012, 421). This is a third point to highlight.

The consequence of all of this has been a series of events and activities that can hardly be described as a very coherent approach, even though individual parts followed the logic of mitigation projects of limited scope, as negotiated between the PLA and the service contractor. In themselves these were consistent and complied with basic guidance for archaeological documentation in a development-led context. There is no question that the team assigned to the task was fully inspired by the fascinating scientific potential, as well as the challenges of 3D-recording. This prevented uninspired, automated documentation. Finding the ideal compromise between recording speed, accuracy and detail, was not easy, however, if it ever is. Despite a clear recording methodology, it turned out to be a very subjective process. Differences in staff experience led to extreme time pressure, with the effect that the recording of all structures could not be finished to the same standards. Likewise, no phase of data integration and analysis was included with the recording. No feedback loops were built into the overall project structure, as no such structure actually existed. Analyses were undertaken, but quite separately. One of the very clear consequences of this is reflected in the sampling that took place for the dendrochronology. The central issue to be resolved was the overall dating of the ship, which was still contentious at the time. Samples were chosen so as to get the best guarantee of a result, but sampling was not targeted at distinguishing between an original building phase and later additions, including the furring, as the overall structure had not yet been understood. Obviously, this is now much regretted.

The dendrochronology example clearly illustrates that what one observes is influenced by what one is looking for and is thus dependent on experience and on constant reiteration of research questions to be addressed. Moreover, what one observes is dependent on what one has access to. A precautionary agreement not to dismantle the coherent structure before any decision on long-term conservation made aspects of the construction at least temporarily inaccessible. That can be assessed as wisdom at the time. But only preliminary and temporary measures followed and the hot potato of deciding between research and conservation continued to be shoved around. With hindsight that can hardly be assessed as wisdom. It just illustrates the absence of a clear framework for management decisions. But also it shows that dismantling a carefully chosen part of the construction is perhaps something that should routinely be built into the feedback loops of integrating data collected in an instance like this. It provides for a far better understanding, not just of the construction, but also of the construction's significance in terms of technological history. In the present instance, the opportunity for adequate observation of a range of key aspects was basically lost, without serving a greater good. Likewise, storage in the brackish but warm waters of Horsey Lake was a wise decision for the short term, leaving different options open. The longer it lasted, however, the more the remains degraded and the more long-term conservation was compromised. So yet again, it can only be stressed that a decision mechanism is crucial. Temporary measures will always be attractive, but are not necessarily wise with hindsight. The importance of stressing this is that, where unwieldy archaeological wood finds are concerned, the example is far from unique. Well-meant or half-hearted decisions in the guise of temporary conservation are taken regularly, in the hope that the problem at hand will go away. It does ... and not with any lasting benefits. Even the opportunity for observation and creation of archaeological data has then been lost.

9.3 The Role of Universities

One of the public roles of university researchers is to provide critical feedback on the processes in society that influence data and knowledge generation. It is, as the reader will have noticed, a role we liberally adopt in these concluding remarks. Another general role for university researchers is actively to take part in the definition of research agendas that are such an important guide and reference for the strategic definition of archaeological activities in development projects (Bazelmans, 2006; Ransley et al., 2013).

In a development-led context, the specific goals of archaeological projects, the ways of achieving them as well as checks and balances to warrant proportionality in efforts, costs and outcome are agreed by the developer who integrates the archaeology into the budget, the curator/competent authority and the operator/contractor who tenders for the job or provides a service in its context. As impact on heritage and the historical environment is just one of the factors defining the costs that are to be balanced by the overall benefits of the development project, ear-marked funding for these aspects is not an issue. They are costs that are integral to the feasibility of the development. Funding for self-contained projects is another matter. Such archaeological projects are undertaken for intrinsic reasons and originate with an interested party who needs to organize it and activate funding.

In each case the process will be informed by discourses in society on the value of heritage and by discourses in the scientific community on current research questions. University researchers are part of this and may be the ones who initiate a self-contained project. In development-led processes they may be important propagators for specific aspects, they may be involved in an advisory role and where it fits their particular research interests they may be available to take on the research or part of it. The latter role has a few issues to consider, such as making sure that it does not negatively interfere with the roles of other operators and institutions. But it can have very beneficial effects (e.g. Jongste and Louwe Kooijmans, 2006).

The remarkable thing about the Princes Channel 'project' or 'course of events' is that it was neither development-led, although some parties perceived it as such, nor self-contained, although other parties definitely perceived it as 'the thing of the archaeologists', although basically no archaeologist or principal investigator in the sense of a self-contained project was in charge. Also, there was no public opinion feedback that forced the creation of a project structure and providing a self-contained basis of funding. It was only much later that a Steering Group was created.

Is it the role of universities to then step in and pick up the pieces? Hardly, one might say. On the other hand, universities have a very specific interest, defined by the research interests of their researchers. Even if no research funding can be secured they are interested in particular primary data and fiddling with fragments in order to address them. That is what happened in the present instance. It was because specific information on the technical developments in English merchant ship-building at the end of the 16th century was in such demand in order to try and move on in current discourses and to compare developments with what we are beginning to know about other regions, that it made sense to take the matter in hand. The opportunities that mitigation and rescue operations offer for truly innovative observations are, after all, a very important factor in a sound archaeological research strategy serving pure research interests.

The dataset as collected and as generated through the steps of analysis presented here allowed for the present result. It was not an optimal dataset, not one to congratulate the archaeological process with. And it is truly hoped that at least some of the lessons learned will feed into future channel adjustments and maintenance dredging procedures (Firth *et al.*, 2012, 5; 72). In dealing with incidents that nevertheless occur, providing for a decision-making structure and sufficient feedback loops between documentation, interpretation and analysis will hugely benefit the results. Selective dismantling of a part in order to at least understand what otherwise one tries to preserve is what will benefit research enormously.

As the playing field of university researchers is not confined by the regional boundaries typical of archaeologists with curator's responsibilities or the procedural traditions associated with these, it is not unusual for their research to try to combine observations made in different places and at different times. As a result they are quite used to working with datasets that are hardly compatible or that have other deficiencies and nevertheless to come to aggregation and conclusions (Maarleveld, 2013, 352). In fact, by its very nature archaeological data is never complete or ideal. If the central *dictum* of statistical analysis: 'rubbish in – rubbish out' applied to all archaeological analysis, the discipline would have no reason to exist. Consequently, universities should not be too aloof to step in and do some dirty work if the material and the issues are interesting enough, even if it feels a bit like scavenging on a project for which others have responsibility. But perhaps universities should offer their services more freely and perhaps the curator and the competent authority should find ways of integrating them earlier on in the process. But clearly a decision procedure should be in place for this to have real meaning. Conversely, one should certainly not refrain from optimizing a responsible way of dealing with archaeological contingencies, on the assumption that in the end university researchers will step in anyway.

9.4 Final Remarks

It is hoped that, through this book and the second volume that addresses the cargo, the so-called Gresham Ship and the data that relates to it will gain in significance, scientifically at least. It is also hoped that it contributes to raising the awareness of operators and authorities when they are confronted with heaps of hopeless wreckage and the need to decide instantly on their significance and on a coherent plan of action. Under unfavourable conditions, time pressure and unaccountable contingencies always join forces to limit on-site work and to defer as much as possible to later, sometimes under the guise of potential protection of integrity of the remains. If, however, even a first recording and analysis of the findings is unduly delayed, it may prove extremely hard to make sure that activity is not discontinued altogether. In fact this is what systematically has happened with many a discovery that deserved better. But contingencies such as the discovery of the Princes Channel Wreck never fully come as a surprise. Large budgets are routinely spent on clearance activities and in this case the Port of London Authority clearly took the potential scientific or heritage values on board. That was a crucial step. There is no reason to think that integrating these aspects as a routine would significantly affect clearance costs or would add to any ensuing confusion. But clearly it would, if the interests of research, acquisition and curation are not smoothly attuned and no clear decision-making structure is in place.

Despite all the critical comments throughout the book and in this last section, it was highly stimulating to work with this fascinating material and face the challenges associated with it. We hope that the reader agrees and is prepared to make do with the many remaining uncertainties and deficiencies.

Appendix:
Princes Channel Wreck – Dendrochronological Data

Sample Code	Origin of sample	Cross-section of tree	Cross-section size (mm)	Total rings	Sapwood rings	ARW mm/year	Date of sequence	Felling period/ Comment
PCW01	First futtock 1061, section 2	Quarter	200 x 180	190	20+Bw	1.06	AD1385-AD1574	AD1574 winter
PCW02	Furring timber F65-01, section 2	Quarter	170 x 140	77	+?HS	2.61	AD1481-AD1557	AD1567-1603?
PCW03	First futtock F60-02, section 2	Half	205 x 130	68	+HS	1.38	AD1463-AD1530	AD1540-76
PCW04	Furring timber F102-01 loose	Quarter	255 x 175	207	13	1.13	AD1362-AD1568	AD1568-1601
PCW05	First futtock F1-02 (loose, but was on section 1)	Whole	205 x 130	109	+HS	1.17	AD1450-AD1558	AD1568-1604
PCW06	First futtock F2-02, section 1	Whole	280 x 205	108	15+Bw	1.2	AD1466-AD1573	AD1573 winter
PCW07	Second futtock LF208a	Quarter	175 x 170	132	31+B	1.43	AD1442-AD1573	AD1573
PCW08	Floor timber F1-03, section 1	Half	210 x 185	228	-	0.98	AD1269-AD1496	after AD1506
PCW09	Second futtock F51-02, section 2	Half	265 x 170	105	-	1.43	AD1455-AD1559	after AD1569
PCW10	Furring timber F64-01, section 2	Quarter	190 x 130	105	+20s	1.49	AD1449-AD1553	AD1573-99
PCW11	Second futtock F55-02, section 2	Half	225 x 185	113	-	1.95	Undated	
PCW12	Unlabelled stringer	Quarter	150 x 140	76	+HS	1.92	Undated	
PCW13	Stringer 1188, loose	Half	240 x 170	78	+HS	2.63	AD1473-AD1550	AD1560-96
PCW14	Furring timber 1205, loose	Half	242 x 160	136	-	1.9	AD1409-AD1544	after AD1554
PCW15	First futtock 1164, section 3a	Quarter	235 x 190	237	32++½Bs	0.96	AD1337-AD1573	AD1574 spring
PCW16	First futtock 2011, section 3a. Same timber as PCW18	Quarter	253 x 195	258	+?HS	1.08	AD1298-AD1555	AD1565-1601?
PCW17	First futtock 2010, section 3b	Quarter	260 x 190	297	25+Bw	0.94	AD1278-AD1574	AD1574 winter
PCW18	First futtock 2011b, section 3b. Same timber as PCW16	Quarter	235 x 180	174	16+Bw	1.35	AD1401-AD1574	AD1574 winter
PCW19	Second futtock 3021, section 3b	Half	205 x 200	120	24+Bw	1.66	AD1455-AD1574	AD1574 winter
PCW20	Second futtock 3033, section 3b	Half	240 x 175	94	21+Bw	1.34	AD1481-AD1574	AD1574 winter
PCW21	Second futtock 3037, section 3b	Quarter	220 x 170	291	30+Bw	0.79	AD1284-AD1574	AD1574 winter
PCW22	Second futtock 3038, section 3b	Half	225 x 170	118	-	1.95	AD1444-AD1561	after AD1571
PCW23	Second futtock 3045, section 3b	Whole	250 x 185	129	+?HS	1.18	AD1423-AD1551	AD1561-97?
PCW24	Second futtock 3023, section 3b	Quarter	-	-	-	-	not measured	-
PCW25	Second futtock 1506, section 3b	Quarter	-	-	-	-	not measured	-

Table A-1   List of samples from Princes Channel Wreck. Total rings = all measured rings; HS = heartwood sapwood boundary, s = number of sapwood rings, B = bark edge, Bw = bark edge winter felled; ARW = average ring width of the measured rings

PRINCES CHANNEL WRECK – DENDROCHRONOLOGICAL DATA

Filenames	PCW 02	PCW 03	PCW 04	PCW 05	PCW 06	PCW 07	PCW 08	PCW 09	PCW 10	PCW 13	PCW 14	PCW 15	PCW 16_8	PCW 17	PCW 19	PCW 20	PCW 22	PCW 23
PCW01_2	3.62	3.43	9.66	3.48	5.02	4.2	7.6	3.52	4.21	6.27	-	6.42	11.25	8.84	4.85	3.71	3.03	4.31
PCW02	*	-	3.79	3.63	5.97	5.86	-	3.27	3.09	4.95	3.03	4.49	4	4.55	-	3.98	3.68	4.87
PCW03	*	*	3.16	5.25	-	-	-	-	3.31	3.35	-	3.27	4.61	-	-	-	3.43	3.84
PCW04	*	*	*	3.39	3.84	3.29	4.82	3.24	4.36	4.37	3.5	6.45	10.42	8.48	3.22	-	-	-
PCW05	*	*	*	*	5.03	5.02	-	4.16	5.75	6.56	6.07	4.1	5.61	-	3.55	4.81	-	3.82
PCW06	*	*	*	*	*	6.13	-	3.64	4.27	6.04	3.23	4.06	3.81	3.56	4.29	4.01	3.33	6.01
PCW07	*	*	*	*	*	*	-	3.61	3.87	4.72	-	-	4.82	3.83	-	3.94	-	6.9
PCW08	*	*	*	*	*	*	*	-	-	-	-	-	8.98	7.42	-	-	-	-
PCW09	*	*	*	*	*	*	*	*	-	4.54	3.96	3.88	3.06	-	5.14	3.28	-	4.6
PCW10	*	*	*	*	*	*	*	*	*	4.21	3.88	3.46	6.16	5.33	-	-	-	3.49
PCW13	*	*	*	*	*	*	*	*	*	*	4.27	4.39	4.41	-	-	-	4.44	7.19
PCW14	*	*	*	*	*	*	*	*	*	*	*	4.48	3.17	3.53	-	3.54	-	3.62
PCW15	*	*	*	*	*	*	*	*	*	*	*	*	5.96	6.53	-	-	-	3.26
PCW16_8	*	*	*	*	*	*	*	*	*	*	*	*	*	10.03	5.34	4.2	3.37	4.76
PCW17	*	*	*	*	*	*	*	*	*	*	*	*	*	*	3.26	-	-	3.35
PCW19	*	*	*	*	*	*	*	*	*	*	*	*	*	*	*	5.64	3.26	3.34
PCW20	*	*	*	*	*	*	*	*	*	*	*	*	*	*	*	*	4.44	4.07
PCW22	*	*	*	*	*	*	*	*	*	*	*	*	*	*	*	*	*	6.36

Table A-2   t-value matrix for correlations between ring-width sequences used to make the 306-year site mean 'GreshamS'; | = overlap < 15 years, - = t-values less

Glossary

This glossary lists technical terms and expressions used in the text of this book. Due to the interdisciplinary nature of the study, the terms and expressions belong to different domains varying from naval architecture, archaeology, heritage management and conservation, measuring techniques, data processing, diving and history. The entries aim to explain terminology as used in the present context. The glossary has no claim at being exhaustive. Italics indicate that a term has its own entry.

Acoustic positioning system – Underwater acoustic positioning systems are built up of several transponders and one or more transducers that are fixed to one or more divers or underwater vehicles whose movements are to be tracked or guided. The acoustic signals sent between transponders and transducer are used to derive the distances between them and to calculate the changing position of the transducer in real-time through *trilateration*.

Adze – Wood working tool. It is similar to an axe, but the blade is set at right angles to the handle.

Anomaly – Irregularity in the image of the sea-bottom or subsoil as evidenced through acoustic or other geophysical methods.

Apron – Part of the stem construction, running through the same arc as the stem and fastened inboard of it. It is sometimes called a false stem.

Archive – In terms of archaeology and heritage management, the archive of a site consists of all the documentation of on-site work in paper and digital form, but also includes any samples or finds and the documentation on their treatment, if any.

Astragal – A ring or moulding encircling a gun at about 6 inches from the mouth.

Auger – A large straight wood-boring drill with a simple wooden T-bar as a handle, used to auger holes for bolts and trenails.

Bar shot – Naval ammunition formed of two sub-calibre balls or half-balls, joined together by a solid bar.

Base-ring – The hindmost ring at the breech of a muzzle loading gun with a *cascable*.

Batten – Battens or sheer battens are used to fair the lines, that is to control the run of strakes and the ship's lines during construction. They are light strips of wood attached to the outside of the erected frames. Likewise they are used in model building. The term is also used as synonymous with *spline*, a flexible strip of wood or other material used by a draughtsman in laying out broad but taut curving lines. *Caulking battens* serve a different function.

Beam head – The end of a beam. In several classes of high medieval and late medieval ships the beam heads protrude through the planking. In that case the beam heads are intricately rebated to fit into slots in the planking and the beams themselves are then frequently referred to as head beams in the archaeological literature.

Beam shelf – A thick internal plank running longitudinally along the hull on which the deck beams rest.

Beam trawl – Fishing equipment for bottom trawling in coastal waters in which the mouth of the net is held open by a solid metal beam, attached to two shoes or skids which are solid metal plates, welded to the ends of the beam, which slide over and disturb the seabed.

Bearing – In surveying bearing means compass direction; in navigation as well. But bearing also means comportment and the bearing of a ship can therefore also mean its behaviour at sea, the characteristics that hydrostatics and hydrodynamics try to describe. In Mainwaring the term is used for the widest part of the vessel below the top strake, the loadline, which can either be too high or too low.

Bilge – The lowest part of the hold of a ship or the flattest part of the hull upon which the ship rests when aground. Also the turn of the bilge, the upward curve of the ship's hull approximately at the end of the floor timbers.

Bore diameter – The internal diameter of the barrel of a gun. Although indicative of the gun's calibre, the bore diameter of an excavated gun as found may vary from the diameter of the design.

Bottom-based – Technical term used in ship archaeology for a construction sequence in which the bottom planks are laid before any internal timbers are shaped and in which the sides are added in a next stage. It applies to classes of flat-bottomed barges with swimheads that may or may not have a central element ('keel plank'). It is also applied to hard-chined flat-bottomed vessels with plank-keels, notably in the Netherlands. It is less applicable to the round-bottomed vessels in the same tradition, although, just like the bottom-based vessels, these are built *shell-first*.

Box-halved – Cut, sawn or split along the heart of a bole or log, where only the cut face has been elaborately worked or squared.

Glossary

Box-quartered – Cut, sawn or split twice at right angles, both times along the heart of a bole or log, where only the cut faces have been elaborately worked or squared.

Breasthook – Large grown timber that is placed internally across the *apron* forming a strong connection between the two sides of the hull.

Breech – The after end of a gun. In cast iron guns with a *cascable*, the breech is considered to be the part that connects the *base-ring* to the cascable.

Breech-loader – A firearm that is loaded at the breech.

Buoyancy – The upward force that a vessel experiences when afloat. It is equal to the weight of the water that the vessel displaces.

Buttock lines – In a lines plan the buttock lines or butt lines are the lines that represent vertical planes that run parallel to the *centre line*.

Butt – The end of a timber or plank when cut square.

Button – On a gun the button is the rounded or somewhat pointed end of the *cascable*.

Cactus grab – Working bit on a crane with six or more interlocking claws that hydraulically or mechanically crush the material the operator wants to grab, extensively used in scrap processing.

Carvel – A word that has come to mean the method of ship construction where the hull planks are flush-laid against a skeleton of frames and are not fastened to each other at their edges, in contradistinction to *clinker*.

Cascable – The cascable (or also cascabel from Spanish *cascabel* = little bell) is the breech part of a muzzle loading gun, not forming part of the internal ballistics nor strictly contributory to the performance of the gun and therefore not considered in the length of the piece.

Cast iron – Iron with a carbon content between 1.8 and 4.5 per cent. It was used in foundry to make castings such as guns. It is strong in compression, capable of being made into intricate shapes, but weak in tension.

Caulking – The method of waterproofing in which fibrous materials, twisted into strands are driven into a seam with a caulking iron and a caulking mallet.

Caulking batten – A lath affixed over a seam in order to keep the caulking material in place. The laths used for this purpose in medieval shipbuilding and generally fixed with purpose-made staples or 'sintels' figure as 'moss-laths' in the archaeological literature.

Ceiling – The internal structural planking of the hull, i.e. not lining or panelling.

Centre line – Central longitudinal axis of a ship, also called the heart line.

Centre of Buoyancy – The centre of buoyancy is the point where the upward force of buoyancy acts on the total of a floating body. When the centre of buoyancy and the *centre of gravity* are in the same vertical line, the body is in equilibrium.

Centre of Gravity – The centre of gravity is the point where the downward force of gravity for all of a ship's components acts on the ship as a whole. The centre of gravity should be on the *centre line*; bringing it forward or aft along the centre line influences a ship's behaviour. The centre of gravity can be moved by trimming.

Chain shot – Naval ammunition formed of two sub-calibre balls or half balls, joined together by a chain.

Chamfer – The angled surface formed when the sharp corners of a timber are cut back or bevelled for safety or good appearance

Chart Datum – the level of the tide to which charted depths are referred. The chart datum for charts produced by the UK Hydrographic Agency is the lowest astronomical tide (LAT), which is the lowest level that can be predicted under normal meteorological conditions.

Chase – The part of a gun in front of the *reinforce* on which the *trunnions* sit.

Chase girdle – The undecorated part of the chase of a gun immediately in front of the *reinforce* on which the *trunnions* sit.

Clamp – The stringer or *beam shelf* upon which the ends of the beams are supported.

Clench – The method of securing metal fastenings by hammering the end of the nail or rivet over a washer or *rove*. This could either be done by simply turning it over the rove or riveting, i.e. beating it until it had tightened sufficiently not to pull out. Also clinch or clink.

Clinker – The method of boat and shipbuilding in which each strake of hull planking overlaps the one below and in which these strakes are fastened to each other through the overlap with nails *clenched* over washers or *roves*, in contradistinction to *carvel*.

Competent authority – The authority issuing permits and seeing to the quality of the activities carried through. In heritage management and in relation to archaeological services and activities the roles of competent authority and *curator* generally coincide.

Concretion – Term used for stone-like encrusted conglomerates created by grains of sand, shell particles and other material around an artefact as a result of the interaction of metal components, notably iron, with the saline seawater environment.

Crank – A ship that is crank or crank-sided is liable to *heel* or capsize: used when she is built too deep or narrow or has not sufficient ballast to carry full sail.

Crossbeam – Athwartship timber effecting a strong union between the sides of the vessel and in the presently discussed context forming part of the deck structure as a *deck beam*.

Cross-pall – A temporary plank used to tie the opposite ends of frames together during construction prior to fitting the *deck beams*.

Crotch – A fork-shaped grown timber that is placed internally across the *deadwood* or after-end of the keel by way of a frame and forming a strong connection between the planking on two sides of the hull; also crook.

Culverin – The name used for a heavy type of gun.

Curation – Used in heritage management as the whole system of taking care of a matter with heritage significance, also synonymous to curatorship or guardianship.

Curator – Used in heritage management for the person, authority or agency responsible for the best possible care regarding a matter with heritage significance, such as an archaeological site or an archaeological object. The curator of a museum's collection is a specific example, but not the example referred to in this monograph.

Datum system – Reference system used in field studies to correlate size and position of phenomena with the coordinates of a map. It can consist of several more or less random points or of a systematic grid. The third dimension is measured in relation to a set height, for example to *Chart Datum*.

Deadrise – A term referring to the upward angle of the floor timbers as they run out from the keel towards the turn of the bilge.

Deadwood – A solid timber built up over the keel in those areas of a ship's hull forward and particularly aft, where the form is too sharp and narrow to be hollow and fit frames.

Deck beam – Athwartship timber of the deck structure that effects a strong union between the sides of the vessel.

Dendrochronology – The comparative study of the annual growth rings in timber. It allows for relative and absolute dating, hence chronology, but has come to include dendro-provenancing, that is to say the assessment of the area where a tree has grown through the statistical comparison of the pattern of its tree rings with the accumulated data collected in dendrochronology throughout different parts of the world.

Depth of hold – The distance between the deck and the bottom of the ship. In classification it is measured in very specific ways.

Developer – The initiator, sponsor or principal customer of a development project.

Development-led archaeology – Is the system through which in many parts of the world the detection and research of archaeological phenomena in the context of urban, rural, industrial or maritime development is organized in order to prevent unnecessary destruction as well as awkward rescue situations that are not planned for and that will therefore disproportionally affect project management. Outside the UK it is sometimes referred to as preventive archaeology.

Digital solid – see Solid

Double – To apply an extra layer of planking.

Dovetail joint – A fastening or joint composed of a *tenon* cut in the shape of an expanded dove's tail, fitting into a *mortise* of corresponding shape.

Draft – The depth of water which a vessel draws or requires to float her.

Dub – The action of working timber to a smooth surface with an adze.

Dutch flush – Generic term used in ship archaeology for a range of methods to build flush-planked hulls in a sequence in which a substantial part of the shell of planking is formed before any or most internal timbers are shaped. The planks are temporarily fastened to each other by means of clamps temporarily nailed upon them, for which systematic rows of plugged nail- or spike-holes (*spijkerpennen*) are the archaeological proxy. Such a shell-first approach is typical in the (northern) Low Countries, but it is unknown how far it was also practised in neighbouring areas.

Dutchman – A repair to a timber or plank where the flawed or damaged section is cut out so as to form a rebate. After preparing with a luting compound a new piece of wood is let into it and fastened in place.

Early modern period – The early part of the period which in historical periodization of northern Europe follows the middle ages, alternatively also called Renaissance or early post-medieval. In the present context the early modern period refers to the 16th and 17th centuries.

Glossary

Entrance – A name frequently given to the foremost part of a ship under the surface of the water; it can be sharp or bluff.

Fairing – Making sure that the lines or curvatures of a vessel are suitable for its easy passage through water by making them follow smooth curves without irregular wiggles or by adding structure for this purpose.

Falconet – A light piece of ordnance of various calibres.

False keel – A layer of timber fastened along the bottom of the keel, either for protection (being relatively easy to replace when worn) or in order to increase the lateral plane.

False post – A layer of timber fastened along the outside of the (stem-)post, either for protection (being relatively easy to replace when worn) or in order to increase the lateral plane.

Fillet – A narrow flat band used for the separation of one moulding from another on a gun.

Filling timber or filling frame – A timber that is additional to the timbers that are integrated in systematically built-up frames.

Finbanker – Cast-iron mass-produced gun of a particular Swedish design and make.

Flat vertical scarf joint – A joint between planks, in which the ends of the two planks have been tapered in such a way that the two planks overlap over a certain distance.

Floor – A floor or floor timber is the lowest component of a ship's frame running across the keel.

Flush – 1 said of planking to indicate that it is applied with a smooth outer surface, unlike *clinker*.

2 said of a trenail to indicate that it has no head protruding from the surface, nor is set in a recess.

Frame – Transverse timbers to which the planks are fastened. In large vessels frames are made from several components, such as *floors*, *futtocks* and *top timbers*.

Frame bend – The curve of a frame, defined by the ship's planking in a filling frame, defined by geometry in a pre-erected frame, hence 'the *midship bend*'.

Frame-first – Term used in ship archaeology to denote building methods in which the frames are erected first and the planking is added later, as opposed to *shell-first* methods.

Frame-led – Term used in ship archaeology to denote building methods in which the process is guided by one or more predesigned frames, irrespective of the question whether the actual building is predominantly *frame-first* or predominantly *shell-first*. Bottom-based and *Dutch flush* approaches can thus be frame-led or have frame-led elements, despite the fact that they are predominantly effected in a shell-first order.

Framing timbers – Timbers constituting a frame, such as floors, futtocks and top timbers.

Freeboard – The distance between the waterline and the lowest part of the gunwale or sheerstrake.

Furring – A process of broadening a ship, by removing the planking, adding extra timbers to the frames and then re-planking.

Futtock – Futtocks or foothooks are the timbers that together with the floors and the top timbers form a frame. If there are more than one, they are numbered 1st, 2nd, 3rd and 4th, the 1st being the lowest and the 4th the highest.

Garboard – The plank next to the keel. The garboard strake is the lowest strake of planking.

Geophysical survey – A survey with geophysical techniques. The most common ones used for underwater work are based on acoustics, such as *side-scanning* or *multi-beam sonar* to see irregularities at the bottom surface, or seismic and sub-bottom profiling to locate irregularities deeper down. Techniques to measure irregularities in magnetic fields are likewise used.

Geo-referenced – Said of a datum system or a position if it is linked to a global coordinate system such as the World Geodetic System 84 (WGS84).

Girdling – Adding a girdle of extra planks all around a ship so as to strengthen her or increase her beam.

Graving piece – A filling piece added to a timber or to the planking as repair or to fill in a minor section.

Grid-based recording – Recording in grid squares that are physically laid out over the phenomena to be recorded, for example, in the form of lines or more solid material.

Half beam – The small timbers supporting the deck planking that lie between and parallel to the deck beams. They are rebated into the carlings or carlines that longitudinally connect the deck beams and possibly into the *beam shelf*.

Half model – Ship model of which only one half has been executed, from the plane of the *centre line* to one of the sides.

Hanging process – The process of putting on the planking in a frame-first building process.

Head – The top end of a timber (but see also *Beam head*).

Heart rot – Specific type of timber decay caused by fungi or bacteria that affects the inner parts without showing on the surface.

Heartwood – The central part of a tree; as successive rings of new sapwood are formed the innermost cells become too far from the growth and solidify into heartwood.

Heel – The lower end or foot of a timber; e.g. the heel of the sternpost.

Historical environment – Technical term in protection and management denoting heritage values in the context of protection of the environment.

Hood end – The end of a plank that fits into a *rabbet* in the stem- or stern-post.

Hopper dredger – Self-propelled mechanical dredger that collects the dredged material in its own hold or hopper in order to dump it elsewhere.

Hydrodynamic – Pertaining to the forces acting upon an object moving through water and its performance in doing so.

Hydrostatic analysis – Analysis pertaining to the equilibrium of a ship in water and the forces exerted on it at rest.

In situ – Literally meaning 'in place', in situ is used in archaeology to indicate that something is in its original position or rather that its position has not been disturbed by present-day interference.

Iron concretion – Term used for stone-like encrusted conglomerates created by grains of sand, shell particles and other material around an iron object.

Iron minion – A compound containing iron oxides and chalky clay or other calcites, used mostly for priming, as anti-corrosive or as antifouling protection.

Keel – In wooden ships the keel is the lowermost fore-and-aft constructional member, formed of one or more timbers, running along the centre line and joined to the stern post and stem.

Keelson – The internal backbone of a ship. A large timber (or timbers) running parallel to the keel above the floors. It secures the floors by being fastened through them to the keel.

Knee – An angled or curved piece of timber used to connect various elements of a ship's hull through approximately right angles, for instance deck beams and frames. Knees with one arm running down from the side or underside of a beam are referred to as hanging knees. Those set horizontally against the beam are lodging knees and those rising vertically from the top of the beam are called *standing knees* or standards.

Knuckle joint – Term occasionally used in ship archaeological literature to denote interlocked joints between framing elements.

Langrel shot – Shot consisting of sharp pieces of scrap iron or flint packed into a case, used in anti-personnel actions and to damage rigging; also langrage.

Lapstrake – The method of boat and shipbuilding in which each strake of hull planking overlaps the one below; if *clenched* it is called *clinker*.

Laser scanning – A method to rapidly capture shapes of objects, buildings and landscapes through the controlled steering of a large number of laser beams integrated with a distance measurement at every pointing direction.

Laser sintering – see Selective laser sintering

Leaky hose system – Porous tubes or hoses with many constantly dripping holes allow waterlogged wood to be kept in a wet condition just as it allows for neatly regulated irrigation of flower beds.

Lifting frame – A system of spreaders, sometimes rigidly fixed, to allow a complex structure to be lifted by a crane without crushing it between the strops.

Limber hole – A channel for the passage of water to the pumps. They are usually cut in the underside of the floor timbers. Alternatively they are formed by the gaps left between timbers for the purpose.

Lines plan – A standardized way of representing a ship's hull in naval architecture, in which the key is to project the intersection of a series of cross sections in orthogonal planes; a lines plan thus includes the projection of *section lines*, *buttock lines* and horizontal *waterlines*.

Load waterline – The line on the *lines plan* of a ship that represents the intersection of the ship's form with the plane of the water surface when the ship is floating at the designed draft.

Magnetometer – An instrument for measuring magnetic forces and in particular anomalies in terrestrial magnetism at any point.

Maintenance dredging – Dredging with the purpose of keeping a fairway or harbour at depth.

Master frame – A pre-erected frame at a ship's greatest width; by extension also the widest cross-section of the ship.

Midship bend – The outer form of the midship section.

Minion – 1 A compound for priming as anti-corrosive or as antifouling protection. Depending on the composition either containing lead or iron oxides it is also called red lead or iron minion.

2 A small kind of ordnance.

Glossary

Mitigation – A term used in planning for the reduction of negative impacts. In development-led archaeology it translates in measures for protection of sites, in the euphemism 'preservation by record', but also in turning potentially negative effects into positive and creative research.

Mortise – A square or rectangular recess cut into a timber into which the *tenon* of another timber fits, thus forming a mortise and tenon joint.

Mould – A pattern, for instance a thin plate of wood by which something is shaped; a template.

Moulded – The moulded dimension is the depth or thickness of a ship's timber when viewed in section i.e. looking forward or aft, as opposed to the *sided dimension*, which is measured to the inner or outer view of the same timber. By extension, the moulded shape is the shape in section.

Moulding – Decorative feature on a cast iron gun or a similarly shaped carved finish to a timber.

Multi-beam sonar – A sonar instrument used to produce a high resolution image of the seabed. As opposed to the traditional echo sounder or a side scanning sonar, the multi-beam covers a full swath under the surveying vessel, hence the multi-beam sonar technique is frequently referred to as Swath Bathymetry.

Muzzle – That end of a fire-arm from which the shot is discharged; in a cannon it is the part extending from the *astragal* to the extreme end mouldings.

Neck – The narrow part of a gun connecting the *cascable* with the *breech*.

Nogging – Fixing a *shore* in place by means of a trenail.

NURBS – Short for Non-Uniform Rational Basis Splines, which is the technical label used for the definition of a specific type of curve in three-dimensional modelling that gives a high level of freedom and flexibility to the modeller. More specifically a NURBS curve is defined by B-spline vertex points, called knots. The shape of the curve is influenced by the position of the defining vertex points, but it is generally smoother than a curve passing through the defining vertex points, although the curve is not automatically fair.

Oakum – Fibres of old rope teased apart and then twisted together in strands for caulking seams between planking and elsewhere.

Offset measurements – Measurements taken at right angles relative to a base-line or grid.

Ogee – Moulding that in cross-section consists of a continuous double curve: convex above, concave below.

Operator – The person or organisation professionally or officially engaged to perform the practical or mechanical operations belonging to a process, business or scientific investigation, for instance in development-led archaeology.

Ordnance – Military materials, stores or supplies, more specifically engines for discharging missiles; artillery.

Orlop deck – Originally, the single floor or deck with which the hold of a ship was covered (Dutch: *overloop*). By extension the lowest deck of a ship with more than one deck.

Perrier – A ballistic engine or cannon for discharging stone shot.

Plank – In the classification of timber planks are the slabs sawn or split from a bole that are between 4 cm (1½ inch) and 10 cm (4 inches) in thickness. Timber thicker than this is referred to as thick stuff and thinner timber as board. The term planking is specifically applied to the outer planks of the ship's hull.

Polyamide nylon dust – The specific synthetic material used in *Selective Laser Sintering*.

Poly-line – In computer graphics, a poly-line is a continuous line composed of one or more line segments.

Poly-surface – In computer graphics, a poly-surface consists of two or more surfaces joined together. If the poly-surface fully encloses a volume, it is also a solid.

Post – The upright timber at the front of a ship or boat (the stempost) and the upright timber at the stern (the stern-post), on which the rudder is hung (the rudderpost).

Pre-assembled – A frame is called pre-assembled if it is built up of timbers that have been connected to each other prior to integration with the rest of the ship's structure.

Pre-designed – A frame is called pre-designed if its form derives from a theoretical construct rather than from a mould taken from the form of the hull at its intended position.

Pre-erected – A frame is called pre-erected if it has been put in position prior to the hull's planking. There is a considerable procedural difference between pre-erected frames (Dutch: *spanten van oprichting*) and frames that are put in position later (Dutch: *spanten van aanvulling*).

Pre-moulding – The procedure of moulding frames on the basis of a pre-designed construct.

Preservation strategy – The envisaged strategy for short or long term preservation and curation of archaeological material. If the strategy realistically aims at long-term structural integrity of archaeological ship remains, the parameters for research are quite different than if taking apart, sampling, disposal, reburial or conservation of the parts with the aim of later refitting are put up as the goal.

Rabbet – A recessed channel cut in a timber to accommodate another, such as a V-shaped rabbet cut into the side of the keel to fit the garboard strake.

Rabbeted beam keel – A keel consisting of a wooden beam fitted with rabbets for the garboard strakes.

Rake – The slope of a near vertical element such as a mast, the stem- or stern-post.

Reinforce – A sleeve of increased thickness on points of greatest stress in a gun barrel.

Remedial recording – Recording in the context of mitigatory archaeology aiming at recording what gets lost.

Rescue archaeology – Archaeology performed as emergency measure when a discovery is made without having been foreseen. The need to avoid rescue archaeology led to the integration of archaeology into planning and present-day development-led archaeology.

Reverse naval architecture – An expression coined by the Danish ship researcher Christian Lemée to denote the process of inferring the design of a ship (and of the concepts and people behind the evidence) from the archaeological evidence, in essence the reverse of the process whereby the naval architect goes from idea to real ship through design.

Ribband – Lengths of timber nailed along the outside of the frames to bind and support them during construction.

Rising floor – A floor that is not straight is rising towards its ends. The rising increases progressively fore and aft of the midship section.

Rising line – The rising line (of the floor) is a technical term for a line drawn in the plan of a ship to show the increasing rise and depth of the floors (or the height that they are set above the keel). The rising line is a central element in discussions on ship design in which *whole-moulding* and arcs of circles have a part.

Rove – A small metal plate or ring over which the point of a nail or rivet is clenched or beaten down in the fastening of overlapping planks.

Rule of thumb – A principle with broad application that is not intended to be strictly accurate or reliable for every situation.

Run of the strakes – The form of the vessel as expressed by the fair flow of the strakes of planking.

Rutter – A pilot book or seaman's guide.

Saker – A form of small cannon, employed both in sieges and on ships.

Sappy – Said of timber if it has much sapwood.

Sapwood – The outer rings of a tree through which sap is transported and in which food is stored. It is softer than *heartwood*.

Scantlings – The sectional dimensions of a timber or of all the timbers in a ship taken collectively, also expressed in moulded and sided dimensions.

Scarf – 1 End to end joint between two pieces of plank or timber with a tapering overlap, generally so that the width and thickness is not altered. There are many types of scarf joint varying in complexity.

2 To join two elements in this fashion.

3 The amount of overlap in such a joint.

Sea-keeping – Sea-keeping abilities relate to the seaworthiness of a vessel.

Section – 1 Part of the Princes Channel Wreck, section 1, 2, 3a, 3b or 4.

2 A cross section or profile, by extension *section line*.

Section line – In a lines plan the lines that represent vertical planes running at right angles to the centreline plane are called section lines or sections.

Selective laser sintering (SLS) – A method of printing a 3D computer file in which loose polyamide nylon dust is selectively coalesced into a solid mass through the appliance of a laser. As the object printed in this way remains surrounded by unsintered powder the process allows for very complicated shapes.

Service contractor – A person or organisation who contracts or undertakes to perform work or provide a service at an agreed price or rate, for instance in the context of development-led archaeology.

Shank – The shank of an anchor is its straight and central part, to be distinguished from the *stock* in a two-fluked stock anchor.

Sheathing – The layer applied to a ship's hull to protect the planking from attack by marine borers such as gribble and shipworm. In early modern western European contexts a sacrificial layer of pine is the most usual form of sheathing.

GLOSSARY

Shell-first – Term used in ship archaeology to denote building methods in which the planking is assembled to form a shell, into which frames are inserted later, as opposed to *frame-first* methods.

Shore – A timber used as a temporary prop or support for frames, stem and stern post etc., during construction of the vessel; see also *nogging*.

Sided – The sided dimension is the breadth or width of a ship's timber when viewed from the inside out or from the outside in, as opposed to the *moulded* dimension, which is measured to the section or depth of the same timber.

Sidescan sonar – A sonar instrument used to skim the sea-bottom to either side of the surveying vessel and thus to detect material that protrudes from the sea-bottom only to a limited extent.

Significance – A central term in heritage management. Although it is difficult to strictly define, significance is quite easy to understand. In relation to a site, an object or a story, significance is the quality that makes it meaningful or of consequence, for a person, for a group or for humanity as a whole.

Site – The place or position occupied by some specified thing. In the integration of archaeology with planning the definition of the boundaries of an archaeological site has become quite crucial. The same holds true for the protection of a site. In relation to shipwreck archaeology and heritage management it is important to understand that a wreck is embedded in the archaeological deposit of the wreck site. Archaeological objects or artefacts, including the elements of a wreck, are movable; a site is not.

Skeleton-built – Term used in ship archaeology to denote building methods in which all the frames and thick-stuff are erected first in order to form a coherent skeleton to which the planking is added. It is a method where the *frame-first* approach is taken all the way; sometimes this is also denoted as full carvel, as opposed to those carvel or flush building methods in which the planking defines ship shape to a certain extent.

Skid – The shoe or iron sledge that is welded to the ends of the beam used in beam trawling to keep the net or bottom trawl open.

Skills-based rules – The set of rules, including *rules of thumb* that govern the practical mode of operation of a craftsman, including choice and use of tools and application of techniques.

Small arms – Small arms is a term used to denote personal weapons. For the early modern period it includes edged weapons as well as small firearms, such as pistols, muskets and arquebuses.

Solid – In computer graphics, a solid is any three-dimensional object with a volume.

Spanish olive jar – A rough type of pottery container used for long-distance transport of oil and other substances. As the shards are quite recognizable, they have been found in many late medieval and early modern contexts all over Europe. In cargo contexts they have been found in a plaited vegetable fibre protection, much like a traditional Chianti bottle.

Spijkerpen – A small wooden plug filling a hole left by a removed nail or spike in order to prevent the timber to rot at that point. In regular rows on both sides of a seam in the planking *Spijkerpennen* are indicative of temporary clamps fastening the planks in a largely shell-first building technique, such as those comprised under the term Dutch flush.

Spike – A large square shanked metal nail used for general fastening purposes, particularly planking.

Spile – Spiling is the means by which a builder determines and measures the shape of any curved piece that must be fitted to a curved surface. It is accomplished by establishing a line of reference (for which a spiling batten can be used) and by measuring from this line at regular intervals to where the new piece will fit.

Spline – A fairing batten used to draw curved lines on a drawing board.

Spreader bar – A bar or beam used to keep lifting cables, chains or strops apart.

Square tuck – A flat surface at the stern of a ship, departing from the equally flat transom and extending backwards over the stern-post and rudder (see Tuck).

Standing knee – A standing knee or standard is an angled piece of timber rising vertically from the top of a beam and supporting the ship's side.

Stave – Component plank of a cask or other stave built container such as a bucket, by extension the wrought iron component bar in a wrought iron gun barrel.

Stem – The stem or stempost is the large timber scarfed onto the keel that determines the shape of the bow of a ship and into which the (hood) ends of the outer planking are rabbeted.

Stereo-lithography – Solid imaging or 3D printing technology.

Sternpost – The large timber set on the upper face of the after end of the keel to which it is joined. It can be variously formed depending on the type of vessel, but commonly the ends of the outer hull planking or transom are rabbeted into it in the same fashion as they are into the stempost; the rudder is hung on the after side of the sternpost.

Stock – The heavy (wooden) cross-bar of an anchor that sits at right angles of the *shank* and at right angles with the plane of the arms on which the flukes sit.

Stone shot – Stones, cut round to be shot from a *perrier*.

Strake – A run of planking.

Strop – A band used in lifting.

Surface supplied equipment – Surface supplied equipment or SSE is diving equipment in which the breathing gas is supplied to the diver through a hose or umbilical from the surface. Although other forms exist, such as a simple flow hose or a hookah with a mouthpiece regulator, in all commercial settings the breathing gas is led to a band-mask or helmet and the equipment includes a backup or bail-out gas supply.

Swell – The slight widening of the outer diameter of a gun barrel towards the muzzle, having its widest point just behind it. A low muzzle swell diameter for a gun otherwise cast to the same specifications as one with a higher value indicates it is probably cast for naval rather than terrestrial use. Otherwise there is no distinction.

Swivel gun – Small gun mounted on a pivoted rest enabling it to turn horizontally in any required direction, for example on the gunwale of a boat.

Target – In geophysical mapping the word target is used for an anomaly that warrants further inspection or ground truthing.

Tender – 1 A person who attends to the diver, more specifically who holds his tether or umbilical.

2 Said of a narrow ship that has inadequate stability; also *crank*.

Tenon – A projection fashioned on the end or side of a piece of timber, to fit into a corresponding cavity or mortise in another piece, so as to form a close and secure joint.

Timber – 1 Wood that is suitable for or has been converted for carpentry or construction as planks or as thick stuff.

2 A constituent part of a frame or another element in the hull, as opposed to a plank.

Tonnage – 1 The size or capacity of a ship measured according to various formulae, which are a calculation of volume as much as of weight.

2 In an English early modern context, tonnage refers to *tons burthen* plus a factor to allow for the weight of crew and munitions carried.

Tons burthen – Tons burthen refers to the net cargo capacity of a ship, in an English early modern context calculated by reference to the length of the keel, the maximum beam and the depth of the hold. The cargo capacity is an indication of the size of a ship. It is substantially less than gross tonnage, which again is substantially less than the ship's (loaded) displacement.

Tool-marks – Tool-marks are the marks left on material such as wood by an implement. Tool-marks are thus highly revealing indicators of the practical mode of operation of a craftsman and the specific tools used. Hence their great importance in archaeological and forensic studies.

Total station recording – Recording with a total station, which is an electronic theodolite measuring bearings and angles or transits, integrated with an electronic distance meter to read slope distances from the instrument to a particular point.

Touchhole – The hole or channel in the breech of a cannon through which fire is communicated to the charge.

Transom – Transverse beam fastened to the stern-post. Hence also the lower stern if flat.

Trenail – A trenail or treenail (also trennel or trunnel) is a wooden dowel used for fastening timbers together.

Trilateration – A method of surveying analogous to triangulation in which each triangle is determined by the measurement of all three sides.

Truck – Small solid wooden wheel or roller, specifically those on gun carriages.

Trunnion – Cylindrical protrusion on each side of a gun with which it rests almost in balance on its carriage.

T-shaped keel – A keel that instead of being rectangular in cross section such as a beam keel is broader in its upper part and recessed below, so that the garboard strakes are fixed in the corner of the recess rather than in a *rabbet*.

Tuck – The gathering of the ends of the bottom planks of a ship under the stern; the lower stern.

Tumblehome – The characteristic of a ship whose beam gradually becomes narrower from the (orlop) deck upwards.

t-value – The *t*-value is the outcome of a statistical test for the amount of correlation or difference between of two sets of data, the so-called Student *t*-test. In *dendrochronology* it is standard practice to use this test as an indicator of the significance of the correlation between the measured ring sequence and calendars to which it is dated. Reliable dendro-provenancing requires significantly higher t-values than dating.

Underwater lines – On a lines plan the underwater lines describe the form of the submerged part of the hull.

Upperworks – The superstructure of a ship.

Vent – The hole or channel in the breech of a cannon or firearm through which fire is communicated to the charge; the touchhole.

Wale – A thick hull strake providing additional longitudinal strength (and acting as fender).

Waney – Said of timber if it is unsquared or imperfectly squared.

Waterline – 1 The line of floatation of a ship; the line taken to be described on the hull by the surface of the water when a ship is afloat.

2 The proper line of floatation when a ship is fully laden, also load waterline.

3 Any one of the lines in a lines plan that represent the contour of the hull in horizontal planes at various heights above the keel.

Waterproofing – Generic term for all techniques to ensure water tightness, such as caulking, coating, luting, pitching, the application of stopwaters, etc.

Waterway – The outermost deck plank, usually thickened towards its outer edge in order to guide water away from the most vulnerable seams.

Weather deck – A ship's deck that is open to the sky and exposed to the weather.

Whole-moulding – Whole-moulding is a method of drawing the rounded part of all the frames by a sweep of the same radius or with a mould formed to answer this purpose, called the bend-mould.

Wrongheads – The end (or head) of the (rising) floor timbers (Dutch: *wrang*; French: *varangue*).

Wronghead sweep – The wronghead sweep or floor sweep is the curve or arc of circle that defines the turn of the bilge in *pre-designed* shipbuilding that follows the principles of *whole-moulding*.

Wrought iron – A pure form of iron, containing virtually no carbon, and fibrous in texture due to threads of slag. It is the product of charcoal-fired furnaces for the direct reduction of iron ore or of the forge.

3D record – The result of surveying in which each measurement has been taken in three dimensions without having been projected on plans and sections as basis for 3D computer graphics.

Bibliography

Abell, W., 1948, *The Shipwright's Trade*, Cambridge University Press, Cambridge.

Adams, J., 1985, 'Sea Venture: A second interim report – part I', *International Journal of Nautical Archaeology*, **14(4)**, 275–99.

Adams, J., 2003, *Ships, Innovation and Social Change*, Stockholm.

Adams, J., van Holk, A.F., and Maarleveld, T.J., 1990, *Dredgers and Archaeology: Shipfinds from the Slufter*, Alphen aan den Rijn.

Adams, J. and Flatman, J., 2013, 'High to Post-Medieval, 1000–1650', in Ransley, J., Sturt, F., Dix, J., Adams, J., and Blue, L., eds, *People and the Sea: a Maritime Archaeological Research Agenda for England*, CBA Research Report, Bootham, York, 138–63.

Auer, J., 2005, *Princes Channel Wreck, Thames Estuary, Mitigation Strategy: Phase III Recording and Recovery. Summary Report 57330.01*, Wessex Archaeology, Salisbury.

Auer, J., 2012, 'Lessons learned – shipwreck recording in the context of rescue archaeology: the case of the Princes Channel wreck', in Henderson, J., ed., *Beyond Boundaries: Proceedings of the 3rd International Congress on Underwater Archaeology*, Koll. Vor- u. Frühgesch, Römisch-Germanische Kommission, Bonn, 409–17.

Auer, J., and Steyne, H., 2004, *Princes Channel Wreck, Thames Estuary: Report of Archaeological Work. Fieldwork Report 55011.02*, Wessex Archaeology, Salisbury.

Auer, J., and Baggaley, P., 2004, *Princes Channel Wreck, Thames Estuary: Evaluation Work: Dendrochronological Dating, Geophysical Survey and Diving Inspection. Fieldwork Report 56472.02*, Wessex Archaeology, Salisbury.

Auer, J., and Firth, A., 2007, 'The Gresham Ship: an interim report on a 16th-century wreck from Princes Channel, Thames Estuary', *Post-Medieval Archaeology*, **41**, 222–41.

Auer, J., Bangerter, R., and Mallon, F., 2009, 'The Wreck of an Elizabethan Merchantman from the Thames: A preliminary Fieldwork Report', in *Between the seas. Transfer and Exchange in Nautical Technology. Proceedings of the Eleventh International Symposium on Boat and Ship Archaeology, Mainz 2006, ISBSA 11*, Tagungen RGZM, Verlag des Römisch-Germanischen Zentralmuseums, Mainz, 79–88.

Auer, J., Ditta, M., and Logan, M., 2012, *Esbjerg Maritime Survey Reports 1: Survey Report: Cuxhaven BSH-Nr. 1557*, Maritime Archaeology Programme, University of Southern Denmark, Esbjerg.

Auer, J., Schweitzer, H. and Thomsen, C. eds, 2013, *Fieldwork Report: Ågabet Wreck, Langeland 2012*, Maritime Archaeology Programme, University of Southern Denmark, Esbjerg.

Baillie, M.G.L, and Pilcher, J. R., 1973, 'A simple crossdating program for tree-ring research', *Tree Ring Bulletin*, **33**, 7–14.

Barbour, P.L., 1964, *The Three Worlds of Captain John Smith*, Houghton Mifflin, Boston, MA.

Barker, R., 1986, 'Fragments from the Pepysian Library', *Revista da Universidade de Coimbra*, XXXII, 161–78.

Barker, R., 1991, 'Design in the dockyards: about 1600', in Reinders, R. and Paul, K. eds, *Carvel Construction Technique: Fifth International Symposium on Boat and Ship Archaeology, Amsterdam 1988*, Oxbow Monographs. Oxford, 61–9.

Barker, R., 1998, 'English Shipbuilding in the Sixteenth Century'. in Rieth, E., ed., *Concevoir et construire les navires: de la trière au picoteux*, Erès, Ramonville-Saint-Agne, 109–26.

Barker, R., 2003, 'Whole-Moulding: A Preliminary Study of Early English and Other Sources', in Nowacki, H., and Valleriani, M., eds, *Shipbuilding Practice and Ship Design Methods from the Renaissance to the 18th Century*, Preprint 245, Max Planck Institute for the History of Science, Berlin, 33–66.

Bass, G.F., 2005, *Beneath the Seven Seas: Adventures with the Institute of Nautical Archaeology*, Thames & Hudson, London.

Bazelmans, J.G.A., 2006, 'To What End? For What Purpose? The National Archaeological Research Agenda and Quality Management in Dutch Archaeology', in van Heeringen, R.M., and Lauwerier, R.C.G.M., eds, *Berichten van de Rijksdienst voor het Oudheidkundig Bodemonderzoek*, RCAM, 53–66.

Beattie-Edwards, M., and Satchell, J., 2011, *The Hulks of Forton Lake, Gosport: the Forton Lake Archaeological Project 2006–2009*, NAS Monograph Series 3, BAR British Series 536, Oxford.

Bischoff, V., Englert, A., Nielsen, S. and Ravn, M., 2011, 'Recent Advances in Post-Excavation Documentation, Reconstruction and Experimental Maritime Archaeology', in Catsambis, A., Ford, B. and Hamilton, D.L., eds, *The Oxford Handbook of Maritime Archaeology*, Oxford University Press, Oxford.

Bojakowski, P., and Custer-Bojakowski, K., 2010, *The Warwick: New Archaeological Research on the 17th-century English Galleon*, National Museum of Bermuda, Bermuda.

Bojakowski, P. and Custer-Bojakowski, K., 2011, 'The *Warwick*: results of the survey of an early 17th-century Virginia Company ship', *Post-Medieval Archaeology*, **45(1)**, 41–53.

Bound, M., 1998, 'A Wreck off Alderney from the late Elizabethan period: An analysis of the artefacts', in Bound, M., ed., *Excavating Ships of War*, Nelson, International Maritime Archaeology Series 2, Oswestry, Shropshire, 64–83.

Bourne, W., 1587, *The arte of shooting in great ordnaunce. Contayning very necessary matters for all sortes of seruitoures eyther by sea or by lande*, Thomas Woodcocke, London.

Bridge, M.C., 1998, *Tree-ring analysis of timbers from Gosfield Hall, Essex*, Ancient Monuments Laboratory Report 19/98.

Bridge, M.C., 2000, *Tree-ring analysis of timbers from Croxley Hall Farm Barn, Rickmansworth, Hertfordshire*, Ancient Monuments Laboratory Report 25/2000.

Bridge, M.C., and Dobbs., C, 1996, 'Tree-ring studies on the Tudor warship Mary Rose', in Dean, J,S., Meko, D.M., and Swetnam, T.W., eds, *Tree Rings, Environment and Humanity: Proceedings of the International Conference, Tucson, Arizona, 17–21 May 1994*, Radiocarbon, Tucson, AZ, 491–6.

British Archaeological Association, 1846, 'Proceedings of the Association, December 9th', *Journal of the British Archaeological Association*, **2**, 361–2.

Brown, R.R., 2011, ' "A Jewel of Great Value": English Iron Gunfounding and its rivals, 1550–1560', in Beltrame, C. , and Ridella, R.G., eds. *Ships and guns: the sea ordnance in Venice and Europe between the 15th and the 17th centuries*, Oxbow Books, Oxford, 98–105.

Brown, R.R., 1989, 'Identifying 18th-century trunnion marks', *International Journal of Nautical Archaeology*, **18(4)**, 321–9.

Carr Laughton, L.G., 1911, 'Captain Nathaniel Boteler', *Mariner's Mirror*, **1(1)**, 23–7.

Caruana, A.B., 1994, *History of English Sea Ordnance vol. 1 The Age of Evolution, 1523–1715*, Jean Boudriot Publications, Rotherfield, East Sussex.

Caruana, A.B., 1985, 'The parts of a Gun', *Canadian Journal of Arms Collecting*, **23(1)**, 11–17.

Carver, M.O.H., 2011, *Making Archaeology Happen: Design versus Dogma*, Left Coast Press, Walnut Creek, CA.

Castro, F., 2003, 'The Pepper Wreck, an early 17th-century Portuguese Indiaman at the mouth of the Tagus River, Portugal', *International Journal of Nautical Archaeology*, **32(1)**, 6–23.

Cattrysse, A.J.D.A., 2014, 'Deviations in Northern-European Carvel Ship-building, Master's Thesis, University of Southern Denmark, Esbjerg.

Chapelle, H.I., 1967, *The search for speed under sail, 1700–1855*, Norton, New York.

Cleere, H., 1984, ed., *Approaches to the Archaeological Heritage: a comparative study of world cultural resource management systems*, Cambridge University Press, Cambridge.

Cleere, H., 1985, *The iron industry of the Weald*, Leicester Univ. Press, Leicester.

Cooper, M.A., Firth, A., Carman, J. and Wheatley, D. eds, 1995, *Managing Archaeology*, Routledge, London.

Crawford, M.B., 2009, *Shop Class as Soulcraft: an Inquiry into the Value of Work*, Penguin Press, New York.

Crumlin-Pedersen, O. and Olsen, O., 2002, *The Skuldelev Ships I: topography, archaeology, history, conservation and display*, Viking Ship Museum, Roskilde.

Crumlin-Pedersen, O. and McGrail, S., 2006, 'Some Principles for the Reconstruction of Ancient Boat Structures', *International Journal of Nautical Archaeology*, **35(1)**, 53–7.

Davids, C.A., 1985, *Zeewezen en wetenschap: de wetenschap en de ontwikkeling van de navigatietechniek in Nederland tussen 1585 en 1815*, Bataafsche Leeuw, Amsterdam.

Dellino-Musgrave, V.E., 2012, *Marine Archaeology: a Handbook*, Council for British Archaeology, Bootham, York.

Einarsson, L., 2008, 'Ett skeppsvrak i Ronneby Skärgård', *Ale. Historisk tidskrift för Skåne, Halland och Blekinge*, **(2)**, 1–15.

Endsor, R., 2005, 'A Drawing of the Midship Bend of The *Hampshire* 1653', *Mariner's Mirror*, **91(1)**, 67–82

English Heritage, 1998, *Dendrochronology: guidelines on producing and interpreting dendrochronological dates*, London.

Falconer, W., 1815, *An Universal Dictionary of the Marine*, (reprinted 1974), London.

Fernández-Armesto, F., 2006, *Pathfinders: a Global History of Exploration*, W.W. Norton, New York.

Ferreiro, L.D., 2007, *Ships and science: the birth of naval architecture in the scientific revolution, 1600–1800*, The MIT Press, Cambridge, MA.

Firth, A., 2006, 'Old Shipwrecks and New Dredging: An Elizabethan Ship in the Thames', in Grenier, R., Nutley, D., and Cochran I., eds, *Underwater Cultural Heritage at Risk: Managing Natural and Human Impacts, Heritage at Risk Special Edition*, ICOMOS, Paris, 35–38.

Firth, A., Scott, G., Gane, T., and Arnott, S., 2012, *London Gateway: Maritime Archaeology in the Thames Estuary*, Wessex Archaeology, Salisbury.

Fragments of Ancient English Shipwrightry, Pepys Library MS 2820, Magdalene College, Cambridge.

Förster, T., 1999, 'Das Mukranwrack – Ein ungewöhnlicher Schiffsfund aus dem 16. Jahrhundert', *Nachrichtenblatt Arbeitskreis Unterwasserarchäologie*, **5**, 12–21.

Friel, I., 1983, 'Documentary sources and the medieval ship: some aspects of the evidence', *International Journal of Nautical Archaeology*, **12(1)**, 41–62.

Gillmer, T., 1985, 'Evolving ship design technology revealed in wrecks of Post Medieval ships', in Cederlund, C.O., ed., *Postmedieval Boat and Ship Archaeology: papers based on those presented to an International Symposium on Boat and Ship Archaeology in Stockholm in 1982*, Swedish National Maritime Museum Report 20, Stockholm or BAR International Series 256, Oxford, 255–67.

Goodburn, D., 2004, *Notes on issues arising from visiting sections 3a, 3b and 4 of the Princes Channel Wreck 07/12/04 PLA Denton Wharf, Gravesend*, Sittingbourne.

Green, J.N., 1989, *The Loss of the Verenigde Oostindische Compagnie Retourschip Batavia, Western Australia 1629: an excavation report and catalogue of artefacts*, BAR International Series 489, Oxford.

Grenier, R., Bernier, M.A., and Stevens, W., eds, 2007, *The underwater archaeology of Red Bay: Basque shipbuilding and whaling in the 16th century*, Parks Canada, Ottawa.

Guérout, M., Rieth, E., and Gassend, J.-M., 1989, *Le Navire Génois de Villefranche: un naufrage de 1516?*, Éditions du Centre National de la Recherche Scientifique, Paris.

Guérout, M., and Rieth, E., 1998, 'The wreck of the *Lomellina* at Villefranche sur Mer, 1516', in Bound, M., ed., *Excavating Ships of War*, Nelson, International Maritime Archaeology Series 2, Oswestry, Shropshire, 38–50.

Harriot, T., Mathematical and Scientific Papers, British Library BL Add. MS 6788.

Hasslöf, O., Henningsen, H. and Christensen, A.E. eds, 1972, *Ships and Shipyards, Sailors and Fishermen: Introduction to Maritime Ethnology*, Rosenkilde and Bagger, Copenhagen University Press, Copenhagen.

Hildred, A., 1997, 'The Material culture of the Mary Rose (1545) as a fighting vessel: the uses of wood', in Redknap, M., ed., *Artefacts from wrecks: dated assemblages from the Late Middle Ages to the Industrial Revolution*, Oxbow Books, Oxford, 51–72.

Hildred, A., ed., 2011, *Weapons of warre: the armaments of the Mary Rose*, Mary Rose Trust, Portsmouth.

Hocker, F.M. and Ward, C.A., 2004, *The Philosophy of Shipbuilding: conceptual approaches to the study of wooden ships*, Texas A&M University Press, College Station, TX.

Hodgkinson, J.S., 2000, 'Gunfounding in the Weald', *Journal of the Ordnance Society*, **12**, 31–47.

Howard, R.E, Laxton, R.R, and Litton, C.D, 1998, *Tree-ring analysis of timbers from Chicksands Priory, Chicksands, Bedfordshire*, Ancient Monuments Laboratory Report 30/98.

Jongste, P.F.B., and Louwe Kooijmans, L.P., eds, 2006, *Schipluiden: A Neolithic Settlement on the Dutch North Sea Coast c. 3500 cal BC*, University of Leiden, Leiden.

Lavery, B., ed., 1981, *Deane's Doctrine of Naval Architecture 1670*, Conway Maritime Press, London.

Lavery, B., 1987, *The Arming and Fitting of English Ships of War, 1600–1815*, Naval Institute Press, Annapolis, MD.

Lavery, B., 1988, *The colonial merchantman Susan Constant 1605*, Conway Maritime Press, London.

Laxton, R.R., and Litton, C.D., 1988, *An East Midlands master tree-ring chronology and its use for dating vernacular buildings*, University of Nottingham, Department of Classical and Archaeological Studies, Monograph Series, III.

Lemée, C.P.P., 2006, *The Renaissance Shipwrecks from Christianshavn: An archaeological and architectural study of large carvel vessels in Danish waters, 1580–1640*, Viking Ship Museum, Roskilde.

L'Hour, M. and Veyrat, E., 1994, 'The French Medieval Clinker Wreck from Aber Wrac'h', in Westerdahl, C., ed., *Crossroads in ancient shipbuilding: proceedings of the Sixth International Symposium on Boat and Ship Archaeology, Roskilde, 1991*, Oxbow Books, Oxford, 165–80.

Maarleveld, T.J., 1992, 'Archaeology and early modern merchant ships: Building sequence and consequences: An introductory review', in *Rotterdam Papers VII*, Rotterdam, 155–74.

Maarleveld, T.J., 2012, 'The Maritime Paradox: Does International Heritage Exist?', *International Journal of Heritage Studies*, **18(4)**, 418–31.

Maarleveld, T.J., 2013, 'Early Modern Merchant Ships, Nicolaes Witsen and a Dutch-Flush Index', *International Journal of Nautical Archaeology*, **42(2)**, 348–57.

Maarleveld, T.J. and Overmeer, A., 2012, 'Aanloop Molengat – Maritime archaeology and intermediate trade during the Thirty Years' War', *Journal of Archaeology in the Low Countries*, **4(1)**, 95–149.

Maarleveld, T.J., Guérin, U., and Egger, B., eds, 2013, *UNESCO Manual for Activities directed at Underwater Cultural Heritage: a Guide on the Rules annexed to the UNESCO 2001 Convention on the Protection of the Underwater Cultural Heritage*, UNESCO, Paris.

McElvogue, D.M., 1998, 'Description and appraisal of a rudder assemblage of a late 16th-century vessel wrecked off Alderney', *International Journal of Nautical Archaeology*, **27(1)**, 24–31.

McElvogue, D.M., 1999, 'Ordnance from a late 16th century wreck', *Journal of the Ordnance Society*, **11**, 1–17.

McGowan, A.P., 1971, *The Jacobean commissions of enquiry, 1608 and 1618*, The Navy Records Society, London.

Manwaring, G.E. ed., 1920, *The life and works of Sir Henry Mainwaring Volume 1*, The Navy Records Society, London.

Marsden, P., ed., 2009, *Mary Rose: your noblest shippe: anatomy of a Tudor warship*, Mary Rose Trust, Portsmouth.

Martin, C., 1975, *Full Fathom Five: Wrecks of the Spanish Armada*, Viking Press, New York.

Merriman, R.D., 1949, *The Sergison Papers*, The Navy Records Society, London.

Munro, M.A.R, 1984, 'An improved algorithm for crossdating tree-ring series', *Tree Ring Bulletin*, **44**, 17–27.

Nayling, N., 2004, *Tree-Ring Analysis of Framing Timbers from The Princes Channel Wreck, Thames Estuary*, University of Wales, Lampeter.

Nayling, N. and Jones, T., 2012, 'Three-Dimensional Recording and Hull Form Modelling of the Newport (Wales) Medieval Ship', in Günsenin, N., ed., *Between continents: Proceedings of the twelfth Symposium on Boat and Ship Archaeology, Istanbul 2009*, Ege Yayinlari, Istanbul, 319–24.

Nayling, N., and Jones, T., 2014, 'The Newport Medieval Ship, Wales, United Kingdom,' *International Journal of Nautical Archaeology*, online preview.

Nelson, A., 2001, *The Tudor navy: the ships, men and organisation 1485–1603*, Conway Maritime Press, London.

Ní Chíobháin, D., 2011, 'The arming of a late 16th century merchantman', Master's Thesis, University of Southern Denmark, Esbjerg.

Oertling, T., 2001, 'The concept of the Atlantic vessel', in Alves, F.J.S., ed., *Proceedings: International Symposium on Archaeology of Medieval and Modern Ships of Iberian-Atlantic Tradition; Hull Remains, Manuscripts and Ethnographic Sources: a Comparative Approach*, Lisbon.

Oppenheim, M., 1892, 'The Royal Navy under James I', *The English Historical Review*, **7(27)**, 471–96.

Oppenheim, M., 1896, *A history of the administration of the Royal Navy and of merchant shipping in relation to the Navy from 1509 to 1660*, John Lane, London.

Overmeer, A., 2008, 'Schepen van verre kusten? Overnaadse schepen in Nederland in de 15de en 16de eeuw', in Oosting, R., and van den Akker, J., eds, *Boomstamkano's, overnaadse schepen en tuigage: inleidingen gehouden tijdens het tiende Glavimans Symposion, Lelystad, 20 april 2006*, Glavimans Stichting, Amersfoort, Netherlands, 41–55.

Perrin, W.G. ed., 1918, *The autobiography of Phineas Pett*, The Navy Records Society, London.

Perrin, W.G. ed., 1929, *Boteler's dialogues*, The Navy Records Society, London.

Perrin, W.G., and Manwaring, G.E., eds., 1922, *The life and works of Sir Henry Mainwaring Volume 2*, The Navy Records Society, London.

Pomeranz, K., 2000, *The Great Divergence: China, Europe, and the Making of the Modern World Economy*, Princeton University Press, Princeton, NJ.

Port of London Authority, 1967, 'Removing the wrecks: the work of the salvage section', *PLA Monthly*, May.

Puype, J.P., 2000, 'Three-wheeled gun carriages from the late 16th-century shipwreck Scheurrak SO1 near the Texel', *Royal Armouries Yearbook*, **5**, 106–16.

Rahtz, P.A., 1974, *Rescue Archaeology*, Penguin Books, Harmondsworth.

Ransley, J., Sturt, F., Dix, J., Adams, J., and Blue, L., eds, *People and the Sea: a Maritime Archaeological Research Agenda for England*, CBA Research Report, Bootham, York.

Redknap, M., 1990, 'The Albion and Hindostan: the fate of two outward-bound East Indiamen', *International Journal of Nautical Archaeology*, **19(1)**, 23–30.

Redknap, M., 1984, *The Cattewater wreck: the investigation of an armed vessel of the early sixteenth century*, BAR British Series 131, Oxford.

Roberts, O.T.P., 1998, 'An exercise in hull reconstruction arising from the Alderney Elizabethan wreck', *International Journal of Nautical Archaeology*, **27(1)**, 32–42.

Roth, R., 1989, 'A proposed standard in the reporting of historic artillery', *International Journal of Nautical Archaeology*, **18(3)**, 191–202.

Rule, M., 1982, *The Mary Rose*, The Mary Rose Trust, Portsmouth.

Salisbury, W., 1966, 'Early Tonnage Measurement in England', *Mariner's Mirror*, **52(1)**, 41–51.

Salisbury, W. and Anderson, R.C., 1958, *A Treatise on Shipbuilding and a Treatise on Rigging Written About 1620–1625*, Society for Nautical Research, London.

Satchell, J., and Palma, P., eds, 2007, *Managing the Marine Cultural Heritage: Defining, Accessing and Managing the Resource*, Council for British Archeology, Bootham, York.

Schubert, J.R.T., 1957, *History of the British iron and steel industry from c. 450 BC to AD 1775*, Routledge and Kegan Paul, London.

Schweitzer, H., (forthcoming, 'The devil is in the detail – The dilemma with classification and typology', in *Proceedings of the International Symposium on Boat and Ship Archaeology, Amsterdam 2012*.

Shirley, J.W., 1983, *Thomas Harriot, a biography*, Oxford University Press, Oxford.

Smith, J., 1627, *A sea grammar vvith the plaine exposition of Smiths Accidence for young sea-men, enlarged. Diuided into fifteene chapters: what they are you may partly conceiue by the contents. Written by Captaine Iohn Smith, sometimes gouernour of Virginia, and admirall of Nevv-England*, Printed by John Haviland, London.

Smith, R.D., 1988, 'Towards a new typology for wrought iron ordnance', *International Journal of Nautical Archaeology*, **17(1)**, 5–16.

Smith, R.D., 1995, 'Wrought-iron swivel guns', in Bound, M., ed., *The Archaeology of Ships of War*, Nelson, International Maritime Archaeology Series 1, Oswestry, Shropshire, 104–13.

Stanek, A., 2011, 'The Wittenbergen Wreck: An example of flush-planked ship construction in Northern Europe'. Master's Thesis, University of Southern Denmark, Esbjerg.

Steffy, R., 1994, *Wooden Shipbuilding and the interpretation of Shipwrecks*, Texas A&M University Press, College Station, TX.

Teesdale, E.B., 1991, *Gunfounding in the Weald in the sixteenth century*, Royal Armouries, London.

Thomsen, M.H., 2000, 'The Studland Bay wreck, Dorset, UK: hull analysis', *International Journal of Nautical Archaeology*, **29(1)**, 69–85.

Thomsen, M.H., 2003, *Princes Channel Wreck, Thames Estuary: Remedial Archaeological Recording. Fieldwork Report 54135.01*, Wessex Archaeology, Salisbury.

Thomsen, C., 2010, 'Reconstructing the Lines of the Princes Channel Ship', Master's Thesis, University of Southern Denmark, Esbjerg.

Trett, B., 2010, *Newport Medieval Ship: A Guide*, Friends of the Newport Ship, Newport.

Trollope, C., 2002, 'The design and evolution of English cast-iron guns from 1543 to 1660', *Journal of the Ordnance Society*, **14**, 51–64.

Trotzig, G. and Vahlne, G. eds, 1989, *Archaeology and Society: Large Scale Rescue Operations, their Possibilities and Problems: papers presented at the symposium in Stockholm, 12–16 September, 1988*, Nordic Secretariat of ICAHM, Stockholm.

Tyers, I, 1996 *Draft Dendrochronology Assessment: Fastolfs sites*, ARCUS Report 255.

Tyers, I, 1996 *Draft Dendrochronology Assessment: Rosary sites*, ARCUS Report 256.

Tyers, I, 1997 *Tree-ring analysis of seven buildings in Essex*, ARCUS Report 292.

Tyers, I, 1998 *Tree-ring analysis and wood identification of timbers excavated on the Magistrates Court Site, Kingston upon Hull, East Yorkshire*, ARCUS Report 410.

Tyers, I, 1999 *Dendro for Windows program guide (2nd edition)*, ARCUS Report 500.

Van der Leeuw, S.E., 2011, 'Information Processing and its Role in the Rise of the European World System', in Costanza, R., Graumilch, L., and Steffen, W.L., eds *Sustainability or Collapse?: an Integrated History and Future of People on Earth*, MIT Press in cooperation with Dahlem University Press, Cambridge, MA, 213–241.

Van Yk, C., 1697, *De Nederlandsche Scheeps-Bouw-Konst Open Gestelt*, Amsterdam.

Vermunt, M., 1999, 'Opgravingen in de Koepelstraat; Een blik in de middeleeuwse stadsgracht van Bergen op Zoom', *De Waterschans*, **1**, 3–6.

Wagstaffe, C., 2010, 'Furring in the light of 16th century ship design', Master's Thesis, University of Southern Denmark, Esbjerg.

Wallerstein, I.M., 1974, *The Modern World System: Capitalist Agriculture and the Origins of the European World Economy in the Sixteenth Century*, Academic Press, New York.

Wallerstein, I.M., 1980, *The Modern World System II: Mercantilism and the Consolidation of the European World Economy, 1600–1750*, Academic Press, New York.

Weidhagen-Hallerdt, M., 1992, 'I eld och rök', in *Stadsvandringar*, Stockholms stadsmuseum, Stockholm, **15**, 85–95.

Wegener Sleeswijk, A., 2003, *De gouden eeuw van het fluitschip*, Van Wijnen, Franeker, Netherlands.

Winfield, R., 2009, *British warships in the age of sail, 1603–1714: design, construction, careers and fates*, Seaforth, Barnsley, South Yorkshire.

Willems, W.J.H., and van den Dries, M., eds, 2007, *Quality Management in Archaeology*, Oxbow, Oxford.

Witsen, N., 1690, *Architectura Navalis et Regimen Nauticum ofte Aaloude en Hedendaagsche Scheepsbouw en Bestier*, Amsterdam, Netherlands.

Index

3D recording	16, 56–7, 68, 88
Aber Wrac'h 1 Wreck	85
Alderney Wreck	47, 53, 55, 67
Anholt Wrecks	54
Apron	19, 22–6, 34–5, 39, 60, 84
B&W 1 Wreck	18, 57, 83, 84; Table 8-1
Baker, Matthew	55, 67, 71–7, 79–80, 81
Mr Baker's Old Way	72
Basque whaler	*See San Juan*
Beam shelf	20, 36, 38, 40, 42, 85
Boteler, Nathaniel	*See* Butler, Nathaniel
Bourne, William	47, 51
Bow section	*See* Section 4
Breasthook	20, 22–4, 26
Butler, Nathaniel	77–8
A Dialogical Discourse	77
Carvel construction	31, 57, 82, 85
Cattewater Wreck	2, 54
Ceiling planks	11, 19, 27, 29–31, 33–5, 38, 41–2, 61, 66, 84
Clinker construction	57, 85, 86
Crotches	25–6, 39
Deane, Anthony	72, 74
Doctrine of Naval Architecture	72, 74
Deck beams	19, 36, 38–40, 42, 65, 81, 85
Dendrochronology	5, 19, 42–4, 83, 88, 91–2
Development-led archaeology	2, 3, 17, 87–9
Diving	2, 4, 6–8, 11–12, 14, 16, 20
Dredging	2, 17, 20, 86–8, 90
Duke of Buckingham	*See* Villiers, Sir George
Dummer, Edmund	79
Dutch flush construction	83
Elefanten	83, 85
Emanuell	55, 70–2, 81–2
English Heritage	3, 6, 16, 43
European Convention on the Protection of the Archaeological Heritage	87
Filling frames	19, 20, 24, 27, 29, 40, 84
Floor timbers	19–27, 29, 39, 40, 61–3, 66–7, 71, 74, 77, 83–5
Fragments of Ancient English Shipwrightry	55, 67, 71–2, 76, 79, 81–2
Frame-based construction	24, 79
Frame-first construction	84–6
Frame-led construction	83–4
Framing	
Pre-assembled	39–42, 83–5
Pre-designed	80, 85
Pre-erected	39, 80, 83–5
Furring	23, 27–9, 31, 33–6, 38–9, 41–3, 46, 59, 61, 63–6, 70–1, 73–81, 86, 88
Furring timbers	27–9, 34–6, 39, 41–3, 59, 63–4, 73
Futtocks	19–20, 24, 26–9, 34–6, 39–42, 44, 47, 59, 61–4, 66, 71, 77, 83–5, 87
Garboard strake	19, 22–3, 32, 40, 62, 67, 85
Girdler Sandbank	1, 2, 20
Girdling	75, 78–9
Great Divergence	86
Gresham College	16
Gresham Ship Project	16, 17
Steering group	16
Gresham, Sir Thomas	1, 49, 76, 81
Gunports	19, 38–9, 42–3, 47, 53–5, 61, 64, 66, 69
Half-beam clamp	20
Hampshire	44, 71
Harbours Act 1964	2
Harriot, Thomas	73, 75–7, 80–1
Henry VIII	75
Hood-ends	20, 22, 35–6, 40, 64, 67
Horsea Lake, Portsmouth	1, 16–17, 56
Hull fastenings	
Iron bolts	22–3, 35–6, 39
Iron nails	22, 31–6, 38–9, 41, 85
Spijkerpennen	83
Trenails	16, 22–4, 26, 29, 31–6, 38–43, 58, 59–60, 79, 84
Joints	
Butt	36, 42, 85
Dovetail	26, 84
Interlocking	39, 61, 66
Scarf joints	22, 31–3, 35–6, 39–40, 60, 64–6, 73, 77, 83–5
Keelson	41
Knees	23, 38–9, 41–2, 84
Kravel Wreck	54
Lampeter Dendrochronology Laboratory	43
Laser scanning	14
Lomellina	54, 83, 84, 85; Table 8-1
Magnetometer surveying	2
Mainwaring, Sir Henry	28, 42–3, 75–81
Seaman's Dictionary	28, 75, 77, 78
Mary Rose	22, 44, 54–5, 74, 83–5; Table 8-1
Mary Rose of 1623	75
Master frame	66–9, 71, 73–4, 81, 84
Merchant Shipping Act 1995	3
Midsection	*See* Master frame
Midship bend	*See* Master frame
Model, wood and cardboard	56–8
Modern World System	86
Mould	*See* Master frame
Mukran Wreck	83, 85
Multibeam sonar surveying	11
Museum of London	16
Nautical Archaeology Society	16
Newport Ship	57
Nomenclator Navalis	
See Mainwaring, Sir Henry: *Seaman's Dictionary*	
Norwegian Barcode Project	58
Nossa Senhora dos Mártires	83; Table 8-1
Pepper Wreck	*See Nossa Senhora dos Mártires*
Pett, Phineas	76–7, 79
Planking	19–20, 22, 24, 26, 29–36, 39–43, 47, 57–62, 64–66, 68–9, 71, 73–4, 78, 81, 83–5
Surface treatment	36
Port of London Act 1968	2, 3

Port of London Authority	1–4, 6–8, 11–12, 16, 20, 26, 51, 88, 90
Prince Royal	76, 77
Princes Channel	1, 2, 4, 12, 20, 86–7
Princes Channel Wreck	
Anchor	2–3, 20, 46–7
Armament	1–3, 11–12, 20, 47–55, 72, 78–9, 81
Carriages and mountings	47, 53–4
PC1	48–9, 51
PC2	49–52
PC3	51–3
PC4	52–4
Shot	20, 49, 51–2, 54
Cargo	
Iron bars	2–4, 11–12, 81
Lead ingots	12
Red lead	20
Spanish olive jar	4
Tin ingots	12, 20
Deck construction	19, 33, 36–8, 40, 42, 47, 84
Excavation	1, 3, 6–7, 10–13, 16–20, 33, 47–8, 54, 87
Lines plan	56, 66–70
Rigging	81
Protection of Wrecks Act 1973	3
Receiver of Wreck	3, 16
Repairs	14, 16, 32–3, 35, 44, 58, 85
Reverse naval architecture	57, 68, 69
Rhinoceros 3D	17, 57–9, 69, 71
Riddarholmen Wreck	54
Royal Armouries	3, 50, 53
Royal Armouries, Copenhagen	49
Royal William	78–9
San Juan	22, 67, 83; Table 8-1
Scheurrak SO1 Wreck	53–5, 83; Table 8-1
Sea Venture	62, 83, 84; Table 8-1
Sections	
Section 1	4, 6, 12, 14, 19–20 28, 31, 59, 62, 63
Section 2	4, 6, 7, 14, 16, 19–20, 24, 27, 36, 56, 60, 63–4, 66, 87
Section 3	6–9, 11–12, 22–3, 42
Section 3a	12, 16, 19, 21, 24, 26–7, 30, 32–3, 35, 39, 41, 58, 61–4, 66–7
Section 3b	8, 12, 16, 19–20, 24, 27–8, 32–6, 38–9, 44, 46, 54, 59, 61, 64
Section 4	6, 7, 11, 16, 19–24, 26, 30, 35–6, 57, 59–62, 64, 66–7
Selective dismantling	17, 89–90
Selective laser sintering	56–7
Self-contained archaeological projects	87–9
Sequence of construction	39–41
Sequence of furring	43
Sergison, Charles	78–9
Shell-first construction	57, 82–3, 85–6
Shipbuilding traditions	76, 82, 84
Shipbuilding traditions (cont.)	
British Isles	82, 86
France	82–3
Germany/Scandinavia	82–3, 86
Ibero-Atlantic	82–3, 84
Islamic	84
Mediterranean	83–5
Netherlands	73, 82, 85–6
Shore-side recording	7
Sidescan sonar surveying	4, 6–7, 19–20
Skeleton-built	83, 85
SL4 wreck site	17
Smith, Capt. John	77
Sea Grammar	77
Sovereign of the Seas	77
St Ekön	54
Stempost	19, 22–4, 34–6, 39, 43, 57, 60, 62, 64–8, 73–4, 84
Stereolithography	60–1
Sternpost	39, 57, 62, 64–5, 67–9, 74
Stoney Cove National Diving Centre	1, 46
Strakes	19–20, 27–8, 30–2, 58–9, 61–6, 68, 75, 77, 85
Susan Constant	73
Thames Estuary	1–3, 20
Theoretical design	79, 80, 86–7
Conflict with traditional craft practice	86–7
Tonnage	66, 71–3, 81, 83
Tons burthen	3, 72–3, 81
Total station recording	14
Transom	64–5, 67–9
Treatise on Shipbuilding	66–8, 73–4, 77, 80
Tumblehome	64, 69, 71, 78
Underwater recording	8, 11, 14, 56
Universities, role of	89
University College London	1, 12, 16
University of Southern Denmark	1, 16, 56
Vejle Hafnia Wreck	83, 85; Table 8-1
Viking Ship Museum	57
Villiers, Sir George	75
Virginia Company	47
Wale	19–20, 29–30, 32–6, 41, 43, 61, 63–4, 67, 78, 85
Wall-raised	78
Wall-reared	78
Warwick	47, 77, 83–4; Table 8-1
Waterproofing	31–4, 40, 42–3, 85–7
Caulking	24, 31–5, 38, 41, 43, 83, 85
Waterway	20, 38
Wessex Archaeology	2–4, 6–16, 19–22, 31, 43, 46–8, 53–4
Wittenbergen Wreck	48–9, 54–5, 83, 85; Table 8-1
Wrongheads	27
Wronghead sweep	62
Wynter, Sir William	49, 51
Yassi Ada Wreck	84

www.ingramcontent.com/pod-product-compliance
Lightning Source LLC
Chambersburg PA
CBHW041705290426
44108CB00027B/2863